BASEBALL AND LESSER SPORTS

Baseball

AND
LESSER
SPORTS

Wilfrid Sheed

HarperCollins*Publishers*

Acknowledgment is made for permission to reprint the following:

"Mellowing Out." Excerpt from *The Face of Baseball*. Essay by Wilfrid Sheed, copyright © 1990 by Wilfrid Sheed, reprinted by permission of Thomasson-Grant, Inc.

"Movie Baseball." Copyright © 1989 by The New York Times Company. Reprinted by permission.

"Book Baseball." Reprinted with permission from *The New York Review of Books*. Copyright © 1989 Nyrev, Inc.

"Outtakes: Computer Baseball." Reprinted with permission from *The New York Review of Books*. Copyright © 1989 Nyrev, Inc.

"Sports Talk." Reprinted with permission from *The New York Review of Books*. Copyright © 1982 Nyrev, Inc.

"Unnecessary Roughness." From *The Good Word & Other Words* by Wilfrid Sheed, copyright © 1971 by Wilfrid Sheed. Used by permission of the publisher, Dutton, an imprint of New American Library, a division of Penguin Books USA Inc.

"The Unknown Football Player: No. 65 Replacing No. 63." Reprinted with permission from Harry N. Abrams, Inc. from *Athletes* © 1985.

"The Vanishing Tennis Brat." From *Essays in Disguise*. Copyright © 1990 by Wilfrid Sheed. Reprinted by permission of Alfred A. Knopf, Inc.

FIRST EDITION

Designed by Cassandra J. Pappas

LIBRARY OF CONGRESS CATALOG CARD NUMBER 90-55941

ISBN: 0-06-016531-6

91 92 93 94 95 WB/RRD 10 9 8 7 6 5 4 3 2 1

Contents

Introduction

As a child, one of my most reliable pipe dreams had me retiring into sportswriting, after the longest career in baseball history. When the corn silk reached my brain, I probably imagined doing both at once. Games were short, off-seasons were long—heck, I might as well run for the Senate too.

The gods, who probably know what they're doing, denied me all these wishes in spades, and my envy for my two favorite professions has cooled sufficiently to live with over the years. Writing against deadline between 11 P.M. and 1 A.M. night after night now seems like a particularly grim penance for having enjoyed sports too much as a kid, while everything I've learned about the think tank intensity of modern baseball convinces me that it is no place for the wandering mind of the writer. (In grade school, one of the priests could pick me off first base at will simply by staring at me good-naturedly. A smile from this man was so rare that I thought he must be congratulating me for reaching first base. "Yer out kid." And this kind of thing gets worse with age, not better.)

But whatever I've lost in envy I've gained in respect for those who've kept the torch lit and pursued the dream all the way. Because sports and sportswriting are among that choice handful of adult activities that kids actually think are worth doing. There must be good reasons for becoming a patent attorney or a proctologist but they don't strike you right away or light your way through high school—or, if you don't make it, haunt you slightly for the rest of your life.

Baseball haunts you—at least until your heroes begin to retire. I remember watching Willie Mays stumbling around the Mets outfield in the 1973 Series and thinking, well, if he's too old so am I, and so is my memory and so is my whole psychic apparatus. And I know for sure that if I tried to imagine myself out there now, it would be as an old man, a displaced fifties player swinging a heavy bat with a thick handle and looking sadly at sea among the AstroTurf gazelles of 1990.

So it was time for my astral self to retire to the imaginary press box where I still had years ahead of me. I had always done a little sportswriting with my left hand—in fact, the first real piece I ever published was on sports, just to keep the candle flickering; but it wasn't until my late thirties, when my real self would have retired from playing anyway, that I began to think seriously about making a second, or shadow, career out of it, with the result you are even now wiping sand off or trying to keep from getting wet.

The point is, I don't think the timing was accidental: the urge to play and the joys of reflection are slightly different animals, and it was like a midlife rebirth to find that one could prolong the pleasure of sports indefinitely simply by writing about it and letting the reflections roll. To be asked to cover a sports event from time to time (and without those kill-joy deadlines) is almost as good as being asked to play again, and I spent a happy fortieth year trekking around the country doing TV stories for *Sports Illustrated*, and trekking all the way to England for SI to cover the new hot story over there, soccer violence.

It was the perfect time of life to be discovering new worlds, whether it be Scotland Yard, where old detectives reminisced fondly about the soccer violence in *their* day, or in a TV truck with the inmates howling about having to stay an extra day in Jacksonville, Florida. "What luck—an eighteen-hole playoff!" chirped the announcer outside. "Twenty-four more hours in this hellhole" moaned the groundhogs within. "My effing luggage must be in Chicago by now."

A bubble of excitement forms around sports events—old friends yakking it up at the bar, famous athletes trundling through the lobby, rumors and speculation everywhere—on which a man could live forever. At any rate, it offered a much richer life than the one that just now seemed to be opening up, or closing, in front of Willie Mays. Willie's memory was already frozen forever a few yards in front of the Polo Grounds' center field clubhouse as he hurtled under Vic Wertz's fly ball—and Willie was all of twenty-three at the time, an age when many kids today don't even know what they're going to do for a living yet. Although the "Say-hey Kid" still had many great years in front of him at that point, nothing *better* was ever going to happen to him—nothing the public would remember anyhow. And if he were to go to a big event today, there would probably be no bubble in it for him, only regret one imagines, and possibly vexation at the sight of lesser men playing his game, and stealing his headlines.

By contrast, Red Smith, who played nothing but the English language (at which he had even more moves than Mays) still seemed like a young fellow, sort of a say-hey kid himself in fact (although he would have phrased it better), in his late fifties, and would until the very day he died. And now I began to see why. Although a major sports event might seem like a Dickens Christmas to a new boy with a long lead time I could see how real sportswriters might find it a chore after a while, looking for the best restaurant in Cleveland one more time or, if your tastes run that way, calling up last year's playmate and praying not to get her new husband on the phone instead. But Red Smith was never bored by anything, and he blew into every town on a gale of laughter and anecdote—he might be saying something like do you remember the night Kid Mulrooney fought in this town? He was so surprised when he heard he'd won that he fainted dead away and the ref absentmindedly began counting over him. The story was that the fight was fixed, but in the confusion the ref couldn't remember who was supposed to win.

Red could seemingly charge his enviable batteries this way— and all the other batteries in the vicinity, in any tank town to which his calling sent him (he would, come to think of it, have made a fine parish priest or country doctor) and, to cut a long story short, I had the great good fortune to plug into Red not once but several times myself, picking up in the process not only maybe a Dixie cup full of his boundless enthusiasm, but a sense that a first-rate man could express his whole self, his whole talent in writing about sports, and consider his life well-spent at the end of it.

Like most of his readers I knew Red Smith inside out before he met me. Furthermore, I had actually met him once in person when I was sixteen and he endeared himself to me forever by laughing at one of my lines (there is no more exacting form of courtesy than laughing at a teenager's lines); but there was no reason for him to remember that.

Our next meeting was probably a little more conscious on his part. I was in Cleveland, trying to track down the elusive Muhammad Ali—elusive to me anyway: I had been given precisely three-and-a-half months to write and research the text of a picture book about the great one, and he had been forbidden by his publisher (*everybody* has one these days) to cooperate with me in any shape or form. And even though it took the strength of ten to keep this man away from *anyone* who wanted to write about him, there were more than ten men in his entourage and some of them were mean-looking mothers. So at that early stage I was pretty much down to lobby sitting and checking my mailbox—where I found to my glee a note from Red saying, in effect (I wish I'd kept it), I hear that a fellow member of the Bobo Newsom Memorial Society is in town and I think we should drink to that. And we did, again and yet again over the next few years, as much of this book either was being written or thought about.

Although Red Smith had missed the first meeting of the curious society referred to in his note, he wouldn't miss many more, and in no time he became its centerpiece and finally its chief reason for existence, such that none of us could quite bring ourselves to convene again after he died. The Bobo Newsom Society consisted of some bright, funny men spitballing about an inexhaustible subject, baseball, so it could have gone on forever: but the drop in excitement would have been too sharp, we would have felt like Dr. Johnson's circle without Dr. Johnson, and we dispersed (apparently) forever.

Since none of us had ever wanted the club to be talked about—we were writers and knew better than anyone how exposure can kill delicate things—Ira Berkow continued to respect our privacy in his biography (and I in my review, reprinted here), and the whole episode seemed to have disappeared from history, which was fine with us but perhaps slightly shortchanges Red's memory: so here goes with a partial list in no particular order of the baseball scholars and kibitzers this least pretentious of spellbinders held in the palm of his hand right to the end: Ray Robinson, Jim Bouton, Joel Oppenheimer, Don Honig, Larry Ritter, Vic Ziegel, Joe Flaherty, John Leo, Ted Hoagland, Al Coblin of the Lion's Head, Ross Wetzeon, Eliot Asinof and our commissioner David Markson, whose good nature we would strain to breaking by straying from the agenda—or even straying from baseball altogether, if we really wanted to drive him crazy.

Honig used to transport Red down from Connecticut for the meetings and home again later, taking the most circuitous routes each time in order to prolong the pleasure and maybe hear one more story about Ping Bodie (Red's favorite baseball name) or Connie Mack. And once toward the end, we all trooped up to Red's house for a meeting on a crisp pre-winter night, and I remember autumn leaves everywhere, all over the lawn and driveway, and thinking what a strange and yet correct setting this was for this man of a thousand hotel rooms. Unlike many sportswriters, Red Smith was a solid bourgeois who seemed to relish family life, and it was no great stretch to imagine him raking those leaves himself—if he could find the time between bouts and games and races.

Anyway, that is my last mental picture of Red. The next thing I knew, it seemed, was Tom Seaver standing tall and still at the altar of St. Patrick's Cathedral as if he were about to fire his high hard down the aisle and eulogizing his old friend thus. "In the league he played in, Red Smith was the best there was."

Well, perhaps he was: would that one's friends were always the best at what they did. But that was a tough league Seaver was talking about and honesty, which has its cold-blooded side, compels me to admit that nobody ever covered a game better than Dick Young of the New York *Daily News*, or wrote a funnier column than John Lardner, or a more sportswise one than Larry Merchant. Fortunately honesty does not compel one to downgrade all one's friends—some of them really *may* be the best—so I'll quickly throw in the name of Vic Ziegel, also of the *News*, as a contemporary contender, with perhaps an asterisk for Mike Lupica of *The National* for making me laugh in the teeth of his rabble-rousing opinions. Every second young journalist wants to be a Mencken, but it's harder than it looks, and Mike comes a lot closer than most.

Unfortunately, this kind of judicious pencil-chewing struck the wrong note—it even sounded wrong to me—when I was asked to review a couple of posthumous collections of Red Smith's writings soon after his death: *somebody* had to bury Caesar, but I realized too late that it probably shouldn't have been any of the Knights of Bobo, we all owed him too much. So I tried again, with the mixed results you'll see in here (both pieces are in the book), before giving up completely. The book review is probably not a suitable form for a valentine and years of practicing the form had left me incapable of bending it enough to say goodbye properly; so I'm saying it here.

Although the Newsom Society should never be confused with Shakespeare's Mermaid Tavern, it did set several birds singing about baseball who were not normally known for doing so: Leo wrote about the Hall of Fame, Markson about Pete Reiser, Oppenheimer more than ever about his beloved New York Mets. We were encouraged in this by the obliging fact that the market for baseball writing suddenly seemed to be opening up to unprecedented widths. When I started doing these essays, the outlets seemed to consist entirely of magazines like *Sports Illustrated* and *Sport*—specialty books for specialty readers. But by the eighties, everybody was asking for sports stuff, specifically baseball, and I am struck now by the different number of magazines represented in here, including three different sections of the *New York Times*—none of which is the sports section.

But the number also indicates that nobody wanted very *many* sports pieces—just a few words for our April issue on what baseball means to you, or a roundup of sports books for Christmas, or how about baseball and the American dream, or baseball and the arts, or just *you* know, a piece about BASEBALL?

Everyone suddenly seemed to feel there was something more to be said about baseball, but they didn't quite know where to scratch next. So George Will tried over here and David Halberstam had a go down there, and before you knew it the new guys had doubled and tripled a body of writing that already surpassed the literature of any other sport played with a ball any time anywhere except for my other favorite, cricket—a game which incidentally I learned to love and in a rudimentary way play from print and still pictures during World War II. Other sports may be more fun to play than baseball or cricket— water polo looks like more fun than anything—or more exciting to watch, if you excite easily. But when it comes to reading or writing about them, the more "fun" they are, in the water polo or even basketball sense, the less trace they leave on the left brain or consequently the page.

Baseball writing and thinking occur mostly in the interstices, the spaces between the fun, and some of the latest thinking as exposed in books and movies isn't really about baseball at all, but about how nice America used to be (we've got movies to prove it), or how great it felt to be young—Reaganism at its purest and most justifiable. Still, I sometimes wish they'd leave baseball alone and pick on bowling or horseshoes for a while. Although I can't go all the way with George Will's new puritanism which would throw out all the statues and incense from baseball and replace them with murals of heavy labor and furrowed brows, its central thesis is surely right—you have to remove the "poetry" from baseball to discover the real poetry. (The proof is in the eating: Will's book *Men at Work* fairly spills over with poetry, with a sense that there's more where it came from. The movie *Field of Dreams*, which can stand in for all the other "Look ma, I'm being poetic" effusions of the past few years, does not.)

My own view of baseball begins with something I said to Bryant Gumbel the only time I was ever on a morning TV show. The question was, did I think of baseball as a metaphor, and the answer was, "No. A metaphor means it reminds you of something else [I am not responsible for my grammar on talk shows]. Baseball doesn't remind me of anything else. It is not a representational art."

Baseball and the other sports are alternatives to life, stories we tell ourselves to take our minds off life but also to add something to it, as art itself does. The fact that I think our Summer story incomparably the best was not enough to trap me into denouncing football though, as Mr. Gumbel's ensuing questions seemed to invite me to. The heresy that to like something you have to dislike something else has no place in the sports calendar. If you like the things people do with a ball, you always want to see what they're going to do next. And besides, football breaks the fall wonderfully well between the baseball season and the Abyss, or Black Hole of February.

But even football isn't as good to write about.

The one defection I have to note sadly from my list of admirations is boxing. While he was still fighting, my favorite subject Muhammad Ali used to poke harsh fun at punch-drunk boxers and swear he would never get like that himself: but even then, his cerebral cortex probably knew things it wasn't telling him. The last time I saw him, he whispered in my ear and I wish

I could say it made sense. Well, maybe I missed something. And then we had the great Sugar Ray Robinson dying and turning out to have been a vegetable for the last fifteen years of his life—the same Sugar Ray who used to drive around in a pink convertible with tiger skin seats, laughing at the world. And then in the same week, Sandy Sadler and Rocky Graziano both turning up empty, unable to remember who they were or what town they were in. Too much.

My defense of boxing in the last section is still the best I can make, and it's one I will probably use when Mike Tyson fights Evander Holyfield, or the next great fight after that. But I'm no longer quite sure that it's good enough.

As for the other sports both in and outside of this book— I've never felt that being a sports fan meant that you had to love them all indiscriminately, any more than an arts fancier has to love all the arts: even with such simpler categories as cats and babies, I prefer to judge them one at a time. The word "sports" in itself covers such a disparate array of activities and atmospheres, from cross-country skiing to skeet shooting to Ping-Pong, that to love them all is surely to love none of them, but simply to love competition for its own sake, the way a soap opera nut loves romance, *any* romance: which is okay when you're fifteen, but kind of desperate by your forties and fifties.

Of the sports that have made the cut from my omniverous teens into my averagely greedy mid-life, I'll say quickly that I'd like to have covered a little more tennis and a lot more golf. But for golf you'd have to know the courses better than you can learn them from those dreamy TV visitations (much as these help to pass the winter). The course *is* the competition in golf, so leaving them out reduces the sport to shadow boxing. As for tennis, you have only to listen to the announcers at the U.S. Open to realize how little words actually add to this sport. "Steffi should be coming into the net more often . . . Gabrielle seems to be exploiting that suspect backhand"—your only excuse for not having noticed these things yourself already is a deep coma, which is always a possibility.

It is no knock on a sport to say that its pleasures are self-evident. Tennis generates moments of fire and beauty that match anything in the world of games: Tony Trabert jousting with Ken Rosewall in the Davis Cup and with Pancho Gonzales in Trabert's professional debut (don't be fooled by the man's announcing: Trabert was always one-half of a great match waiting to happen)—these will stick in my mind until the last cell is burned out in there, alongside Arnie Palmer strewing the course with cigarette butts on his way to the Masters title in 1960 and Willis Reed hobbling onto the court to jerk the 1973 championships around with his very presence. What's to say about these things?

One turns from these fevers to the cool subterranean caverns of baseball with a certain relief. Here there is plenty to talk about—so much so that for some fans the year is divided nicely into a playing season and a talking season with no need for any other sports at all.

Whether all this babble is worth writing down is, of course, another question. Until recently, eggheads and highbrows who wrote about baseball were invariably greeted by catcalls from the gallery and accusations of slumming and posturing. It seemed to be a law of American life that you could write about other sports any way that you liked, but for baseball you had better write like William Bendix or the Fonz to be taken seriously (a tough assignment for Roger Angell and an impossible one for Jacques Barzun, the good-humored pioneers of two-dollar baseball writing).

One thing that writers like David Halberstam and Mr. Will have made decisively clear is that they are not slumming when they write about baseball, but have given the game their very best shots, according it an uncomplicated respect that they wouldn't dream of wasting on politics. And the subject has rewarded them with some pretty fair books.

This is probably no accident. If, as the saying goes, chicken is the great chef's palette, enabling him to shoot the works and show everything he can do, then baseball is the chicken of subjects. Halberstam's gifts for writing driving, pounding narrative are seen in clearer, more satisfying outline in his baseball writing than they might be with muddier subjects, while *Men At Work* reveals not only a skill at reportage and anecdote that I hadn't suspected but a characteristic of Will's that I hadn't fully understood. Readers of his political writing will recognize that it is never enough for this author to have an idea, he must also find some degenerate idiot who holds the opposite and heap him with scorn. But I had put this down to a blind hatred of liberals until I saw him doing the same thing in a milder and sunnier way to opponents of the designated hitter rule, and realized how much this tic of his was just a rhetorical device and not an act of war.

These and countless other writers, painters, and moviemakers have succeeded by now in erecting a vast and ornate structure of words and pictures around the game of baseball which might conceivably attract someone who'd never even seen a game, the way pyramids mesmerize people who've never heard of King Tut. Baseball is, remember, still the same old game, the one you first encountered on a beach or an empty lot: you still play it with a stick and a ball and you run around in a square, and you're out or you score, and at that level it isn't even pretty to look at. Could this really be what all the fuss is about?

It is indeed but the case is not all that obvious. To many people, recent attempts to mythologize this rather simple activity must seem about on a par with Bob and Ray's legendary turkey dinner made of franks and beans, a triumph of human imagination and foolishness. And they'd be half right.

You have to fill out the game you're watching with your own thoughts and memories, and place it in the rich context of a season and a tradition, in order to appreciate just how much you can do with a ball and a stick. Every game produces as a by-product a heap of imagining and thinking material to be processed over a lifetime: numbers, tendencies, strange plays you never saw before. If you're not collecting any of this, the game empties out quickly and you're back on the beach with a bunch of kids running round hollering.

If so, and if you're reading this book against your better judgment, I can only say—enjoy your turkey.

P.S.: Each of my previous collections has contained one sports piece as a species of calling card: all the rest have been saved up for this one.

1

The Game

◇

Beginnings

hey took away my cricket bat at the age of nine and told me I wouldn't be needing it anymore. Out of kindness they didn't tell me I wouldn't need my soccer ball, either. Otherwise, I don't think I would have come to America at all. I would have lied about my age and joined the horse marines.

Exile is an ugly business at any age. Harold Pinter, the playwright, carted his bat with him all over England to remind him of the past (he must have been eight when he started out). I was forced to hand over mine at the frontier, and with it the long summer evenings, the boys with the dangling suspenders, the whole Fanny-by-gaslight world of cricket; my life for the next few years would be a hunt for fresh symbols, a bat and ball I could believe in.

Baseball dismayed me at first blush almost as much as the big cars and the big faces in the street. In the dictionary of the senses *cricket* stood for twilight, silence, flutter. (See also *Swans.*) *Baseball* equaled noonday, harsh, noise, clatter. (See *Geese.*)

That was how it looked at first—boys milling around dusty lots jabbering and hitching at their pants. But as I kept craning from train windows and car windows in my first days in America, I noticed something promising: that nothing ever seemed to be happening at that particular moment—the same basic principle as cricket. The pitcher peering in to get the sign, the ritual chant of the infield, the whispered consultations and then, if you were very lucky, a foul tip (before you were whisked out of range). Baseball was not as busy as it seemed but lived, like the mother game, on pregnant pauses. This, plus the fact that it happened to be in season and you played it with a bat and ball, made it look like my best bet.

Unfortunately, the place where we first lived was an almost deserted village, so there was no one to play with. There was one boy about a mile down the road who straightened out my batting stance and filled me in on the First World War, too, but he was five years older than I, with his own life to live, so I couldn't bother him too often.

Instead, I became perhaps the outstanding solitary baseball player of my generation, whaling fungoes down the long, narrow garden and plodding after them, chattering to myself and whaling them back again. Anything pulled or sliced got lost, so my first encounter with American botany was staring sightless through it, hunting the tawny baseball. When that palled, I would chalk a strike zone on the garage door and lob a tennis ball at it. Already I had the style, though God knows where it came from: the mock aggression and inscrutable loneliness. Gary Cooper high on a hill, twitching his cap, shaking off the sign: nodding, rearing, firing. Clunk, against the old garage door. The manner came with my first glove.

Another thing that stoked my love affair was the statistics. I like a game that has plenty of statistics, the more inconsequential the better, and I began soaking up baseball records like a sea sponge before I even knew what they meant. I liked the way you could read *around* baseball, without ever getting to the game at all. I devoured a long piece in the old *Satevepost* about Hank Greenberg, baseball's most eligible bachelor, and another about young Ted Williams, who only shaved twice a week. Official baseball sneaked up on me through its trivia. My learned friend up the road took me, at last, to an actual game at Shibe Park, and I was hooked for fair. It was the St. Louis Browns versus the Philadelphia Athletics, hardly an offering to stir the blood, but more than enough to stir mine. The Brownies built up a big lead, but the As, led by Wally Moses and Bob Johnson, staged one of their rare comebacks and pulled it out of the fire. The sandlot games I had seen so far had not been beautiful to look at, only intellectually interesting (I used phrases like that occasionally, a real little snot in some ways); but here we had something as elegant as the Radio City Rockettes—explosively elegant and almost as fussily stylish as cricket.

Baseball became my constant, obsessive companion after that. Up and down the garden, faster and faster, first as Dick Siebert, the A's first baseman, then as Arky Vaughan, whose name and dour appearance I fancied, then right-handed as Jimmie Foxx. And at night I played out whole games in my head, in which I was always the quiet, unobtrusive professional (I detested show-boating) who hit the penultimate single or made a key play in the *eighth* inning. It was as if I'd brought my cricket bat with me after all.

The point about this was that it was all what D. H. Lawrence would have called "baseball in the head." When I came to play with other boys in the next few years, I continued my solipsistic ways, trotting out quietly to my position, chewing all the gum that my mouth would hold and gazing around with mild, shrewd eyes; or, for a time, grinning like Stan Hack, the Cub third baseman—a steady player on a steady club, the way I wanted to spend eternity.

A sociologist might (and I would probably agree with him, having just made him up) explain my choice of this particular type of athlete quite simply. Baseball was my social passport, and a slight averageness is good on a passport. It means that the officials look at you less closely. Who is that guy over there? Maybe he'd like to play. Say—he's quietly efficient, isn't he? I remember standing around picnic sites and county fairs, wistfully, with my glove half concealed under my arm as if I didn't mean anything by it. I was slightly ashamed of my accent and bitterly ashamed of my first name; but baseball did not judge you by those things. The Statue of Liberty, bat in hand, said, "Try this, kid."

Sometimes, magically, it happened. I was rather light for a ballplayer in spite of weighing myself a lot. I knew the names of all the light ballplayers (the Waner brothers were a special comfort), but still, eighty pounds was eighty pounds, and even with the most graceful swing in town I could rarely nudge the ball past second base. However, I waited out numerous walks, if there happened to be an umpire, fielded as well as the pebbles allowed and always looked a little better than the clumsy lout they had buried in right field. Afterward they went their way, into houses I knew nothing about, to a life that contained other things besides baseball; and I went mine.

In the fall of '41 I left for boarding school. Although the baseball season was still raging, I found that it was all over as far as my new school was concerned. I felt as if I had lost a friend. My companion of the long, silent summer was replaced by a harsh, grunting affair, where people shouted like drill sergeants and made a big thing of getting in shape, being in shape, staying in shape. Suck in your gut, get those knees up.

I saw right away that football was the enemy. If eighty pounds was of dubious value in summer, it was downright ludicrous in fall. Beyond that I distrusted the atmosphere of the game, all that crouching and barking. It was a side of America that might have appealed to a little German boy, but hardly to me. The essential solitude of baseball gave way to a false heartiness, a just-feel-that-stomach toughness. We only played touch football that year, but even so managed to make a military thing of it.

God knows how, I came to love football anyway. The finished product, the game itself, transcended all the midweek drivel. I had seen the previous winter one game, in which Whizzer (now Sir Whizzer) White scored two touchdowns against the woebegone Eagles of Philadelphia, and I guess I liked it all right. I

drew some crayon pictures of it, anyway, showing little Davey
O'Brien being smothered by Lions.

But there was an actuality to the game as played that was
quite different from the game as watched or the game as planned.
I became second-string quarterback in our rather peculiar school
and got to run back a kickoff in a quasi-real game. Huddled in
the lee of a gland case, a 250-pound eighth-grader, I made our
only considerable gain of the day. I relished the swooping, shift-
ing patterns that had to be diagnosed instantly, the hilarity of
each yard gained, the pleasure of doing something you've practiced and getting it right.

It was quite different from my dreamy, poetic, half-mad relationship with baseball. This was crisp and outgoing, hep-two-
three-four, and based on the realities of the game, not on some
dream of it. Yet it filled the same social purpose. It became a
shortcut, or substitute, for mastering the local culture. I still
didn't know how to talk to these people but while I was playing
I didn't have to. The soundless pat on the back, the "nice going,
Sheed"—you could be any manner of clod, or even an English
boy, and it didn't matter. I remember blocking a punt with my
stomach and writhing in agony and feeling it was worth it for
the brief respect I commanded.

This was canceled on another occasion, which is still almost
too painful to describe, and which I write of here only that it
may be of help to others: that is, to any eighty-pound English
refugees who happen to be reading this. The setting was a pick-
up game played in semidarkness. The agreed-on goal line was
a fuzzy patch of trees off in the middle distance, I'm still not
sure where. My team was losing 12–0, and it was understood
that the next play would be the last one: hence meaningless, a
lame-duck exercise. Their man threw a long pass. I intercepted
it and reeled a step backward, someplace in the area of the goal
line.

Triumphant hands were clapped on me, and I was told that
I had just handed two points to the enemy. Would (and I have
woulded this would often since) that Zeus had smitten my

tongue at that moment. The game would have been forgotten—
12–0, 14–0, who cared—and I would have been spared three
lousy years. As it was, I said in fruitiest cockney, "How was I
supposed to know where the goal line was?"

Wrong thing to say. I heard no more about it that day. The
saying went underground for a while, and when it emerged the
context had been garbled slightly. I was now alleged to have
run the wrong way, like in the Rose Bowl, and to have capped
it, in what was now a horrible whine, " 'ow was aye suppowsed
to know which why the gowl was?" Well, okay, I was used to
that by now, in an Irish school. But this legend so grabbed the
popular imagination that I was still hearing it three years later
from boys who had just entered the school.

The moral of this tragedy is that sport as a Julien Sorel passport has its treacherous side. It can bestow curses as carelessly
as blessings, and the curses stick. However, those first two years
would have been grim without sports, which played an unnat-
urally large part in my life, and still do in my mind, because
they were, at times, all I had.

As to my life as a fan, that, too, was a social passport, and
therefore doctored slightly. "Hey, how come you know so much
about baseball?" could be a friendly question or it could be
weighted with menace. Like a dumb blonde who has artfully
bleached her brain, I found there were circles where it paid to
keep my knowledge to myself, even though it burned in the
mouth and even though some smug fool was deluding the crowd
with wrong statistics.

It was, though, an acceptable subject, and there weren't too
many of those. I did not understand cars, had not been camping
last summer, had a noncooking mother: subject after subject
broke in my hands. Only sports could be trusted. Fate had
presented me with three frowsy teams to talk about: the Phillies,
As and Eagles, all usually cemented into their respective last
places. (I was foolishly pleased when a friend said, "Don't the
As usually finish around sixth?" The As never finished anywhere
near sixth.) Pennsylvania University was some small consolation—I saw it beat Army, Harvard, Cornell on various week-

ends—but hardly enough. My own social position was too sensitive to burden with three risible teams, so I decided to diversify. I took on board the Brooklyn Dodgers and the Washington Redskins. Sammy Baugh was a man I could identify with. Lean and steel-eyed, my winter self.

On balance, I would say that playing games didn't do much for my character. It gives one a highly specialized confidence and a highly qualified cooperativeness, but in return it makes one incurably childish. Intellectually, it teaches you that you can't argue with a fact, a mixed blessing. However, being a Brooklyn fan was useful. It taught me to suffer. The Dodgers immediately and definitively broke my heart. I had barely become a fan when Mickey Owen dropped the third strike and gave a World Series game away. Then the next season, 1942, Pete Reiser banged his head on the wall and they blew a ten-game lead over the Cardinals. The Dodgers came to Philadelphia on July 4th strutting like gods and pasted the local scarecrows 14–0 and 5–4. Reiser hit the neatest, mellowest little home run you ever saw. Medwick, Camilli—players twice as big, twice as regal as any since.

On the Sunday after Labor Day the Cardinals came in. They had beaten the Dodgers the day previous, on Whitey Kurowski's home run, to reach first place for the first time. The Dodgers were playing two with Cincinnati. There was strangling doom in the air. I knew, everyone knew, what was going to happen. All afternoon I watched the scoreboard. The Phillies were managing to split with the Cards, an unlikely reprieve, but the Dodgers went down slowly, inexorably to total defeat.

I was insane with grief. It was worse than the fall of France, and the feelings were not dissimilar: the same sense of irreversible momentum and crushed dreams. It seemed strange even then that a misfortune suffered by a random collection of strangers could hurt so much. Yet for days I was sick with sorrow and actually tried to forget about baseball: a trick I wasn't to master for another twenty years. I recovered in time to root lustily for the Cardinals in the World Series. A defeat for the Yankees was already sweeter than a victory for anyone else. Hence there was an element of vindictive nihilism in my baseball thinking, which was to run riot when Walter O'Malley took his team from Brooklyn to L.A. some sixteen years later, and which has dominated since that time.

In the fall of '43 we moved to New York. The Philadelphia hermitage was over. No more mowing lawns and hoeing vegetable beds in our victory garden to pay my way to Shibe Park, no more early-morning trolley rides to Frankford and long subway rides from there in order to get the whole of batting practice and two games for my buck and a quarter. I had not realized what a grueling regimen this was until I took a friend with a medium interest in baseball along for company. Even though we saw Ted Williams strike out three times on the knuckle ball and then hit a home run in the tenth, my friend never once mentioned baseball again.

But now I was in New York, the capital of baseball, and my appetite raged wantonly, like some Thomas Wolfe character in Europe, prowling the streets and roaring. In those days every barber shop had a radio, every butcher shop—the whole block was a symphony of baseball.

To be young in Paris, to be coming up for thirteen in New York! Unfortunately, the game itself was not in such hot shape right then. The stars were wafting, or drafting, away and being replaced by squinting, shambling defectives like the ones I had left behind in Philadelphia. The Dodgers tried out a sixteen-year-old shortstop. The lordly Yankees were reduced to the likes of Joe Buzas and Ossie Grimes. The St. Louis Browns actually had a one-armed centerfielder. The hottest player in town was an aging retread called Phil Weintraub. You had to love baseball to survive those years.

But I liked going to the parks anyway. They offered the cultural continuity of churches. You could slip into one in a strange city and pick up the ceremony right away. College football stadiums made me nervous with their brutal cliquishness, and professional football stadiums always gave me rotten seats—the same one, it seemed like, high up and to the left, in back of the goal line. But ballparks were home and still are, a place where I understand what my neighbors are up to, even after a year abroad.

The football scene was a slight improvement over Godforsaken Philadelphia. The wartime Giants must have been one of the dullest teams in history, with their off-tackle smashes and their defensive genius. But they were usually able to make a game of it. I saw Don Hutson *throw* a touchdown pass off an end-around reverse, and my hero, Sammy Baugh, quick-kick sixty-six yards to the Giants' four. You didn't seem to see things like that in Philadelphia.

My own playing career mooned along all this while, striking me, at least, as promising. I had become a spottily effective left end, running solemn little down-and-outs and tackling with bravura (I found I wasn't afraid of head-on tackles, which put one in the elite automatically). I discovered that basketball yielded to humorless determination better than most games and I once succeeded in sinking seventeen foul shots in a row. But the game had no great emotional interest; it was more like a bar game of skill that whiles away the evenings. I liked the hot gymnasiums and the feel of the floor underfoot, and it was fun fretting about the score, but the game left no resonance afterward. Fast breaks and the swishing of the strings—a thin collection of memories.

Baseball continued to intoxicate, worse than ever; tossing the ball among snowdrifts at the beginning of spring, the sweet feeling in the hands when you connected and sent it scudding over the winter grass, the satisfaction of turning your back on a fly and turning round in more or less the right place to catch it. I had grown off my eighty-pound base and was now a gawky fanatic of 105 or so, willing to field for hours, taking my glove everywhere, pounding an endless pocket into it, scavenging for a game.

This sport, which I had needed so badly on arrival, was now making me pay for its favors. I was enslaved to it, like Emil Jannings to Marlene Dietrich. My life had become seriously lopsided. I refused to go swimming because it interfered with my career—tightened the skin on the chest and all that. I looked

at the countryside with blank eyes. My father admonished me
to throw away my baseball magazines after one reading, but I
hid them like an addict. I don't recall reading anything else at
all. Nothing, not even the war, interested me anymore.

In my new neighborhood my passport was honored handsomely. I was the best shortstop, in an admittedly skimpy field,
and I was always sure of a game. I didn't bother to make friends
in any other context, seeing myself as an aloof professional who
never mixed business with pleasure. I took an ascetic view of
people who goofed off and had a mortal horror of games de-
generating into horseplay. "Come on, let's play ball," I would
say austerely, like some Dominican friar behind on his *autos-
da-fé*. My father, who spent half the war in each country, took
me to see a cricket match in Van Cortlandt Park, and it struck
me as a vague, ramshackle game. We got into a discussion over
the concept "not cricket." It seemed to me ridiculous not to
take every advantage you could in a game. The slyness and bluff
of baseball were as beautiful to me as the winging ball.

How long this would have lasted, I have no way of knowing.
I might have snapped out of it in a year or two, under pressure
of girls and such, or followed it glumly until some awakening
in a Class A minor league. I contracted polio at the age of
fourteen, and my career was over just like that. I ran a fever
and for the first couple of nights I could see nothing in it but
sports images: football highlights, baseball highlights, boxing (I
was the only boy in school who had rooted for Louis over Conn,
so I had the films of the fight in my repertoire), all rushing
through my head like the Gadarene swine on their way to the
sea. I was allowed to switch sports, but not the main subject.
My obsession had to play itself out.

When calmness returned, I found my interest in sports had
fixated, frozen, at that particular point. I was to remain a four-
teen-year-old fan for the next twenty years. I continued thinking
that the life of a professional ballplayer was attractive long after
a sensible man would have abandoned the notion. I returned to
England for a while and became a cricket nut all over again.

Yet it wasn't really the same. I knew now that my bat had

been taken for good and I had better find something else to do. Sports still raged, but in one lobe only. The other was liberated, free to grow up if it could. And my interest in sports was more house-trained and philosophical: no more wrist-slashing over defeat, no more hero worship, an occasional thin smile while losing at pool—all in all, about as much maturity as you can expect from a hardened sports addict.

But when I see some black or Puerto Rican kid making basket catches or running like an arrow, breaking the language barrier and waving his passport, I feel like saying okay, but don't take it too seriously, don't let this be all. Sports are socially useful, up to a strictly limited point. I stopped being a foreigner the moment I blocked that kick, and a moment is sometimes all it takes. But blocking kicks or whacking baseballs only gets you so far. (Don't bring those muddy boots in the living room.) The mockery starts up again the minute you leave the park.

I thought sports had made me an American but in some ways they actually retarded the process. I played them like an English colonial officer, exhausting himself with some amusing native game and missing too many other things. Having said that, let me double back on it: If you had to limit yourself to one aspect of American life, the showdowns between pitcher and hitter, quarterback and defense, hustler and fish would tell you more about politics, manners, style in this country than any one other thing. Sports constitute a code, a language of the emotions, and a tourist who skips the stadiums will not recoup his losses at Lincoln Center and Grant's Tomb.

Mid-Life Crisis: Memoirs of a Philandering Fan

or Mets fans of a certain age, the Mets are perforce a second marriage, a condition which is rightly frowned on by the Church of Baseball, which believes that if you stray once you can stray again. But God knows, we gave it our all the first time around. I would have sworn on a stack of Carl Furillo cards that I would never leave the Dodgers, and Giants fans for whatever pathological reasons seem to have felt the same way about their guys.

So picture us all standing tear-drenched on the platform as the train pulled out, forced to face life for the first time as baseball bachelors. Maybe, let's face it, one would someday find companionship with another team—celibacy was a bit bloody much to ask—but commitment was definitely out. (I mean, supposing the first girl came back? There isn't a one of us who wouldn't to this day drop everything and go panting back.)

To be sure there are a few fickle souls who never really got the hang of things, and who actually seem to feel thirty years is about long enough to wear black and scuffle slightly when

you walk and have become 100 percent Mets fans, even committing the unthinkable heresy of living in the present. But the
rest of us have become typical second husbands, or wives, almost
too detached and critical at times to be real fans at all. For
instance, we expect our team to be good now, something we
never asked of the old one, and when it loses, we don't suffer
nobly the old way, we just get sore. The Mets were put on earth
to give us pleasure, dammit, not to break our hearts; and if it
doesn't work out this time, *we're* not the ones who are going
to get jilted.

However, even a Graham Greene or Eugene O'Neill marriage
must have its high spots, and although I for one will never bleed
*any*body's pinstripes, there have been moments, in '69 and '73
and '86 of course, but between times as well, when I could have
sworn that this was the real thing—all the better for the bumpy
road we've traveled.

But Lord, it was hard at first. To begin at the beginning, I
was damned if I was ever going to root for a team named after
an opera house. (For some reason, giving my soul to a bunch
of Trolley Dodgers had seemed perfectly reasonable.) And to
top off this insult to all that's holy in the way of baseball names,
they proceeded to disappear into the first of the anonymous
space-age stadiums to hit New York. The Restoration Theater-
like intimacy of Ebbets Field, which had made anyone who
played there automatically colorful, and the sheer kinkiness of
the Polo Grounds had given way to one of those Three Riverfront Coliseum agglomerates, where the planes vrooming overhead seemed part of the decor and the only neighborhood was
a parking lot stretching to infinity.

Floundering around in this urban sprawl, the Mets rapidly
lost the one attribute that had made their first year, 1962, mildly
diverting: namely, their gift for slapstick. As a Dodger purist, I
was never as amused as some by the humor of incompetence—
we'd done all that; but if one had to have bad baseball, the
Polo Grounds was not a bad place for it. In my twisted bitter
heart, I even derived a certain atavistic pleasure from watching
the home team bleep up in that particular setting, and besides,

there was the stadium itself, which had an odd, idiosyncratic cheerfulness about it, as if it were only pretending to be a ball-park.

In Shea Stadium, a bad team was just a bad team, in equal parts remote and desolate, and even the incomparable Casey Stengel was slightly diminished, visually at least, although he battled the elements like a titan to remain our one vibrant, noncounterfeit link with tradition. (The patchwork uniforms were, by contrast, more like cheap souvenirs of Old New York, shown up cruelly each time our ex-wives came to town sporting the real thing.)

For a counterfeit link that actually held up for a while there was also the parade of the walking dead, old stagers like Duke Snider and Gil Hodges and Yogi Berra who had indeed come back to New York to die. The beauty part of this, from a management point of view, was that the corpses could be re-placed every year, or almost as fast as they dropped, by ever fresher corpses such as Kenny Boyer and Roy MacMillan and Warren Spahn, all still good for at least one last twitch and a brave little stagger step, and all mouthwateringly available at 1960s prices.

For a brief glint of time, history seemed to stand still: every day at Shea was Old-Timers Day, and the museum curator in us (old-timers by now ourselves) rejoiced. But, of course it was too good, not to say just a little too dead, to be true, or even that enjoyable (as Tim McCarver might say, "Does necrophilia become necromancy when you get lovey-dovey? I'm only *ask-ing*"). The old men out there were just making *us* feel older and the little boy who lives alongside the curator in even the crustiest of us began to howl for some action by the late sixties: we wanted the feel of a pennant race once more, and to hell with these old farts.

At about the same time, the linchpin of our faith, undying hatred of the Yankees, began to come unstuck. It's unfair to blame Horace Clarke for everything that went wrong in the sixties (in fact he was probably the best of them) but suddenly all the majesty began to drain out of the Yankees and just like that they weren't worth hating anymore. That saintly bumbler Michael Burke had somehow managed to create instead some of the same effect as the Maras in football: that of a good old Irish boy in charge of a tasteful operation, which only its fans could hate. Talk about museum keepers: how could we ever hope to compete with a man whose crowning glory had once been bringing the old circus to the old Garden year after year?

With the Yankees stacked over in one corner with the dead-wood (Giants, Rangers, Columbia football, and Edith Wharton novels), the Mets began to feel their youth for the first time. Joe Namath had hit town and the Knicks were beginning to stir in their sleep and Bob Dylan seemed to be singing about all of it; and lo, the Mets were born again as a sixties team, a bit awkward at first, and manifestly unsuited to the role, but then suddenly swept away by it, as by the beat of a peace march, in the incredible year of 1969. And lo (yes, lo again), the lame could walk and the blind could hit and the old Giantdodger fan found his raspy old voice once more.

Sitting at Shea the night the Mets clinched against the Cards I felt the same unearthly bubble in the throat that I had last encountered in 1955 when Gil Hodges gloved the last out of the Series: but when I looked around for a little mindless ca-maraderie, I noticed that all the "now" people were rushing toward the field with a view to dismembering it.

Gloating wasn't enough that year, you had to rip and tear and "be me"; and it occurred to me these weren't baseball fans at all, but results fans, the exact opposite. So. "Listen, you guys," I thought to myself stonily (and entirely without justification), "I *earned* this pennant the hard way. Just tell me this: Who was it who hung in there during the bad days?"—well, not me, actually, except in the sense that I hadn't physically left town during the period, but the words had been spoken now, or mouthed. I'd been trapped into saying "I do."

And what a honeymoon it was. As the Mets alternately walked through walls and on water for the rest of the season, I can only say that I never knew it could be this good. Gil Hodges, our new manager, seemed to have the whole world in his glove this time, and if the Series had gone on till New Year's Eve, the Mets would have been good until midnight (after that I don't know).

What was easy to miss in the throes of this love feast was the sobering fact that I had fallen in love with a miracle, not a team, and that when the Holy Ghost, or Mr. Applegate, left town at the end of the year on his mysterious errands, the Mets, Jets, and Knicks of 1969 would all turn back into pumpkins, or whatever their fruit of choice.

In the Mets' case, what we saw when the moondust cleared was a slightly inferior version of what we have today; namely, a championship pitching staff attached to a second-division chassis. "Ya gotta believe," howled Tug McGraw over this gim-crack contraption, and somehow a last drop of 1969 magic was squeezed out of the old tube and a pennant was snatched in 1973, as dishonest a one as I can remember, like a second honeymoon in Jersey City.

After that, it was strictly back to paying bills and sorting laundry. It became painfully clear that M. Donald Grant, the Mets' general manager cum old sofa cushion, had simply been waiting all along to make like Wellington Mara himself, pre-siding over his very own decaying dynasty, however miniature; and in no time the Miracle Mets had come to rest at a level of staid mediocrity hauntingly familiar to New York fans, except that our equivalent of Horace Clarke was the sight of Steady Eddie Kranepool grounding eternally to second base.

And this is where true second husbandly exasperation set in in earnest. We didn't have to take this, by God. We could always become, well, Red Sox fans, couldn't we? And some of us did, but it never felt right. It's a myth that baseball fans have free will. Giantdodger fans, for instance, were never put on earth to be dilettantes, sending out of town for our baseball: we have to go with the neighborhood for better or worse, which meant in this case either the unthinkable Yankees or the old ball and chain herself, the former Miss America of 1969, who might have gone a bit flaccid and suburban on us but who still put her pants on one leg at a time, God bless her, and who at least

played in the right league—and who above all lived close enough
to boo. Only this time, she better shape up.

So we rooted for Tom Seaver, until he was taken away from
us (presumably on the principle that we were having too much
fun) and we rooted for Jerry Koosman (my all-time favorite)
and for Jon Matlack, and Tug McGraw wherever he went, and
after a while for all the souls in the Mets' diaspora, everyone
who M. Donald Grant had the grossness to trade. And we also
made our peace with the immutable fact that if you want to be
a Mets fan, you'd better like pitching an awful lot. The little
gusts of wind that once blew Joe Namath's passes about Willy-
nilly (and kept his statistics human) have made Shea the shrine
in perpetuity of the well-pitched game, and the rest of the team
will probably never, till the end of time, look quite as good as
its pitching staff.

Meanwhile, something strange was happening over at the
Stadium. The Yankees seemed to be changing once more before
our eyes—but into what? The face in the glass contorted hid-
eously and the banker's uniform began to sprout gravy stains—
but you had to have been there the first time to place the new
image precisely. What the Yankees were turning into—and I
didn't believe this myself at first—was nothing other than the
Brooklyn Dodgers of 1941! Uncanny, you say? Well, draw your
chairs closer to the fire and listen to the stranger's story.

Once upon a time, the Dodgers had a choleric owner named
Larry McPhail, whose pleasure it was to fire and rehire his
favorite manager, usually in the course of one night (McPhail
liked *fast* action). And this manager by chance happened to be
a feisty ex-infielder named Leo Durocher, who alternately threw
punches at people and tantrums at umpires, and was even, I
believe, the first to kick dirt on one of the latter as a species of
compromise between the two modes of assault. As for the staff,
the actual players, these were hired guns to a man. The entire
league championship team of 1941 had started life someplace
else.

And it was to this mob of misfits, this variorum of vagrants,
that I first plighted my troth, at an age (a perfect ten) when a

man's troth still stands for something; and ever since, I have
been plagued by a passion for slightly shopworn ballplayers,
factory seconds, guys with the luggage labels still on them—in
short, the Hernandezes and Ojedas and (sob) Ray Knights of
this world (for some reason, Gary Carter doesn't quite make it:
too pink and shiny from all that soap).

So imagine my dismay when virtually the whole French Foreign Legion began to file one by one into the wrong stadium:
Catfish Hunter, Dave Winfield, the incomparable Reggie, and
Tommy John himself, surely the patron saint of this sort of
thing, a man whose very pitching arm is store-bought. If aesthetics had anything to do with it, I'd have become a wetback
on the spot.

Except for one thing, of course: George Steinbrenner, God
bless him, who must be the best antidote to the roving eye since
pre-Vatican II nuns' costumes. Criticizing George at this point
is like punching the heavy bag in the gym: your arms get tired
before he does. So suffice it to say that Larry McPhail, for all
his lip-frothing frenzies, was a real baseball man: he hand-picked
those players himself, not because they were the best or most
expensive, but simply because, like Branch Rickey, he *saw* something. Picking and choosing among the migrant workers of the
thirties like a rag-picker sorting through garbage cans, McPhail
had already put together two crazy-quilt pennant winners in
Cincinnati before he ever got to Brooklyn, and at a time of life
when George was still playing with his daddy's boats.

In short, McPhail earned his bankability the hard way, by
working for it, while Steinbrenner earned his the old-fashioned
way, by inheriting it—and it shows in his work. A man really
prizes the players he discovers himself, and goes the last bloody
mile with them, but the ones he bought on somebody else's say-
so better be good right away, Goddammit. Thus we arrive at
the weird phenomenon of an owner bawling under his tree every
year because he didn't get the presents he expected, and the
even weirder one of fans actually feeling *sorry* for the Yankees,
as they live out their jumpy lives as characters in a *Daily Worker*
cartoon circa 1935 (and if anyone grunts that they get well paid

for it, don't they, just ask Yogi Berra, or Goose Gossage, how much money it would take to get him back to New York).

All of which adds up to a terrible game to play on the battered New York psyche. Everyone down to Maggie Thatcher knows that you can't feel sorry for the Yankees; it goes against nature. In fact, the very thing we loved to hate most about those creeps was their freedom from pain, or from any human feeling whatsoever. This was the team that, according to legend, didn't even bother to have a victory party one year, presumably because celebrating had become such a bore.

But that was before the owner began to take the air out of his own players before you could even get to them, criticizing them like John Simon if John Simon had no talent. Once upon a time, if you didn't draw the Yankees in a World Series, the whole thing was a spitback, it didn't count. One's whole object in life in those days was to see those lordly guys howl just once. But what can you do when the owner has already made them howl for you?

Dave Winfield, for instance, ought to be the perfect Yankee to hate, regal of movement and proud of face (which may be why Steinbrenner can't stand him), but all this season I have been rooting for the man helplessly; it's the only decent thing to do [this was written in 1988]. And then there's Don Mattingly, with his damn perfection—prime hating material if ever I saw it. But as I'm about to get down to business, Steinbrenner calls him selfish—next stop Mother Teresa—and my own efforts simply shrivel. I can never on my best day hate the Yankees as much as he does.

Which brings us back to the Mets one last time, and I'll try to hurry. It has been almost too easy for the Mets to be popular in a Steinbrenner town: you can almost feel the fresh air coming off the page when a sportswriter moves from one clubhouse to the other. But without the contrast, the air isn't that fresh. Too many of the Met players seem alternately overeager and bored out there, as if they weren't much interested in baseball as such but only in hitting, which they worry about *too* much—but then do stupidly anyway. But we can continue this discussion in the runway: your quarter is as good as mine on this one.

The real story is, of course and forever, pitching, and thank God we have been taught the hard way to appreciate it. In the curious highlighting of Shea with the spot trained eternally on the mound, this year's staff actually oversteps its appointed bounds of glory by fielding better than several regulars, and occasionally hitting better too.

It may feel it has no choice. Imagine working night after night in front of a specter composed of Dave Magadan's feet (when a Met hears footsteps, you can bet they're tangled), Tim Teufel's hands and Gary Carter's arm (a year later, I could have thrown in Gregg Jefferies' brain). You'd learn to field too, the way a drowning man learns to swim. And watching Howard Johnson battle the trauma of finding men on base any time he comes to bat would probably do the same for your hitting.

In fact, it's my impression from squinting into the dugout that the pitchers even have to turn to each other for conversation—either each other or Keith Hernandez, an honorary pitcher who, against all reason and precedent, actually succeeds in making first base the most interesting position on the diamond. Hernandez occasionally buckles under the weight of egghead expectation, and I'm not talking about his hamstrings but his dialogue, which can be discouragingly banal (a few hours a day with Ortega y Gasset would do wonders); but in the field, he is nothing less than a complete baseball team unto himself, a wizard who at his best can make the whole stage teem with life, like a theatrical illusionist.

It's enough. In fact, with Strawberry's swing and Doc's Sunday curve, it's almost more than enough. But I don't want a Subway Series this year. The Series is no place for emotionally troubled teams, not to mention fans. Just suppose that Dave Winfield were to come to bat with the bases loaded in the ninth inning of the seventh game (so far, so good) *and* you happen to catch George Steinbrenner out of the corner of your eye glaring at him venomously, well, could you stand it, old fan? Or might the ghosts of Walter O'Malley and Horace Stoneham rise up and darken the screen once more as they once darkened all of baseball in New York?

To end on at least a semiserious note, George Steinbrenner's many sins against baseball include not least allowing real-life considerations to enter and dominate the game. And a fan doesn't take kindly to being woken from his dreams.

So until the Yankees get an owner who is old enough to know the difference between baseball hatred and real hatred, I frankly just wish they'd go away for a while. One of the pleasures of being a Yankee-hater (in the baseball sense) is that it makes you a fan of at least five other teams in the other league, any one of which—but perhaps especially the Boston Red Sox, who break hearts as methodically as the Dodgers used to—would do very nicely for an enemy (in the baseball sense) until the Yankees clean up their mess.

P.S. When George Steinbrenner finally got the axe in 1990, I didn't know whether to laugh or cry. Did I really *want* the old Yankees back? I decided to laugh while I still had the chance. It could be years before the next one.

Mellowing Out

his began as the text of a picture book, illustrated by the fine baseball photographer, John Weiss. I consider picture books a license to celebrate, and it's possible I may have overindulged a little here. But every fan should be allowed his primal scream from time to time, and this is mine.

1. The Dream

Forget what you have seen on TV; nothing in life so far has prepared you for that first squint down the ramp—at the impossibly green grass and the golden patch of infield and the figures in white skimming across it. It is your first glimpse of perfection, and from then on even the rank smells of mustard and grade-Z beef will be transubstantiated by it, and the hum of the crowd will sound like a choir of angels, every time you enter a ballpark. And perfection only becomes more so as the home team explodes out of the dugout and the play begins.

It is a great stage set, of a kind that extracts prolonged applause from first-night audiences and, incidentally, sets certain
writers to gibbering whenever they hear the word baseball. Rumor has it (rumor, Hell—I've felt the damn stuff) that sometimes
they use fake grass these days, and that certain infields have
been reduced to white lines and postage stamps of dirt—but
not here. This writer is such a fanatic on the point that he
actually believes Ping-Pong should be played on grass too; so
there will be no Astroturf in this essay.

Because Astroturf, for all its chemical charm, is not the stuff
that dreams are made of, and baseball *is*—more so than almost
any activity I can think of. Where football dreams tend to jerk
you awake and tennis dreams can deepen your sleep to coma,
baseball is just right, not too fast or slow; monotonous, maybe,
but not *too* monotonous.

And there is so much of it. A ballplayer's life contains a million
scenes to slip into the projector, starting in Peewee League,
where our hero first hitches up his pants and learns to spit like
a professional, on up through the lower depths of pro ball where
the lights are barely fit to read by, or maybe the college ranks
where they use tin bats to save money (Charles Dickens would
have thrown up his hands at the stinginess), and everywhere
buses—not glamorous trains with parlor cars or airplanes with
stewardesses you can marry when you land, but regular, down-
at-heels, no-frills buses, bumping along exactly the same as they
did in the Depression when they carted the elite of the nation's
bums and sharecroppers to their next appointments; a means
of transport so boring and uncomfortable that you are almost
forced to dream in self-defense.

And all the dreams could probably be filed one way or another
under the words "big league": big-league baseball dreams, of
course, but as the bus grumbles its way through the night, no
doubt visions of big-league meals as well, not to mention big-
league girls in big-league hotels, and, for the pure of heart, even
a big-league house for the parents. Playing in the minors must
be something like serving as an intern in an inner-city hospital
or doing the dirty work in someone else's law office: all you

can think about is having your own practice uptown someday. And for a ballplayer uptown means Yankee Stadium, or something like it; that is to say, a ballpark you can remember even from the television snippets and not one of those anonymous sports factories that turns into a football stadium every time you turn your back.

Yankee Stadium is particularly dreamworthy because, not so long ago, the World Series used to turn up there as punctually as Wimbledon, and by the time the bus reaches Altoona, our hero is undoubtedly deep into the seventh game of some future classic. No one has yet taken a poll of rookies' fantasies, but young guys reporting for duty in the Bronx for the first time have been known to go into something like shock upon finding themselves standing where Babe Ruth stood in right field, or DiMaggio just in back of second, or Gehrig at first. (To compare lesser things with greater, I once sneaked out to center field myself as a youth to see how things looked from Mickey Mantle's point of view and felt the same tingle some people get from Civil War battlefields.)

Ballplayers have a sense of history like no other athletes, if only because baseball *has* a history, and not just a collection of famous names and faded photos. A football player has nothing to measure himself against because his game is constantly changing and obliterating its past, so that if you asked one how he would defend against, say, Ernie Nevers or Steve van Buren, he'd probably wonder who the devil you were talking about, and why.

But a young pitcher today who's so minded can easily imagine throwing to Jimmie Foxx or the Babe; we not only know exactly what their swings looked like but what kind of pitchers they hit best. And we know their statistics so well we can almost see their faces in them. Everything in baseball is recorded, down to the meanest sacrifice bunt, and the records still vibrate. When Pete Rose broke Ty Cobb's record for base hits, he wasn't competing against some antiquity or curiosity; that was a real barrier he had to run through, made of real base hits, and everyone on the field including the bat boys knew it.

Which is not to say that every major league player has a head stuffed with numbers, or is even a baseball fan. (Just last week, as I write this, Mookie Wilson, the exuberant ex-Met, was reported saying, "I could never watch that stuff, I have to play it.") Ballplayers come in many shapes and sizes. But the flakiest of them knows that this is a sport in which the word "immortality" actually means what it says, and doesn't expire every five years or so.

When Ted Williams drops in on a spring training camp, he doesn't have to introduce himself—and neither would Ruth; they are baseball royalty and always will be. And a young player might reasonably figure that if he too hopes to go down in history, he might as well know what history is. Politicians who wish to be remembered almost invariably become students of history, just to get the feel of the stuff. And the aforementioned Pete Rose probably knows as much about the past as a history major or your average U.S. president.

And speaking of Rose, the man is also walking, or running, proof that studying history is good for the soul, because it has left him with at least one pure desire, stronger even than his desire to get back in the game professionally, or to cash a triple exacta; strong enough possibly to make him a living saint if necessary—and that is his craving to be enshrined in the Hall of Fame at Cooperstown, the baseball equivalent of Abraham's Bosom or Valhalla, where the game's heroes live together forever along with their impedimenta of gloves and bats and hats.

Now there is a museum for you. If the measure of such places is their ability to bring a whole civilization to life, item by item, so that you can practically hear the crowd sounds and feel the atmosphere on your skin, then there is no more thorough one in the world than this unpretentious hideaway in the middle of nowhere in upper New York State. Although I am no believer either in ghosts or in the movie *Field of Dreams*, Cooperstown is different; I would not only expect to hear voices if I got locked in there some night, along with the clack of spikes on the floor, but would have a crisis of faith if I didn't.

So this is the pot of gold, the coronation, that lies at the end of the road for ballplayers who do their job well; and although

ballplayers—young ones at least—probably are not as sentimental as fans, slavering over bric-a-brac, everyone who makes
the big leagues has probably given Cooperstown at least a
thought. And the neat thing about it is, you don't have to be a
Grand Master to get your foot in the door; one hitting feat
allows your bat in for you, and an errorless streak can do the
same for your glove. Or you can enter as a team. Each of the
great or just plain unusual outfits has a glass case to itself, so
all you have to do is make sure you belong to one of those. Or
failing anything else, just wear an unusual sweatshirt or use a
bottle-shaped bat like the (very) late Heinie Groh and hope for
the best—nothing related to baseball is too small for the museum's generous attention.

   And finally, for those who can't even get a sock or an unusual
belt buckle in the Hall, there is still a form of immortality to
be had even by you, because baseball also has its own Good
Book, in which your deeds are inscribed forever, or at least as
long as you and print and baseball are around to care. Whether
your name is Aaron or Zwilling, whether you have been to bat
in the majors ten thousand times or just once, there it all is in
The Baseball Encyclopedia to be discovered and committed to
memory by insomniacs yet unborn. (In fact, if you change your
last name to Zyzmanski, you might even find your name mentioned in essays like this.)

   So. If the first sight of a major league ballpark is daunting to
a fan, imagine for a moment how it must look to a rookie, with
all this in front of him; the noise is deafening and the lights
must seem blinding, brighter than high noon, and the moment
he steps out there, he knows that the meter will start running
on his record, his shot at glory. One of the actors from the
movie *Major League* reported afterward that he had never experienced such pressure; and that was just from *pretending* to
play baseball, in front of a few thousand people that the pro-
ducers had rounded up to fill one grandstand. Imagine, then, a
three- or four-tiered stadium packed to the sky and roaring like
an animal. And a real Nolan Ryan on the mound. And you.

   So imagine further the unbridled glee of the rookie upon

discovering that this atmosphere actually suits him, and that this is just the place for him to be; as he trots out into the noise and glare, he is coming home and going to work all in one, and he will be checking into this office every night for a long, long time to come. "It's great to be young and a Giant" said laughing Larry Doyle back in 1912. And then, as now, he said a mouthful.

2. The Dreamers

Watch a troupe of basketball players loping through an airport sometime and you'll think you've died and woken up in Flamingo Park; turn them into football players and the scene becomes a convention of nightclub bouncers. Sharing an elevator once with a group of both types, after a party for Joe Namath, I felt I was alternately gazing up Mount Fuji and being crushed to death. And I found myself wishing that Joe only knew a few baseball players, so I could get my bearings.

In other words, ballplayers, alone among Big Three athletes, come in regular Earth-sizes that the ruck of us can identify with and dream along with. The Elias Sports Bureau reports that they are currently two inches taller than they were fifty years ago, but then maybe we all are; at any rate, they don't need to be. Lenny Dykstra of the Phillies looks as if he would fit in your pocket, yet I have seen Lenny hit impressive home runs, while his former teammate Howard Johnson hits them "over buildings," in Casey Stengel's happy phrase, with a physique that looks like precisely the national average.

Gazing round a specimen locker room (the San Diego Padres), I get the impression that the pitchers may be responsible for the extra two inches; but even this is traditional. The legendary John McGraw, on whom even movie baseball managers are based, wouldn't look at a pitcher under five feet ten inches, which would be six feet now—presumably on the same principle that used to prompt groundskeepers, before all the mounds were leveled to ten inches max, to raise the mound in the interests of a dominant home pitcher, so as to exaggerate the downward swoop of his pitches. Dwight Gooden used to look like twice the pitcher on a high mound (L.A.) than he did on a flat one (Chicago).

Other judgments vaguely attributed to McGraw, who was kind of a *Poor Richard's Almanac* of baseball smarts, were that "pitchers are not ballplayers" and "ballplayers are not athletes," and even if my memory made one of these up, old photographs would seem to bear out both propositions. Scrawny, bowlegged, potbellied—no physique was too bizarre for some of the old-timers, Ruth included. It seems as if the only way one could tell they were ballplayers at all was that they couldn't possibly have played anything else.

This is only glancingly true today. The likes of Kirby Puckett among outfielders and Rick Reuschel among pitchers are probably as eccentrically designed as ever, and all bets are off with catchers, who still reserve the right to look like fireplugs. But in general, today's ballplayers are manifestly athlete-athletes, with well-tended physiques and wholesome faces, who could easily pass for track stars or squash players and not just for the first team at McGonnigle's Saloon, as their forebears usually did.

Two revolutions are responsible for the change, the first happening forty-some years ago when baseball pretty much gave up on daylight and became a sport for night people. One by one the wrinkles disappeared from the players' faces and their eyes reemerged from their eternal squints; and they automatically began to look a good ten years younger—although a few, like Robin Yount, continue to look as if they've fought in five different wars, on both sides. (On the other hand, some also took to stumbling around under fly balls like blind men when they were obliged to play in the sun; "better," as an old Brooklyn Dodger fan might have put it, "they should sleep in coffins all day.")

The second revolution occurred just the other day, and if one had to put a name on it, I'd say Steve Carlton, with Nolan Ryan seconding. The sight of these two aging flamethrowers outliving their spans, like creatures in mythology, snapped baseball's head around on the subject of conditioning. Up to then, players had tended to view this issue with superstitious caution. "Very few injuries are caused by falling off bar stools," said Casey Stengel, who was the fountain of wisdom in residence through the forties to sixties, and, incidentally, the favorite disciple of McGraw; and the great Joe DiMaggio made virtually a fetish of avoiding exercise in the off-season, and had every injury known to man to show for it.

In those days, hunting and fishing might be okay if you were a fanatic. But weightlifting, the current rage, would have been unthinkable: you didn't need all those muscles, in fact they got in your way; and no one had yet come up with a method, prior to Nautilus equipment, for touching up muscles selectively. So perhaps the Nautilus people deserve a footnote of their own in *The Baseball Encyclopedia* for their contribution to that un-heard-of phenomenon, the forty-year-old superstar.

Sitting, or rather, standing, in the clubhouse (civilians sit by invitation only), I am struck by how much the personnel resem-ble young executives arriving for work. The fact that many of them are black seems to pass unnoticed by now, either by them or by me: in fact, I only thought about it later, because people always ask about race, and it occurs to me that the outside world has been infinitely slower to integrate than the supposedly less real one of sports.

What one does notice, though, is that the players are better dressed, in more expensive-looking clothes or even suits (for lunch with their publishers no doubt), than the guys I used to wait for outside the Polo Grounds and Ebbets Field years ago. These are not workmen clocking in for duty, but relatively wealthy young men—some wealthier than others, but nobody seems to worry about that. There is no visible class resentment around here, i.e., the rich guys do not hang out in one corner and the underclass in another, because these guys are dreamers through and through, and each of them hopes to hit it big himself someday. So Roger Clemens won the jackpot this year. Great. Maybe I'll get mine next.

The other danger that was feared when free agency was es-tablished in the seventies and salaries flew through the roof was that players with that much insulation from life's chances would dog it, subconsciously or otherwise, and this may have happened in a few cases; but it is in no wise epidemic. The Dream was never primarily about money anyway, but about playing base-ball in Heaven, and this the guys still do with the abandon of kids playing for nothing. I can't remember ever seeing more home-plate collisions than I have this past year, and you would never guess from watching these simulations of train wrecks that the legs and arms tangled up in there are worth millions of dollars apiece.

All the same, today's players are probably cooler customers than their forebears. They have spent less time in the minor leagues getting broken in to their trade, and on average, more time in college. And free agency has tended to make them free-lances, whose attachment to the team they play for is strictly year to year and renewable (though it's amazing how intense it can become in the course of a single season; a championship team is like a platoon that has come through a long war intact, buddies forever).

If they fight and scratch eyes less than they used to, it's partly because they have less riding on each other than they used to—and partly because they simply don't see as much of each other. The heat of train communication has given way to the coolness of air travel, and it's possible for a selfish player to live entirely in-side his own skin, treating his locker as a private office and his teammates strictly as business associates; and it's possible for one or two such misplaced yuppies to sink a team without a trace, or at least be suspected of it (e.g., the New York Mets in 1989).

Yet even these flowers of the eighties are nothing new to baseball, which has seen it all by now, several times over. The Selfish Player is as old as the game itself, and what's interesting is that there are so few of him these days, considering the temp-tations. After the haggling of winter has ceased and the dismal rattling of coins, and after the last agent has slunk from human sight, most of the players revert happily to type. Once they're out of their million-dollar sports shirts and into their monkey suits, you wouldn't know them from Ty Cobb or Lefty Grove or the characters in Ring Lardner, except that the pants are tighter these days, and the physiques look better maintained; these are ballplayers, a species as unmistakable and indigenously American as buffalo, and even the century doesn't matter much.

Leaving the clubhouse and entering the field, my photographer friend and I come upon a bunch of Phillies cavorting around the batting cage. Roger McDowell, the sinker-ball pitcher and world-class cut-up, is at the center of it, and McDowell has a tendency to reduce, or elevate, things to the sandbox level wherever he goes. So the players laugh as they bunt and jockey each other like frat brothers around him.

Somebody points out a lady in red who comes to watch batting practice each day, and whom they've nicknamed "the Cat Lady," and the photographer says, "I'll bet she only comes to see you, Roger." And McDowell dimples prettily and says, "Well, she's only human."

And so he is, and so are all of them.

3. The State of the Game

Every age in baseball is a golden age, and this one is no exception. Old-timers complain that players today are not as steeped in baseball as they used to be, and make more mental errors, and this may be true. Those long hours on the train and in the pre-television hotel lobby were mostly spent talking *base*ball, *base*ball, *baseball*, to the sound of train wheels and the whir of overhead fans, while the extra years in the minors were like the equivalent in violin practice; the old players were note-perfect at their craft and could throw to the right base, or hit behind the runner, in their sleep, where they sometimes were (day games left you a lot of time to play at night).

Yet the best of them probably never fielded more impeccably than Keith Hernandez or pitched more shrewdly than Orel Hershiser or hit more knowingly than Wade Boggs. If the average of competence is lower these days, the peaks may be slightly higher, as today's geniuses avail themselves of technological aids that simply didn't exist in the other golden ages. Tony Gwynn, the young master, is famous for traveling with videotapes of pitchers pitching, and of himself hitting against them, which he studies before each game (unlike some of his free-swinging colleagues, Gwynn also uses the batting cage as a lab); while Davey Johnson, the Mets manager, would be lost without his computer. A student of the game has much more to study these days, and the bull sessions between catchers and pitchers, batters and coaches, and slumping players and anyone who'll listen are correspondingly more nutritious.

But this is merely garnish. No one has built a computer that comes close to matching Casey Stengel's head (1890–1975) or Keith Hernandez' today. A good baseball mind comes with a built-in feature that computers will never have, namely, hunch capacity or the instinct that tells a great card player to go for it on this hand regardless of the data, or a manager to switch to a left-hander against a right-hand hitter—or, as famously happened once, to bring in a hungover old Hall of Famer to pitch with the bases loaded in a World Series. It would take the manager all day to explain the move, even to himself, but half of a split second to know it's the right one.

And while such accurate illuminations may actually be so rare in cards that it might be wiser to ignore them, they are the very essence of baseball, with its constant fluctuations of circumstance and profusion of possibilities. A computer might, for instance, know exactly what a given batter is likely to do in every conceivable situation—where he hits curves, where fast balls, and how both against this particular pitcher—and still not know that his bat looked slow on that last pitch, maybe from the heat wave, or from worry about his divorce (gossip helps at times), or just from thinking too much; and that's just to list *his* problems—you should hear the pitcher's.

The good baseball mind has all this stuff and more stored where he can get at it, faster than an Epson could print it out; and on the strength of it, Hernandez or Ozzie Smith or Willie Randolph moves back just a few feet—just for this pitch. When and if the count goes to three and one, or two and two, it will be a whole new ball game, and he'll have to rethink the situation (while the computer collapses with exhaustion).

Now more than ever, intelligence *is* skill in baseball, and glancing through John Weiss' cast of photographs, I was impressed by the sheer brain power he'd assembled, a veritable think tank and powerhouse of baseball cunning. Orel Hershiser's brain cells alone, when turned on full as they were at the end of the 1988 season, could light up a whole city block if one knew where to plug them in.

But I was also impressed by the sheer animal talent and pure physical skill of these particular men. No baseball fan is happy unless he gets to pick an All-Star line-up now and then, and it was easy enough to pick one from the Weiss collection—one that I felt one could match confidently against any squad from any time in the past. My only problem then and now was an embarrassment of immortals, particularly at shortstop. How in God's name does one leave out Ozzie Smith? Or Cal Ripken, Jr.? Or Alan Trammell? Or the Robin Yount of 1982? And then there was the Mike Schmidt versus Wade Boggs problem at third... okay, that went to Schmidt, but what about Lou Whitaker and Ryne Sandberg at second? Or Clark and Hernandez at first?

The one position I did feel clear about—the manager's—I now feel I was probably wrong about, and I'm glad to have a second shot at it. As it happens, Weiss had included a particularly epic portrait of Sparky Anderson looking like the Duke of Wellington as I imagine him, and I couldn't for the moment picture anyone outsmarting this man. But I, and Weiss too, had overlooked at least two men who very well might have—Tony LaRussa and Whitey Herzog. Since LaRussa has not yet passed the (quite arbitrary) test of having managed successfully in both leagues, or even of having figured out quite how National League teams play when he meets them in World Series, it comes down to Anderson and Herzog, and it's anybody's ball game.

For my money, Herzog is the more obviously brilliant but Anderson may have the better rapport with his players. So I'd rather play for Sparky, but, if *big* money was on the line in a series between the two, I'd probably bet Whitey. Anderson can win with great teams, but Herzog proved in Kansas City and St. Louis that he can win with any kind of team at all.

Sliding for Dollars:
The Split Season of 1981

*T*he *other side of the coin. The last chapter was written between strikes—and in the heart of winter—when everything about baseball looks as good as you want it to. This one, on the other hand, came right after baseball's only out-and-out strike, and could have been written again, only more so, after the lock-out of 1990. Baseball had better stop doing this, or someday the reflexes* won't *come back.*

For baseball fans, it was a tense spring training. Are the reflexes still there? Will the heart still lift with the first glint of grass (or that plastic stuff) and stay lifted through the doldrums while one's team remains eternally glued to fifth place? What about the vocal cords? Will they still groan like Pagliacci over loud fouls and snigger when the umpire gets hit in the foot and has to hop like a bunny? Or will we perhaps not bother to go at all?

The thing is, we've had a scare. After the baseball strike last year, the reflexes didn't come back, at least for some of us. The game had lost its fizz; the grass was just, if that, grass. It couldn't just be the greedy owners and selfish players, could it? In that case, baseball would have died in infancy. While the strike was on, I kept telling myself there was nothing a little baseball couldn't cure.

Just as you don't need a good priest to perform a valid marriage—any old hack will do—so, in its humbler sphere, any scoundrel who can run, throw and hit with power is authorized to perform baseball. When the players came back halfway through the season, they looked and played like the first day of spring training. But it *was* baseball.

Yet something was wrong. Maybe the strike had bitten a little deeper than we thought. After all, the players were fighting specifically for the right to leave their teams, which is perfectly reasonable but does not go down well in dreamland where the fans hang out. To find your very favorite player demanding extortionate ransom just to stay in your neighborhood hurts a fellow after a while.

Then there was the practice of naming the player rather than his agent in the endless headlines (fans will read anything). "Joe Blow demands an arm and a leg" seems to smite one right through the bubble-gum card, but it isn't an exact account of what most likely happened. Joe may not even know what he is demanding today. He has acquired an agent, because it's the thing to do, so that he can keep his mind on higher things, like warning kids off alcohol abuse and giving his money away. Unlike the old-timers who did their own haggling all winter and wouldn't give a dime to a blind waitress, today's superstars need never think of cash at all.

Unfortunately, it all seems upside down to the fan. Why leave your own team to make more money, which you're going to give away anyway? Never mind. It is the nature of agents, who are only really happy when all their clients are playing in New York and Los Angeles, where commercial opportunities tumble over each other in senseless profusion.

Still, this does not quite scratch the itch. Although the fan would probably prefer to pay less for his seat than to support the Joe Blow Foundation or whatever pious undertaking the latest free agent gives his salary to, I don't think he minds the players getting the big bucks so long as it hurts the owners enough. (The villainy of owners is a baseball tradition not to be tampered with.)

What he minds is that the concept of "team," which is a mighty act of imagination in the first place, becomes harder than ever to sustain. We've always known in theory that the random collection of out-of-towners who currently represent our city could all be gone tomorrow. Owners have bought and sold whole teams in the past, and the faith has endured. The fans themselves have to provide the glue, the continuity that makes, say, the Boston Red Sox an idea rather than just an employment office. A team's personality lives on in the stands, regardless of who's playing out there (which is why there is no such thing as a dull Red Sox team).

But it does not live on regardless of the fans. When they go, all the TV revenue in the world can't buy you back your personality as a team. And the glue doesn't exist that will make a team out of guys who'd rather do after-shave commercials than stay put in our dream.

Another trouble with last season was that the numbers came out all wrong. A home-run leader is supposed to hit so many, the RBI man so many more—and a Cy Young winner is *not* supposed to be 13–7. I hadn't realized how much one depends on these things coming out right. With our diamond-like minds, fans demand things orderly.

Which means no more double or triple playoffs ever again. Any playoffs are bad enough—they don't belong anywhere, being neither season nor Series, and their records just dangle. "So-and-so's record in post-season play" is an ersatz, anemic phrase. Other sports may exist for their playoffs, but not baseball. The season must be cut to measure, so that Babe Ruth and Hank Aaron may appear to do roughly the same thing and we can have something to talk about through the black winters.

This at least is the view of the old breed, who want an asterisk put after *everything*. Pete Rose plays eight more games a year than Ty Cobb—give him an asterisk. The last man to hit .400 did so before the real onset of night baseball—asterisks all around. Call us the last of the grass brigade (Astroturf is the ultimate asterisk), but we come in all ages. Baseball is the home of young fogies who never grow up.

But a new breed may be upon us who, still jangling from their electronic games, want excitement right now and to hell with the old numbers. The designated-hitter rule, which enables decrepit athletes to trundle on rubber legs past better men's records, simply soups up the action for these wild-eyed newcomers. The electronic mind does not fret about things like team loyalty: it would be like getting sore at the figures in a video game. Winning is the only thing.

Baseball is really not designed for such people, though George Steinbrenner is trying. But if the old-timers become disaffected, the game may have to be restructured like a hot rod to produce artificial hysteria. Players might be persuaded to fight each other every few minutes, flailing their bats like hockey sticks. Olympic sprinters could enter the game at will, jumping up and down on home plate and hugging each other. Chorus girls might carry signs announcing the number of the inning.

Right now, the Atari generation has to settle for exploding scoreboards, excruciating organ music and ridiculous uniforms. Is it enough? I know it's more than enough to depress the pants off the fogies, but does it also perform the modern miracle of making this stately sport *exciting*?

It could be that the very things that have cooled my own baseball fever and slowed my reflexes to a crawl are the heralds of a new era sweeping *me*, not baseball, into the dustbin of history. It may even be necessary to purge the old-timers in order to get the revolution in gear.

...I woke from that last paragraph sweating. Oh, Ghost of Baseball Past, say it ain't so. The rustic graces of the old game must eventually work their magic on even the savage Yankee fan. The essential game is so unchangeable that even under a ton of makeup it looks good. And it is the nature of the baseball fan in spring to be afflicted with hope.

The free-agent thing seems to be calming down, as more and more guys with long-term contracts pile up on the bench, crowding out talented kids. Baseball skill is not a fixed commodity but a continual gamble, and a scout with a good eye can still outsmart a rich myopic; i.e., Baltimore beats out most of the big spenders.

And as for the playoffs, even the owners (whose denseness is also legendary—we need it) must see that a little extra boodle at the end of the season cannot make up for the cheapening of the season. Baseball is not a set of isolated explosions like football, but a steady, timeless pleasure that builds as gracefully as it plays—and can only have one climax.

Do not mess with it, gentlemen.

Movie Baseball

A couple of baseball movies have come to town recently on the coattails of last year's hit *Bull Durham* in the timeless tradition of bad to so-so movies chasing good ones until you never want to see another of that particular kind as long as you live. In the forties it was bildungsroman musicals (or sons of *Yankee Doodle Dandy*), and in the fifties it was westerns—at which point sociologists with a license to babble declared that America obviously saw itself as a frontier once again, though all it had really seen was *High Noon* and the best of John Ford.

What it has seen this time, besides *Bull Durham*, have been several dazzling (and largely unnoticed) improvements in the technique of televising baseball that have given the game a face lift and made it worth telling stories about. And suddenly everyone is a baseball fan, including, significantly, women—which is roughly the equivalent of being allowed to trade with China for the first time, from a movie maker's point of view. Already publishers' lists groan with baseball books in recognition of this, so why shouldn't the movie houses groan too? At any rate, the "box-office poison" label seems to be up for inspection one more time.

Although they are ostensibly part of the new wave, neither *Field of Dreams* nor *Major League* follows *Bull Durham* in its true originality. The first is about baseball as myth (that old thing) and the second about baseball as joke, but neither has the breathtaking gall to deal with baseball as it actually is, in all its subtle monotony. *Field of Dreams* is actually a threnody to the sixties when all the yuppies were very young, and the yippiest of them had adopted baseball if only because it wasn't football, the Sport of Hawks; and it is told with a sentimentality that would shock Barry Fitzgerald. But it's not really about baseball, only the idea of baseball as perceived by a brief but ardent attention span. For every two minutes of catch we get an hour of talk.

In fact, the closest ancestor I could find for *Field of Dreams* was not a sports movie at all, but either *Joan of Arc* or conceivably *The Song of Bernadette* (if you want to know where the religious movies went), except that the protagonist hears voices telling him to build a shrine to *baseball*, to await the second coming of those latter-day saints the Chicago Black Sox. Among baseball fans in general, the dreamers have been gaining ground steadily on the hard hats, and this, in a word, is their movie with gossamer tassels on.

Superficially, *Major League* might be described as *Bull Durham* without the wit. The swearing, for instance, is hopelessly uncreative and heavy and the locker-room repartee lacks all the gritty particularity of our prototype; "Porky Plays Baseball" would not be quite a fair title, but it crossed my mind (I should add that after you've been slightly stunned by its limitations, *Major League* might conceivably grow on you; the pennant race has a nice rhythm to it).

However, the crucial distinction between *Bull Durham* and most of its children is in its attitude toward the game as played. Although it is a comedy, the film treats baseball itself with reverent accuracy; the Baseball Annie character (Susan Sarandon) refers to the Cathedral of Baseball (Americans can make a religion out of anything) and humor stops at the church door. Perhaps *Bull Durham* sins slightly by making its wild pitcher *too* wild at the beginning (wildness in baseball being measured in inches; it doesn't mean throwing the ball fifty feet up in the air). Otherwise, the film's respect for the probabilities is so sweeping that it actually shows two batters hitting pop-ups, a form of out almost unknown to baseball movies, in which strike-outs outnumber everything else by at least nineteen to one. (The only other pop-up I can remember rounds out the action in *Bang the Drum Slowly*, and as I recall, the dying catcher, played by Robert De Niro, staggers around under it woozily, and small wonder: he has obviously never seen one before.)

The strikeout may in fact be said to symbolize where most baseball movies go wrong. In *The Natural*, you know that Roy Hobbs (Robert Redford), the Lazarus figure who has come back from an apparently fatal shooting, is in a slump because he does nothing but strike out, and you know he's out of it when he hits nothing but home runs: his bat has no edges. And in *Eight Men Out*, when a pitcher decides to go straight, he automatically becomes unhittable; it's the least he can ask. Of the rich gray diet of bleeders and ropes and humpbacked liners that constitute the real game, a movie fan would know nothing. Nor would he begin to guess the magic chasm that lies between connecting safely 20 percent of the time and 30 percent, or between winning two games out of five and winning three. It's hard to film modulations, and baseball is made of modulations.

The Natural is a perverse movie because half of it knows better. A couple of times it actually defies tradition by showing whole sequences of plays instead of unrelieved highlights; and Robert Redford's swing is maybe the best acting he's ever done. But the film violates baseball reality in too many other ways. Roy Hobbs, the mythic hero, has no teammates to speak of, his bat never breaks, and, since he is too ethereal for statistics, we don't even know where he stands in relation to Babe Ruth's record, which was a fixation until 1961, long after this story takes place. And on and on. As Hobbs rounds the bases hem-

orrhaging from his old bullet wounds to win the playoff game
and the pennant, all I could think was, "No wonder the National
League loses so many World Series"—which was not what the
movie wanted me to think, I know, but that's the difference
between a fan and a movie.

However, a fan shouldn't grumble too much, I daresay, because the good news is that there is at last some real baseball
in the baseball movies, which previously had been as suspect as
wartime sausages. Gone, it seems, are the days when Gary
Cooper, swinging like a nervous housewife who just wants to
get it over with, could be flopped from right-handed to left-
handed and palmed off as the great Lou Gehrig in *Pride of the
Yankees* (1942). For *Major League*, Steve Yeager, the ex-
Dodger, sweated the actors until they looked like the real thing,
and for the admirable *Eight Men Out*, D. B. Sweeney actually
took the trouble to learn to swing left-handed, though pedants
might note that his character, Shoeless Joe Jackson, would probably not have lifted his hand on the follow-through. Babe Ruth
didn't, and he claimed to be a Jacksonian.

Baseball fans are pedants, there is no other kind, and it's a
pleasure to have something to be pedantic about for a change.
To wit: I noted with glee that Eddie Collins in the same movie
not only swings from the wrong side—Hollywood seems to have
a devil of a time finding left-hand batters—but is endowed with
a strong chin, which, if the real Collins had been, might have
altered the course of history. And the same Shoeless Joe in *Field
of Dreams* not only bats from the wrong side but throws with
the wrong hand, a kind of "Baseball Through the Looking-
Glass" effect.

And it isn't only appearances that have been spruced up to
the point of quibble. In *Pride of the Yankees* Gary Cooper
reaches out for a bad pitch in the crucible of a World Series
game because he has promised *two* home runs to the inevitable
kid in the hospital. In real life, of course, such egomaniacal
philanthropy would violate the game's integrity as badly as
anything the Black Sox ever dreamed of, besides deceiving the

luckless child forever as to the nature of baseball, and of reality itself.

Anyway, it wouldn't happen now. Somebody in the Dream Factory must have realized that those are real baseball fans out there, and that if you throw in the Japanese and sundry Latin Americans, you might have the makings of a market worth reckoning with. And baseball fans are a querulous, frequently apoplectic lot who are used to watching the real thing, which their forefathers in pre-television mid-America were not.

Once upon a time it was assumed that while Americans by and large loved baseball to distraction, they couldn't stand more than a few seconds of it at a time, and if you put together all the actual action from the Dark Ages you wouldn't have wound up with more than an inning or so, or less than a football game without the huddles and time-outs. The few fanatics who wanted more would, it was reasoned, come anyway, because any baseball was better than nothing; so the film was free to concentrate like a politician on the flabby center and the hostile left.

"More than a baseball movie" was what the ad always said, and for once you could believe it. More than half the old baseball films were, in fact, what used to be called women's pictures. *Pride of the Yankees* took no chances at all by being about a terminal illness, that foolproof crowd pleaser (later, *Bang the Drum Slowly* would show how to do this right, with maybe the best baseball movie yet made).

But farther down the ward you could find *The Stratton Story*, featuring a one-legged pitcher, *Fear Strikes Out*, a study in psychosis, and *The Winning Team*, in which Ronald Reagan battles double vision with the gritty assistance of Doris Day. In each case, the afflicted player has had the good sense to hook up with a woman who looks more like a trained nurse than a sex object—June Allyson and Teresa Wright being to real wives what these movies are to baseball—and together they generate so much character that who needs two legs, or even talent?

One's only consolation at the time was that Hollywood was

equally cavalier toward every occupation it touched, and William Bendix, who couldn't even manage a decent home-run trot for *The Babe Ruth Story*, was no more at sea than Don Ameche inventing the telephone or Robert Walker frowning over "Ol' Man River." Since it was understood that all professional lore is boring, we never actually learned how anyone did anything.

Finally, besides the baseball movies that were really about something else, there were the baseball-as-whimsy specimens, that feeble subdivision of baseball-as-joke. *The Absent-Minded Professor*, *Angels in the Outfield*, the pencil falls from my hand. Not that these are necessarily bad movies, it's just that there's nothing to say about them. And I find that other fans of my vintage cannot even remember for sure which of these movies they actually saw, so slight was the movies' hold on one's consciousness.

But I remember quite a lot from the latest batch, and I just thought I'd jot down a couple of items for consideration in some possible Bobo award ceremony (I prefer this to Babies) sometime in the future.

1. The Prettiest Scene—and this is discouraging right here. *Field of Dreams* shows a view of Fenway Park from behind first base that is infinitely comelier than anything the technicians have come up with so far, which might leave one asking, why bother?

2. The Second Prettiest Scene, also from *Field of Dreams* (there isn't much baseball in this film, but as Spencer Tracy said of Miss Hepburn's flesh, what there is of it is "cherce"), and also from behind first base, though this time it's a fictional scene, tells you, perhaps, why one should bother. The primal scene most fans first fall in love with is the panorama from behind first or third, so it's surprising how few movies use it, let alone dozens of other great angles that television can't even afford to waste cameras on, which might, in ensemble, piece together the whole mosaic for the first time anywhere.

3. Best Double Play. Movies love these because they convey the beauty and complexity of fielding in seconds: on the screen

as in real life, they save time. Anyway, the slickest by a hair comes in *Eight Men Out*, courtesy of the funny little 1919 gloves which make the difficult seem impossible.

4. Feast of Plenty Award. *Major League* features not only a grounder that *isn't* a double-play ball, but a carom off the out-field wall and some honest-to-God base running. Well, it's a beginning.

5. Best Blending of the Big Game With the Undulations of the Season. The rhythm of these is the whole point of baseball, its dramatic edge: in no sport are the small games so small or the big ones so big, and a movie can build to a screaming crescendo simply by tightening the screws as the games get bigger. If memory serves, *Bang the Drum Slowly* wins this one by blending its hero's concerns with the quickening of a very good, and completely authentic, pennant race.

6. Best Myth of Baseball Movie (if one must have them). Still *Damn Yankees*, by a mile. Whether he is just standing by, like Woody Allen's Zelig, or doing it himself, like Oscar Levant playing all the instruments in *An American in Paris*, the Fan wants to be where the myths are. Only this time he is allowed to be the myth himself. And the music is marvelous.

7. The Best of Everything Award belongs to the sequence in *Bull Durham* where Kevin Costner, the Johnny Bench look-alike (and no actor has ever looked more like a ballplayer than Costner), attempts to think along with the pitcher, ending with the words "quick hands, quick hands" (crunch). Not quite *Spellbound*, nor yet Molly Bloom's soliloquy, it nevertheless is something new in interior monologue for sports movies. Football and boxing should do it so well someday.

It could be quixotic to offer suggestions to a fad that may just as well be on its way down as up. At the last real movie award ceremony, *Bull Durham*, which is a good movie whatever your interests, got only one grudging nomination, reminding one that people who don't like baseball don't like it very much indeed, and that even neutrals tend to consider it a hopelessly parochial amusement, not worth bothering Telstar with on its global rounds. If westerns have gone out of style, it takes faith to give baseball a better chance.

However, baseball fans have faith to burn; they feel that their subject has a natural edge over the winning of the West, or even the Civil War, because we know how those turned out. So why not our very own *Gone With the Wind*? Only next time, no more corner-cutting (strikeouts are low budget, and look it; all the more elegant scenes in baseball contain extras) and much more adventurousness with the camera than we've seen so far. Then simply hire a film man with the historical sense of John Sayles and Ron Sheldon's feel for the game's dailiness, and tell him to shoot the works.

...And trust to future audiences in Japan and Kiev—yes, Kiev—to pick up the tab and make it worth everybody's while.

Book Baseball

*W*riting is not usually one of my hobbies—it's too much like real life. But baseball is different. When the New York Review of Books *gave me permission to review some baseball books, I took off like a butterfly collector. I was surprised and delighted that they ran as much as they did.*

It could be a coincidence, but as each of our major wars winds down we seem to become more and more mesmerized by baseball, and the cold war so far has proved no exception. To a nervous system set on high, peace can be an awful anticlimax; suddenly a section seems to be missing from the papers and there's nothing special to wait for. This is *it*, the thing you've been praying for. So what do you *do* with it?

In this troubled state, baseball seems to constitute a quite serviceable halfway house to the *longueurs* of peacetime: alternately laid back and explosive, riveting and dull, it also comes to you every day like a soap opera (our other games would kill you if you played them every day), bringing a fresh mouthful of information each time, for six mind-numbing months on end. And it bears the further overwhelming recommendation of being considered terrifically American, though this I've never quite figured: it is one of those dogmas one accepts without fully understanding.

The mere fact of books on the subject by David Halberstam and George V. Higgins, and one to come by George Will, suggests the spectrum this baseball mania cuts across. Conservatives, having done so much in recent years to kill or stun political enthusiasm in America, might be presumed to have a special interest in finding some other focus of attention, a playtime equivalent of disarmament and reconversion, but liberals like baseball too, possibly because doing so proves that they're as American as anyone else: it is like having an alternative pledge of allegiance, complete with a backup anthem that even a Bolshevik can sing along with. Ethel Rosenberg in her last days talked about her "beloved Dodgers" in what I take to be an informal plea bargain, though the poor woman probably meant it. Her fate suggests that maybe one can overrate the importance of baseball in America, which brings us to our first witness.

David Halberstam is a loud writer, he can't seem to help it. When he tries to lower his voice, it reminds one of Jiggs trying to sneak past Maggie on a moonlit night, with every floorboard betraying him. All Halberstam's effects are big, which can lead to great bathos, not to say occasional risibility, when the subject is too small for him, but he can be unlaughably powerful when he hits it right, as he did with the Vietnam War in *The Best and the Brightest.*

Nor do all his best subjects have to be quite as ostensibly major as that: his book *The Amateurs* was a small-framed study of a group of oarsmen bent on making the U.S. Olympic team, and for the occasion his hyperintensity precisely matched their own. Rowing is an exhausting, hard-breathing affair, and one sensed Halberstam's own heart bursting as he crossed the finish line, a thrillingly appropriate performance.

And even when his subject is perhaps not quite as big as he thinks it is, his heavy brooding can still generate queer and interesting effects, as in the portraits in his new book, *The Summer of '49*, of baseball's *capo di capos*, Joe DiMaggio, whose morbid shyness translated into an air of overwhelming authority, and of the reprobate Red Sock, Ellis Kinder, whose idea of prepping for a big game was to drink till dawn the night before. In other cases Halberstam seems to be beating his chops over nothing much, as when he feels duty-bound to recite the subsequent careers of every single member of both the Boston and New York teams of 1949: enough auto dealerships is enough. And in all cases, the reader has to shoulder the task of deciding for himself what's important and what isn't: the author, one feels at despairing times, would be the last to know.

Baseball is, of course, a far cry from rowing (in baseball, to breathe hard is to have failed), and on the face of it, its pleasures might seem rather understated for Halberstam's sledgehammer methods. But he has a knack of inflating things to his measure, somewhat in the manner of a March of Time newsreel, and within pages one has no doubt whatsoever that the American League pennant race of 1949, that cusp year in the reign of King Television, was one of the major turning points in our history.

And why not? My only quarrel is with the season he chooses: obviously our great watershed was the National League pennant race of 1942, as the brash upstarts from the West (St. Louis) toppled the old-money Easterners (Brooklyn and the Yankees), President Roosevelt gave baseball the green light, and the "Star-Spangled Banner" was sung for the first time at ball games (or was that the next year?)—and above all I was almost the same age as David Halberstam was in 1949 if one allows for the fact that Dodger fans matured faster in the crucible of defeat.

In other words, any number can play at this game, and so long as it is understood to be just that, a game, Halberstam plays it uncommonly well, recapturing as few of us still can the fevers of prepuberty and rephrasing them as a sharp-eyed, occasionally ironic adult (Halberstam's boyishness cohabits with a fitfully sophisticated mind: he can never be dismissed out of hand). As an old investigative reporter, he is also accustomed to drilling somewhat wider and deeper than most sportswriters, and he comes up with a richer lode of gossip. (Where else would you learn, for instance, that Johnny Lindell, the Yankee out-fielder, used to whap unwary teammates with his member as they reclined on the training table? The sports pages just don't cover stuff like that.) As for his baseball writing proper, I believe it on the whole profits from being aimed at a general audience rather than outright fans, and for sounding, if you will, just a little amateurish at times.

This may not seem like much of a virtue, but other kibitzers should make note of it. Most outsiders writing on this subject tend, out of piety, to adopt the stock phrases of newspaper accounts, as if there were no other way to describe a ball game. But the only justification for publishing books by outsiders (and I suppose for reviewing them) is to hear it told freshly. And in this respect *The Summer of '49* is a modest sort of landmark: a book by a generalist who brings his own weapons of gusto and doggedness to the event and doesn't rely on hand-me-downs (or bad poetry) to see him through.

And the result is some very satisfactory swashbuckling. A pennant race is not unlike a military campaign, so it gives Hal-berstam's fearsome concentration plenty to play with, and few specialists if any have ever done more justice than he to the variables: namely, the big game vs. the small one, the crucial series that proves inconclusive and the minor one that turns out disastrous, and all the streaks and slumps and injuries that curl their way through the season; and behind and around all this, the alternating rage, boredom, and glee of the personnel, which here includes not only the gypsies who play the game, but the alcoholic manager (Joe McCarthy) and man-child owner (Tom Yawkey) of the Red Sox, and the pixilated manager (Casey Stengel) and Scrooge-like general manager of the Yankees (George Weiss), and what seems like hundreds more. Halberstam has a voracious appetite for characters and he crams them in here with a savage excitement that can be contagious, if you feel like playing today. Otherwise, the treacherous question intrudes: all this about a *game*?

Possibly Halberstam wonders about this too, because he shows a regressive tendency to drag the outside world in by the tail in order to place the mere game in a larger context. "It [1949] was the last moment of innocence in American life," he quotes the announcer Curt Gowdy as saying, thus giving his stamp to at least the fifth date for this recurrent ritual that I've heard so far this year. Foreigners must be puzzled at how often we seem to lose our innocence around here, but it's just something we do: if we ever *really* lost it, we probably wouldn't go on about it so much (and we certainly wouldn't make movies like the recent *Field of Dreams*, in which the denouement consists triumphantly of the hero playing catch with his dad).

Halberstam's apparent approval of this inanity indicates that he isn't thinking terribly hard for the occasion (what the hell, it's only a baseball book). And this impression is confirmed a couple of other times. To wit: although the Red Sox lost the 1949 pennant heartbreakingly to a bloop hit by Jerry Coleman which left them almost catatonic with grief, he quotes without criticism Tommy Henrich's obiter dictum that the Yankees actually won it because they wanted it more, and they wanted it more simply because they were underpaid.

This, after the author has just wrung our withers describing the tattered pitching arms that had tried to bolt the door for Boston, is a bit hard to take, even from an aside. Not only does it make no sense in terms of what he has just described so well himself, but its accuracy also depends on reducing all baseball history to a single year: otherwise one is left having to suppose that the Yankees were also paid less than the Indians and the White Sox, the Giants and the Dodgers, and all the other teams they humbled in those years, and the correct phrase should read, "Rich guys finish last," a formulation that doesn't even completely cover George Steinbrenner.

*   *   *

But this illustrates one of the less salubrious aspects of trying to write baseball books for a non-baseball audience: reflexively one reaches for explanations outside the game itself—economics, character, anything will do. By contrast, George V. Higgins in *The Progress of the Seasons* attempts to explain the same enigma—what's wrong with the Red Sox, a question that every generation must answer in its own way—in purely baseball terms, and I doubt if there's a non-fan left in the house after the first sentence (although there are other reasons for reading, or not reading, the book).

(*The Progress of the Seasons* is a good elbows-on-the-table, Here I Stand kind of baseball book, which sometimes leans a bit clumsily on the new numbers racket: for instance, the attempts to collate Red Sox performance with hours spent traveling—but in that case shouldn't one first subtract the opponents' flying time, not to mention the relative jet lag caused by flying east to west? And do we really want to go on with this? But insofar as baseball is used simply as background music to the passionate reticences of an Irish upbringing, the book has the effectiveness of a small, precise truth. This is exactly how it was.)

An investigation into the relative merits of carrots and sticks in baseball might be rewarding, but it would also be technical, and a mass-market author simply wouldn't have the time for it. Such a one must pick up his major insights on the run, which may account for the slapdash sermonette that Halberstam tosses in toward the end of his book in order to give it a message it has in no wise prepared us for or earned.

> Those five championships [1949–53] marked both the dawn of an era and ... the end of an era as well. [The Yankees'] failure to sign blacks brought with it a penalty so severe that not only would the Yankees' dominance end but the American League by the late fifties and early sixties would become a lesser league.

Now while the second half of this thought may squeak by as a fairly respectable truism (although Hank Greenberg maintains in *his* book that the American League owners were "imbeciles" across the board, race being only the half of it), the first part, the bit about the death of the Yankees, surely cries out if anything does for the kind of mordant analysis that Halberstam would have brought to, say, the causes of a war or even the rise of the *Los Angeles Times* (but how seriously is one supposed to write these books anyway? and how seriously does one review them?). As it stands, the sentence reminds me of a coda attached, as I recall, to the movie *Spartacus*, to the effect that the slaves' revolt marked the beginning of the end of slavery. What the coda didn't say was that there was no point holding one's breath for the end itself: at that point, slavery still had nearly two thousand years to go.

So, too, the Yankees after 1953* would go on to win another nine pennants and four championships in eleven years, before collapsing into the arms of CBS and Mike Burke, who could have lost with the Negro All-Stars. Right now the Yankees have a profusion of black players and nothing special to show for it—almost as if it made no difference.

In his rush to slap a liberal moral onto his tale, Halberstam has scanted one of the most remarkable phenomena of American sports history, to wit, the uncanny ascendancy of this one baseball team from 1921 to 1964, in a sport whose checks and balances and susceptibility to pure chance would seem to render such a thing impossible. "Yankee luck," we used to call it despairingly. And as I read again of Jerry Coleman's wretched bloop hit that fell in to end the chase in 1949, I felt the same pang I'd felt as an infant when Mickey Owen dropped the third strike. Halberstam mentions earlier that although successive

---

*The year is artfully chosen: if the subject is to be the Yankees and the black factor, surely we have to start counting from 1949. But if one makes that post–1953 instead, it works out that the Yankees "only" went on to win four more championships out of nine. Even so—no other (non-Yankee) team has ever won that many World Series in that short a time in the entire history of baseball.

Yankee teams were known for their bombing and murdering, their real secret was pitching and fielding, which suggests that at some point he may have had the real story in his grasp, only to let it slip away: why *did* those things happen to the Yankees?

In this same brief lapse of concentration—too brief to damage his book fatally—Halberstam may also have missed a possible chance to advance the question of race and sport maybe another inch or two. Blacks already dominate basketball and to a lesser extent football, but so far they don't quite dominate baseball, and significantly liberals, whose preferred stance is that race makes no difference in sports, seem to sense that there must be something wrong about this: voices have recently been raised against the New York Mets for not hiring enough blacks, even though the Mets are conceded to have the most talent in baseball with what they've got. Clearly, the Mets, like Halberstam's Yankees, are riding for a fall, sometime in the indefinite future.*

If only because of the unholy length of the season, assembling a great baseball team is as tricky as casting a play, and the best of them do not necessarily contain the best athletes. And what's mildly frustrating is that Halberstam seems to know it. His discussion of "Yankee pride," which the older ones passed on like samurai to the new recruits, is so acute that it's a pity to see him lining up for even a moment with the fraternity of social scientists in missing what is under his nose.

Surely it must have occurred to these people who are paid to think about such things that the current boom in baseball interest might conceivably have something to do with the fact that it is not dominated by blacks. But if it *has* occurred to them they would no doubt put it down to a collusion of racisms between owner and fan, and let it go at that. Yet surely the actual message of the Yankees and Mets, as opposed to the approved one, is that white boys and girls can still hope to win something in this life, and that perhaps it is even plausible for them to dream of succeeding in this particular sport themselves.

---

*Probably sooner rather than later. Free agency and the annual baseball draft have rendered the construction of dynasties, white or black, almost impossible now. All the same, I wouldn't bet that the old Yankees couldn't have done it.

Baseball *feels* like something they can play with the best, football and basketball don't. And if that be racism, it's a very pure child who isn't afflicted with it to at least some small extent.

But have blacks any edge at all in baseball? So far the people asking this not particularly pressing question have proved much more entertaining, and instructive, than the question itself, because the subject reveals a classic split in the pants of the liberal (and I use the word here in its humorous sense) sensibility. On the one hand, liberal dogma has it that all races are created athletically equal,* and that hence any apparent edge of one over another must ipso facto be temporary and artificial, if not downright illusory; but the tradition has it that the black man is forever being kept from reaching his true potential, so that hence, and equally ipso facto, black athletes must really be even *better* than they seem, and we'll worry about the "edge" another time.

Two current books represent the respective trouser legs of the dilemma. The first, *Necessities*, by Philip Hoose, comes dressed in a cover featuring a black man chained to a basketball, which should tell us, I suppose, where the author is coming from: this will be *libéralisme noir*, in which even having fun will turn out to be a cruel joke ("tote dat ball, block dat kick"). For all I know the author may be right: there may indeed be a dastardly white plot to keep blacks from being quarterbacks and major league catchers. But if so, and if they start to outnumber whites at those positions too, mightn't—and one almost hesitates to ask—that mean that they're simply *better* than whites?

Not necessarily. In *Blackball Stars*, a useful little book about the old black baseball leagues, John Holway executes an entrechat on the subject that would make a Jesuit proud. Having unearthed the apparently crushing statistic that in exhibition games played between 1900 and 1950 professional black teams

---

*Before one makes any more fun of the sports egalitarians, it could be argued that over the years they've been more right than wrong and that their far-fetched assumption that anyone can do anything has proved surprisingly fruitful and one of America's glories. The danger now is that by imposing their will on the evidence, they give the impression of being afraid of it, as if admitting that blacks are better at one thing were tantamount to calling them worse at something else.

beat professional white ones 268 to 168, he first crows about it for a moment or two, then seems to recollect himself and backs off politely, leaving the white man a loophole to crawl through.

"But," he writes,

> even granting the argument that the whites could have won more if they had really wanted to, then one must wonder: How many more? Twenty more? Thirty? Fifty? If they had won fifty more than they did, they would have won 218 and lost 218. Could they still argue that the blacks were not their equals on the field?

Assuredly not: because they would then be *perfect* equals, and we would be in liberal heaven.

But in the more or less real world they didn't win fifty more, and we're left with the number, which just sits there, one of those rocks of fact that sport casts up for theorists to scamper around as best they can.* Athletes, for their part, know what they know, or at least say what they think. The all-star line-up of the black outfielder Dick Allen consists quite persuasively of seven black players and one white (Mike Schmidt), who "is the baddest white boy I've ever seen play the game"—in other words (unless there's some other way of construing this), he plays just like a black.

Baseball, it will be noted, gives one ample opportunity to talk about something else if you'd prefer, and Dick (better known as Richie, a name he hates) Allen's book *Crash* (with Tim Whitaker) may actually be more interesting in its tangents and grace notes than in its story proper. Although Allen was known as a free spirit in his playing days (1963–1977), his opinions here seem quite studied and sly, and, if my reading is a fair guide, reasonably representative of the latest protocol in sporting race

---

*Before a white supremacist can retort that what makes a big leaguer a big leaguer is how much he learns from each encounter, and that the whites would probably prevail if the races played each other more regularly, I suggest we all fall as silent as Galileo until the subject is declared fit for honest discussion. On a recent TV special about race and sport, Tom Brokaw declared that it was almost impossible to get scientists to testify on behalf of genetic explanations: which, TV exposure being what it is, suggests a wave, if not of fear, then of unprecedented timidity.

talk, which seems right now to permit blacks to be slightly more bigoted than whites, so long as they don't go overboard.

To wit: Q. "Do you think the black ballplayer and the white ballplayer share a similar work ethic?"

A. "As a rule, the white and the black ballplayer work equally hard. Difference is, the black ballplayer only lets it show when it makes good baseball sense." And more to the effect that whites show off (example—only example—Pete Rose), while blacks (except for Reggie Jackson) never do—a harmless if cranky enough opinion, but a white athlete probably wouldn't allow himself even such modulated bigotry as that. (Blacks are too laid back, too elaborately cool? Forget it. If you allow a race to have any characteristics whatever, you are felt to be opening the floodgates.)

In a similar vein, Allen states flatly that "the black ballplayer is the innovator in sports," which sounds like a promising topic for an all-night debate; but Allen gets no debate from his white coauthor, or straight man, who merely asks meekly, "Why are the black athletes the innovators?" Which in turn gives Allen a perfect chance not to boast. "When you are poor," he says, tipping his hat to the sociologists, "you have to improvise your time." And if he believes that's all there is to it, then he's the baddest black liberal I've ever heard.

Dick Allen, in short, is obviously a bright man who eats polite interviewers for breakfast, but the ease of this makes him condescendingly slapdash at moments. For instance, in *Crash*, he passes on as if for the first time the accusation that black athletes are always called "naturals," and never given credit for hard work and intelligence, an observation which I thought arresting the first time I heard it, but which has since been so well circulated that even the dullest redneck probably wouldn't use quite those words anymore.* If someone like Allen wants to

---

*The charge that everything comes easily to them has dogged graceful athletes for as long as anyone can remember, and one of my own earliest memories is of Joe DiMaggio wearily defending himself against it—perhaps on behalf of all Italians. But it could be that blacks have been picked on once too often with this compliment. In which case, salvation may eventually arrive from the direction of basketball in which

pursue the thought to its latest hiding place, he should at least break out a new phrase for it: cleverness may be easier to play than baseball, but it makes *some* demands.

On the other hand, another of his haymakers may land a little closer:

Q. "Why does baseball have such a hard time dealing with free spirits?"

A. "They don't—only with the black free spirit."

And before one can say there he goes again, he illustrates the point quite convincingly with the case of one Alex Johnson, who seemed impenetrably surly to whites, but was apparently a sweetheart *in camera* with blacks; and one thinks quickly of other cases, where the colorful black "character" strikes whites as slightly too ominous to be amusing—and in this one might include Allen himself, although discerning whites tended to find him a congenial exception to his own rule.

What Allen seems to have trouble deciding, in his own case and maybe the other blacks' as well, is whether being misunderstood is altogether such a bad thing or whether perhaps it might not simply be the mark of a superior man; and one senses that he would like to keep both the grievance and the pleasure he got from making white men sweat a little over it, as they tried desperately to figure him out and placate him. Certainly nobody ever got more mileage out of being misunderstood than Crash Allen, turning up for work drunk or not at all, and harboring curious ailments that only he could cure, to the fury of his coworkers. Managers had a way of catering to him, to keep on his good side ("You don't treat a man with the baseball skills and intelligence of a Dick Allen like an ordinary baseball player," says one of them) even as he sneered at them for trying to "handle" him.

But although sometimes this game of wits was obviously fun, at other times our hero seems to be just plain lost in his curious

---

Bill Russell, Lenny Wilkens, Isiah Thomas, Magic Johnson, and countless others have always been prized expressly for their intelligence and craft.

situation and improvising rather wretchedly. Allen's sweet-sour predicament, whiplashed between too much love and too much hate, too much praise and too much contempt, underlines one of the peculiar irritations of any black star's life, namely the lopsidedness of the attention he receives. Allen passed his first baseball year, 1963, in Little Rock, Arkansas, just in time for the vicious death throes of Jim Crow, and from there was moved to left field in Philadelphia, which was reputed to be an even more primitive cauldron in those days: the White Man never did anything more vicious to him than putting him in front of the Phillies bleachers, and perhaps no amount of pampering could ever make up for the cretinous abuse he heard out there.

But things did get better, and he lived to receive a standing ovation from those same bleachers, and he seems still at a slight loss as to what to do about the improvement. "I want you to walk in my shoes," he instructs his white coauthor, but most of the time his shoes sound pretty good, particularly to those who haven't had to stand in them on a rainy night when the cabs won't pick him up after, perhaps, a banquet in his honor.

Dick Allen was simply not a clock-puncher or drudge, as the great record setters have to be in the night-game era, but he did quite enough to establish for all time what he *could* have done, which is more than can be said for most of us, whatever our profession; he always had as much character as he wanted to have.

Beyond that, one senses that he is willing to play along, up to a point, with the liberal expectation that he turn out to be yet another victim of racism (blacks have been accused of doing that a lot lately, but some white audiences make it irresistible), but only insofar as it enriches his accomplishment. Any attention is sweet when you're retired. But at one point he quits dancing for a moment and admits that he mightn't have been half the player he was if he'd fit in better. "Somebody," as he tells it,

> once said to my brother Hank, "If Dick had gone along, instead of bucking the system, he could have had 700 home runs and a

.400 lifetime batting average." And Hank answered, "If Dick had gone along, he might have had 100 home runs and batted 220."

To which he adds, "I'll go along with that."

That sounds about right. Although it probably isn't what he had in mind, his quirky little book actually reflects a period in which race may have ceased once and for all to be an excuse, unless whites start using it someday from the other direction.

For another angle on bigotry, from another time, consider Hank Greenberg's *The Story of My Life*. Even more so than Dick Allen, who was raised in a comparatively integrated town in Pennsylvania, Hank Greenberg grew up not knowing that there was anything funny about him; being a Jewish kid in the Bronx was no big deal in the thirties, and young Hank added to that cushion of confidence the extra dose that goes with being extra-large physically, always the quickest if not the best answer to bigotry.

Later, as he rolled triumphantly through the big leagues, hitting fifty-eight home runs in his best year, two short of Babe Ruth's record, that same height and width would give Greenberg the serene air of being above the noise, a giant harassed by pygmies, and the type of impregnable hero that every minority craves. But as Dick Allen reminds us, it's usually a mistake to think that things come easily to anyone. Big athletes have been known to feel more rather than less vulnerable, as if more of them were exposed, and as if they might be missing something up there. Greenberg's triumph was his complete mastery of his large frame: the same command system that enabled his brain to move his hands at the lightning speeds of baseball told him, more slowly but just as decisively, how to deal with social situations; and the same doggedness that kept him practicing until it was too dark to see taught him how to put even anti-Semitism to good use.

"I found it [anti-Semitism] to be a big help," he writes:

Many times during a long season...you had an inclination to kind of drag a little bit. Whenever I was having a bad day... somebody would yell out from the stands, "Come on you big Jew, can't you do better than that?" Or something to that effect. It would always hit me like a cold shower. It would make me angry, but it would also put me on my toes again. Just *anticipating* a barb from the stands did the same thing.

That last sentence surely has to be the last word in positive thinking. Instead of dreading the next blow, put it to work before it even lands: it was no harder than mastering first base or learning to read the pitchers, both of which Greenberg had done by sheer application, as if the game were played in Carnegie Hall. And the obvious corollary was that the moment anti-Semitism stops working, stop using it. "Don't ever use the term 'because you're Jewish' if you don't do well," he told a young Jewish teammate—not because the term is never accurate but because pouting over it is such a waste of a good insult, which "should be more an incentive to be successful."

Unfortunately, the same qualities that made him a great ballplayer make Greenberg an inadequate chronicler: having consigned useless anti-Semitism to oblivion, he has trouble remembering it at all, and, since the perpetrators usually can't remember it either, we'll never know for sure how much he was up against, which would've been fine to him: like Jackie Robinson, he did not wish to be remembered as a saint, but as a great ballplayer—that part, he *did* insist on.

However, one episode perhaps gives us some idea of what we're missing—a scene on a team bus involving a fight between Hank and the pitcher Rip (for R.I.P., as I write this) Sewell: Greenberg gives one version of the fight, and Sewell gives another, but only a third party, Billy Rogell the shortstop, actually recalls the word "Jew" being central to it. "It always starts with that Jew thing again," Rogell told Ira Berkow, the skillful editor and coauthor of Greenberg's book. And perhaps that "always" can stand in for Hank's missing memories.* For his part, the great pragmatist was content to insist, with some truth, that the gentiles were equally rough on each other, while preserving the code of *omertà*, or manly silence, about the rest, and incidentally making the world a safer place for Sandy Koufax and other Jews.

Greenberg's book also suggests in places that he may have had the defects of his virtues: he tended to be tunnel-visioned and stubborn, and a slow take if life sent him a pitch he hadn't seen before. Since he had been given so much grief over being Jewish, he did his occasional best to find out what this thing was that he was, but he never got very far with it. Religion remained for him something that people went to war over, a source of nothing but friction, and certainly it had been in his case; but one somehow wishes the noble creature could see beyond his own stall.

Since he never quite knew what Jewishness was, Greenberg was also quite at sea with the nuances of anti-Semitism, most especially with the anti-Semites' fixation about Jews and money. Throughout the book, he recalls with relish and at length the ferocious bargains he drove with the Detroit management over his salary, blessedly unaware that the Jew who would ingratiate himself with rednecks must appear to be *less* interested in money than they are, at least in his memoirs, where it's easy.

As it is, management had a ready-made weapon to use against him when they were ready to release him. In 1946, he asked for deferred payments on his income in order to lessen the tax bite, a maneuver already common in business but new to baseball, and they either misunderstood or pretended to misunderstand and in any event conveyed indignation over it. "Maybe they didn't like Jews coming up with such ideas," writes Hank, as if it has only just dawned on him, but I think he misstates

---

*Curiously enough, Dick Allen also reports next to no racism from his teammates, but you never can tell with Allen. Although he is no stoic in other respects, he tells *his* coauthor, "I'm not telling stories about my teammates," so we can't be quite sure with him either. But since half of his teammates and opponents were black anyway, it seems safe to assume his worst troubles began where Greenberg's ended, outside the ballpark.

it. If my reading is correct, they *loved* him to come up with such ideas: it was just what they needed to get a popular hero out of town while he still had some value.

Today's pioneer is tomorrow's mossback: not long after leaving Detroit Greenberg became an owner himself and began to bargain just as hard from the other side of the divide; and Al Rosen, the young Jewish player who was about to go through the same cycle and become management himself, describes how Hank was at his new sport. Rosen had done prodigiously well one particular season, but that winter "when I walked out of there [Greenberg's office] I felt like I had had a bad year. He reduced me to ashes. It was absolutely devastating."

One shudders to think what Greenberg would have had to say to our next author, who also happens to be today's champion at financial thumb-wrestling: Orel Hershiser, the muscular Christian who pitches baseballs and products alike with the unflagging enthusiasm of a missionary. A lifelong user, so he tells us, of Johnson's Baby Shampoo who recites hymns to himself between innings, Hershiser must be about as far from the foul-mouthed tobacco chewers of Greenberg's day, or even Dick Allen's more recent one, as you can get; yet at the bargaining table he is a tiger to their tabby cats, and as such a haunting symbol of the Reagan years, family values, profit motive, and all.

"The Lord wanted me to bargain as hard as I could," were his approximate words after he had extracted his latest contract, worth $7.9 million for three years' work, from the Los Angeles Dodgers. The Dodgers had already offered him, as I recall, a mere $7.6 million the day before, but the Lord must have told him there was more money in the room, because at that point he allegedly threatened to leave Los Angeles altogether and peddle his wares elsewhere. Yet when he got the 7.9, he admitted he hadn't the faintest idea what to do with it: he had just wanted to realize his market potential, and here he was, stuck with all this money.

In such cases, modern ballplayers usually add that the lower offer "wouldn't have been fair to my family," but in this instance, we find a player apparently willing to uproot said family from friends, schools, and any hope of having a hometown, and take them to any city, however dismal, in the U.S. or Canada, which will raise his fee from one unimaginable figure to another; willing also to perplex the hearts and minds of countless small fry in the Los Angeles area who might have trouble grasping the fine point of principle that obliged their hero to do it. (Even if he was only bluffing, he was at least letting them *think* that he held their affection cheap.) In the arch little book *Yogi*, Yogi Berra describes having lunch (not a free one I trust) with Milton Friedman. But Friedman obviously met the wrong ballplayer.

What differentiates Orel Hershiser from a score of other scheming athletes of the day, aside from the fact that he does it all himself and can't blame it on his agent, is that he doubles on the side as baseball's showcase Christian, the good example pious people juxtapose most often to that of Pete Rose, the infernal riverfront gambler. Yet Pete, for all his sins, once had a whole city full of fans willing to die for him, while it's hard to imagine what combination of cities would die for a transient like Hershiser, if he ever starts making good on his threats.

There would be no excuse for flogging Orel Hershiser further than that (although he who would be an example should be prepared to take his lumps) if he weren't so representative not only of Reaganism but of much of born-again America. He is obviously a model young man with a curious but admirable detachment about possessions: one feels that if the Lord instructed him, as He instructed the rich young man in the Gospel, to sell all he has and give to the poor, he would do so without a whimper; it's just that he receives other instructions.

No doubt, the Bible being what it is, profit-minded born-againers have long since compiled their own arsenal of texts, telling them in sum to keep what they have and double it. And no doubt also, Hershiser in particular will gladly obey the unarguable command to charity and in fact already has. What is striking is that he can think of no other gesture, no symbolic act, witnessing to his Christianity, be it even so simple as bargaining with the Dodgers to lower their ticket prices so more kids could get in, and to hell, for one shining moment, with free-market mechanisms.

In a theology, deduced from Hershiser, the only gesture left is precisely and entirely being a good example—but of what, besides keeping your nose clean, he doesn't say. The ultimate kernel is obviously just too private to pass on, and Hershiser's public Christianity boils down feebly to high-minded self-help, someplace between auto-suggestion and kissing the Blarney stone. And there it all sits until such time as concupiscence about money is again seen as at least a slight character blemish, not to mention a menace to society—and curiously hard to give up (smoking is a snap in contrast)—and that Christianity might conceivably have something to say about this.

And if this takes us almost too far from baseball, it is only where the players have taken us themselves. Try talking baseball with some of them these days, and they'll come back quick as a blink with God-talk: it seems that the Man Upstairs practically hits the curve ball for them nowadays, so technique doesn't arise. Nor does the Man Upstairs desert them at contract time, at which stage He helps them in very much the same way: not to get what they need, but strictly to beat the other guy. Hershiser wanted that 7.9 in order to be the best-paid pitcher in baseball, and in that sense it was only play money, and it becomes pompous to bring Christianity into the matter: the players probably have more fun getting it that way than Ivan Boesky ever did (unless, as seems possible, he played in the same spirit), though they'd probably enjoy it even more if they had to dive for it or wrestle each other.

All that Hershiser files sternly away under the rubric "business decisions," which he keeps as separate from real life as a mafia chieftain at a daughter's wedding. In real life, he has co-hosted a quite passable baseball book, written, as such books always used to be, for a bright twelve-year-old who might, in this case, want to learn what it's like to pitch in the big leagues and then, more specifically, what went through the author's mind, ball-by-ball, as he pitched to the Mets in the 1988 National League playoffs. Hershiser's astonishing string of sixty-six scoreless innings last year seems to have been a mental prodigy as much as a physical one, and no doubt a vivid example of Christianity in action. "Do what thou doest." I've read a great deal worse during my recent immersion in this stuff.

Meanwhile, back in real life, baseball itself has spent the past summer spinning a story far better, and closer to literature, than any of the above. The endless, timeless showdown between Pete Rose, who bet on anything that moved, including his own team, and the late Bart Giamatti, the baseball commissioner, arrived by stages at the kind of drama that perhaps only our two slowest pastimes, baseball and the law, still have time to stage. Pete Rose is a classical figure in baseball (even his face is old-fashioned): the eternal roustabout who takes the game's natural properties of slyness and bluff home to bed with him and elsewhere. Rose represents the baseball of hidden balls and stolen signs and bean-ball wars and his natural habitat is the second decade of the century, a period which the magisterial Bill James, the baseball philosopher, classifies starkly as "a Decade Wrapped in Greed," and his author is Ring Lardner. Bart Giamatti, for his part, was an *echt* baseball fan, whose love for the game was almost too pure for this world, and whose author, I am tempted to say, in this case, is Giuseppe Verdi. At any rate, Giamatti's final sentencing of Rose could easily be turned into an aria in a tragic opera: both men had the stature for it.

Failing that, the clash of these two mortal rivals for the hand of baseball is at least the stuff of books, and needless to say books under both their names will be appearing shortly. Rose's will presumably tell his side in the case, but Giamatti's (posthumous) volume, *Take Time for Paradise* (even the title sounds like an epitaph), will surely tell about his love for sports—which I guess was *his* side of the case. It will be nice to be reminded of his extraordinary presence just a little bit longer.

Outtakes: Computer Baseball

*A*t that point the meter ran out at the New York Review of Books—*they couldn't very well devote a whole issue to baseball; but I had barely gotten started.*

There is surprisingly little of the actual experience of baseball in any of the books I've read lately, even those co-written by ballplayers. Hank Greenberg in particular gives one the impression he would almost rather be talking about something else, as if he had already *done* baseball, at least the playing part (the structural part still rouses him slightly). I actually met Greenberg once, at a book party for James Kunen's *Strawberry Statement* (which should have told me something right there about yippies, yuppies and the future of baseball); and even then he stolidly deflected questions about his old sport by talking, most earnestly, about the latest version of the crisis in education. And I thought, ho hum, another renaissance ballplayer; but looking back, I don't think he was showing off. He lived (like Fred

Astaire) entirely in the present—an unpromising vantage point for a historian—and I now have the haunting feeling that he was modestly trying to learn from *us* that evening.

At yet a further remove from a bibliography of witnesses lie the sabermetricians, who deserve an article to themselves, though possibly not here. Technically, the term is supposed to cover anyone involved in baseball research, but usage has narrowed it to the numbers people, those whiz kids of the computer generation who have fallen head over heels for the sheer numerability of baseball and the eternal clash it presents between the actuarial and the human. As Stephen Jay Gould has argued, a coin being tossed would undergo streaks and slumps eerily similar in length and frequency to those of a hitter with a .500 average. But suppose the coin *knew* it had just come down heads six times in a row, what then? All baseball can tell us for sure about this is that the coin would quit shaving or changing its socks until it came down tails, because that's what streaking players do; but beyond that the game can only answer, like the book of Job, with further questions.

Because out on the mound is another coin wrapped up in its own numbers, not to mention a sore shoulder and a paternity suit, and around them both the moods of weather and the crotchets of the stadium, which has its own lists of probabilities. One can imagine a computer lighting up like a Christmas tree at the variables: compared with old movies and comic books, here is a fad it can really sink its teeth into. In the same spirit, America's current passion for turning absolutely everything into a potential Ph.D. thesis has already begun to cast a lecherous eye on baseball and its succulent inheritance of trivia, and one can only tremble for the sport, as one does for literature at the approach of a structuralist.

Fortunately, and before baseball disappears completely beneath a welter of printouts and scholarly monographs, a prophet has already appeared to show how both the math and the information explosion can be put to good use without sacrificing the Ring Lardner verities. I have a theory about Bill James which happens to accord nicely with the current shadows-in-the-mist, baseball-as-myth, *Field of Dreams* approach to baseball: namely that somebody made a wish and brought back William James who, reborn under a suitably casual name (and can brother Hank be far behind?), has returned to find that baseball now qualifies as a bona fide variety of religious experience, not to mention the only game in town, even for philosophers.

However he got here, James the younger has already generated quite an industry, at first a one-man one as he started to churn out his annual *Baseball Abstracts* back in 1977—virtuoso prodigies of analysis which are to other stat books roughly what Dr. Johnson is to the latest Merriam-Webster: eccentric, personal, *written*—but lately an industry of imitation as well. *Total Baseball*, for instance, seems to be essentially a James book without the genius, or, at least, the quirks, and the annual *Elias Baseball Analyst* is another, while yet a third actually calls itself *Bill James* in big letters *Presents the Great American Stat Book**, although it is entirely the work of apprentices, as one might announce a painting "from the studio of" Rubens.

What distinguishes a James copy from an original is that the copy would be lost right away without its numbers whereas James wears his so lightly that you barely notice them, but can skip them like footnotes. In fact he has just rescued from the morass of enumeration a perfectly serviceable collection called *This Time Let's Not Eat the Bones*, and if it isn't quite James at his best—he needs *some* numbers, if only to lighten his occasionally oppressive personality and one's sense of being trapped in a phone booth—*Bones* displays something perhaps unique among baseball books, the spectacle of a first-class mind fully occupied with a sport, something a nonbeliever might still consider plain impossible.

---

*None of these are books at all in the serious sense of the word, so there was no occasion to go into them any further in the *New York Review of Books*, but each has its own virtues, and the Elias Sports Bureau is a resource that even the crustiest numbers-haters must find useful, if only because baseball is made of numbers. Come to think of it, baseball numbers are the *only* numbers I have ever really cared for myself and baseball stat books are the only books containing charts and graphs that I have ever been able to read.

Although it isn't so rare to find a first-class wit so occupied, the same nonbeliever might also have trouble with Thomas Boswell's splendid *The Heart of the Order*. Can such a clever man really find all the range and depth he needs in what Scott Fitzgerald once described (in an essay about Ring Lardner) as a "boy's game, with no more possibilities than a boy could master, a game bounded by walls which kept out novelty or danger, change or adventure"?

Yes, he can, it seems, quite nicely; and even if the cake he cuts into again and again is no bigger, in Fitzgerald's further phrase, "than the diameter of Frank Chance's diamond," at least there is always plenty of it, hot off the stove, and unlike most humorists, Boswell never seems to run empty. In these curiously trivial times for Americans, baseball probably has more *to* it than most of our other universal subjects, such as either the celebrity culture or the superficialities of electoral politics; if one can weigh anything so light, Boswell seems not only infinitely funnier, but also to be doing something more important than a satirist of Beltway ephemera such as Mark Russell.

But he has his limitations. His liking for the designated hitter rule, for instance, indicates that he is a pure spectator, and nothing but: no one with a feel for the game as played as opposed to watched, or even managed, can abide the dh rule.

Bill James is a bit of a humorist too, in a hit-or-miss sort of way, and it is very much part of his overall, all-fronts attack; no (baseball) knowledge is alien to him and in his magnum opus, *The Bill James Historical Baseball Abstract*, he stages a bravura display of all of it: not only the numbers, but yellow-press items such as who drank the most and who was the ugliest and even who killed himself and why (as if the all-American game could use a few shadows), along with such more Toynbee-esque matters as where the players came from—Irish in the 1890s, midwestern Germans in the 1900s, Southerners in the 1930s, and much more—and who wrote the books and made the movies that touched on baseball, and on and on.

As a century-plus of "novelty and change" goes clattering

through James' book, Fitzgerald's judgment begins to seem almost provincial, a mere recital of fashionable prejudice. And one can almost picture (while we're reincarnating people) the susceptible Scott "discovering" baseball if he were alive today, as he once discovered Hollywood; it would suit him much better than the Marxism he grimly thought he should do something about in the thirties, and he already had the perfect title for it: forget for now Frank Chance's cake and Ring Lardner's cloister. The image he was subconsciously looking for all along was "The Diamond as Big as the Ritz."

This kind of antic conjecture would be very much of a piece with Bill James' all-the-world's-a ballpark approach in the *Historical Abstract*. While most of his investigations are considerably more business-like and specific to baseball than that one, there is always an air of "your guess is as good as mine" about it, as if he doesn't *want* baseball to become a science, or the discussion ever to end.

As if to ensure that it won't, he gives much more weight to contemporary consensus on old teams and players than most pure scientists would care to, even allowing the tradition to roll over his numbers on occasion—e.g., we *know* that Joe Gordon was better than Bobby Doerr, because everyone thought so at the time—but then worries that he may have given it too much weight in, say, the case of Jackie Robinson, as if he is almost begging the class to state its own opinion. Where other sabermetricians seem to be sealing the game off in the manner of scholars, James opens it up like a teacher.

By letting in the tradition, James also lets in vagueness and life, as if the historian in him were playing a game on the accountant, and all the other accountants, by flooding their worksheets with unclassifiable new data. What are we to do, for instance, with a fact that he overlooks himself, namely that Satchel Paige, who had at various times faced Ruth, Gehrig, Foxx, everybody, called Charlie Gehringer "the best white hitter I ever faced?" Or what about the comparatively late induction of Pie Traynor into the Hall of Fame? James infers from this that the Traynor legend was something of an afterthought, but

I am just old enough to know for *fairly* sure that it wasn't (I heard Traynor talked about reverently the first time I opened my ears, in 1940), and that Hall of Fame inductions, like all-star selections, can be quite inscrutable guides to the past. The uncertainties of historical truth allow everyone with any memory at all to take a whack at the subject, while it allows James to throw away his mortarboard and be as pigheaded as a barfly.*

"Sabermetrics is not numbers" writes James, "sabermetrics is the search for better evidence," and he conducts the search with a mixture of boyish eagerness and Aristotelian thoroughness that might almost cause one to accept baseball's importance the way a bright believer can cause people to accept religion: if it's good enough for *him*...

Such is his sense of mission that he even pauses occasionally along the way to chivy his fellow huntsmen for sloppy thinking or inadequate research. But with all the chivying in the world, it's unlikely that any of them will ever match the originality of James' studies pertaining to such abstruse but crucial matters as the true effectiveness of walks and stolen bases, or to the history of platooning, and much more. Like Hemingway's famous Indian girl, James simply "did first what no one has done better." Unlike the new notaries, who treat baseball as if it had been born in a record book, with the field functioning as a species of lab where experiments are refined, and the archivists, who tend to lose the game's pulse altogether and its necessary vulgarity, James actually writes, accessibly, about the game we thought we knew.

So having begun this marathon discussing books written by generalists, let me conclude by recommending just this one, written by a specialist, to generalist readers, if only because it

---

*If I had been writing this for a baseball magazine instead of the NYRB I would have picked quite a few more quarrels with James, for example, his curious double standard about the old Sportsman's Park, depending on whether he's talking about Rogers Hornsby or Stan Musial; or his rather glib dismissal of the "baseball is 80 percent pitching" theorists (his statistics do not form a fine enough mesh to test the proposition one way or the other). But that, as indicated, is half the pleasure of reading him. Like a good assertiveness trainer, he jerks you out of your seat and almost obliges you to holler something back at him.

reveals so clearly the heart and mind of a fan, suitably enlarged for examination. *The Bill James Historical Abstract* is clearly the work of one who has poured so much of himself, so much pure energy, into the game of baseball that he gets back from it pretty much whatever he wants in the way of life and color and intellectual exercise, which is only what all fans do, only more so.

Bill James is Everyfan, taken to extremes, and his big book, his *Summa Baseballica,* may be the best key now available to what people see in the sport, and to why the current generation of eggheads actually flaunts its love of baseball instead of hiding it as their forebears did. Once recommended as a means of saving low-lifes (like Babe Ruth) from a life of crime, baseball in its new incarnation might now be just the thing to keep young geniuses from spreading computer viruses and starting wars with mischievous messages, proving itself more than ever all things to all Americans.

One disturbing note, though. In a fascinating book called *You've Got to Have Wa,* Robert Whiting reports that the Japanese consider baseball "typically Japanese"—no doubt as Japanese as sushi and fatherland.

I find I have nothing to add to that.

Aspects of the Game

SPRING DAYS AND GRASS ROOTS

*T*he National Anthem seemed to go on forever. And before that, I thought that the line-ups would never end, either; it was like a reading from *The Domesday Book*. Finally, the announcer boomed my name. "Give it all you've got, Bill," he added loudly.

I reached back and fired—only to find that the baseball had stuck to my hand, glued there by stage fright. The thing jerked down and away, like a dog slipping its leash, and the catcher made a graceful stab of it off his shoelaces. My limp thirty-foot effort may have been the weakest ceremonial first pitch since Herbert Hoover: but at least I had thrown it in organized baseball.

The setting was a minor league town where, as in many a town just like it, baseball is being rediscovered on a folk level and even writers get to throw out the first ball. As far back as the sixties, baseball was confidently pronounced dead—and worse than dead, non-linear—mostly by people who didn't care for it anyway. It was too slow, old-fashioned and hopelessly stuck in its ways: in short, a fuddy-duddy, the *Sunset Boulevard* of sports.

Baseball is still, triumphantly, all of these things. Yet this spring, it comes bursting from the pod once again and balls and bats will pop up (and out) like crocuses, in prisons and retirement centers, schoolyards and publishing houses. So what happened? Where did the Death of Baseball theologians go wrong?

One must as always look first to that blank, suspiciously innocent face in the corner of the living room. Television right off did two dubious things to baseball: it made the game rich and it made it ugly. At least it made baseball rich at the top. The bottom could only pray for some trickle down. When the tube first appeared, the game's popularity, on a local level, headed for its death.

On screen, an infielder's throw suddenly shrank to twelve inches, tops, and so did an outfielder's. Balls left the bat in one picture and came down in another—where they'd been in between was anybody's guess.

Football, with its population-intense line of scrimmage actually looked okay in a box. But baseball without its distances was a pitiful, helpless dwarf. A child raised on the old TV game might well draw a picture of it with a pitcher standing practically on top of a catcher-ump-batter (all one blob) with no one else in sight for now.*

Still, such as it was, enough people watched it anyway to wipe out absent-mindedly a host of minor league ball teams, in one of sports history's greatest blood baths. This was really rubbing it in. It seemed that people wanted to see the best, however shrunken and deformed, and after a while, they forgot baseball had ever looked any other way.

Major league ball has a reserved seat in the American psyche

*TV baseball has improved so much over the past few years that it is easy to forget just how ugly it was at first. In fact, I once used the phrase "the missionary position" to describe the unvarying alignment of pitcher and catcher on the old screen. But those times were so different from these that the phrase was cut from my copy as indecent.

and can probably survive anything. The biggies are the city on the hill, the great good place, paved these days with actual gold. Nobody ever dreamed of growing up to play Class AAA ball, but even in the days of radio, boys in Alabama and the outback yearned for the Red Sox or the Tigers or whatever name they'd heard first.

It was wonderfully abstract. Kids from Brooklyn became Giant fans; I, billeted in Philadelphia, became a Dodger fan (one had to do *something* in Philadelphia) just in time for Mickey Owen to drop the third strike and break my heart, which by now is patched over like a wartime baseball. And we knew all about each other. Yankee fans were snobs, embryonic bank managers; Giant fans pressed their pants sideways. Whether we went to the park or not, we had enemies everywhere.

The passion feeds on itself. Baseball is basically a machine for producing statistics anyway, and doesn't even need a season after a while. The hardened fan can rattle on happily through the winter. The cell of deep thinkers I belong to dwells in the past, batting around names like Joe Vosmik and Doc Cramer as if they and their numbers still counted for something. Simply as a religion, baseball could live on indefinitely underground.

But a game cannot depend entirely on its fanatics. The swing voters cannot amuse themselves forever cackling over old bubble-gum cards. They need actual seasons and some real games.

Unfortunately, there is no full-size baseball for them to compare with the wizened television version in many areas. The TV game must by nature remain a montage of disparate events, to which the live game remains the key. Take a Martian or just a run-of-the-mill foreigner to one and see for yourself. TV is an acquired taste at best; the real thing, if it's going to work at all, is love at first sight.

For years, Little League baseball kept the live game alive, but only for the players and their loved ones: it was not pretty to watch, except in Taiwan. What was needed for full recovery was a resurgence of classic grown-up hardball. And this the minor leagues are now scrambling to provide.

Minor league ball is not bad and, at times, is comparable to the very best. I stayed in my sample town of Utica, N.Y., for two games, and the first of them was flawless, a gem anyplace. The second would have disgraced the old New York Mets, from my lamentable first pitch on down (if only the guy hadn't said, "Give it all you've got...").

Inconsistency, of course, is why they're here and not there, in Podunk and not Yankee Stadium. Some of the guys I'm watching might be ready for the bigs right now, but even some professional scouts can't tell for sure until the ante has been raised slightly. Just about every single-season record in minor league history (and some of them are whoppers) was set by a nonentity: or rather by a gifted ballplayer with one weakness. It doesn't show. A hitter doesn't look any less graceful because he can't hit the inside slider.

And meanwhile you have those magical distances back, along with the bazooka throws and the breath-catching fly balls. And you have something else. For anyone who believes that baseball was born in a big-league stadium, the small-town casualness (at least in the towns I've seen) brings balm to the spirit. You are tethered to no particular seat. The usher, if you can find her, doubles as business manager and anything else that needs doing, though she always has time for a chat.

On beer nights, you wander with the gang to that end of the field. Otherwise you watch a bit behind third and a bit behind first, until you have a panascope of the game that television is still striving for. The mood is strictly county fair, with the loudspeaker reeling off an endless list of raffles and lucky winners. The inevitable female camp-followers, or "Baseball Annies," are on hand to check the talent, but they are startlingly young and fresh-looking, and when they make off later with their pink-faced prizes, and with a merry squeal of tires, you feel sure they're heading for ice cream and nothing but ice cream.

However, if not, not. You've had a mellow evening yourself, and let the world do what it likes. This could be the real Middle America at that, as far from book-banning as it is from downtown vandalism. After a last bite of *cordon bleu* hot dog (why do they taste so great outdoors?), you race the flickering stadium lights (which were never that strong to begin with) to the parking lot—where, so help me, you find one of the young athletes still playing pepper with some small fry.

The game is still fun at this stage. At the unaffiliated rung of Class A, the tension hasn't rolled up yet. For some guys, it's just a nice summer job in the open air; for others the big leagues are a crazy long shot—so long that they can afford to horse around while the wheel spins.

So far, the great minor league boom has not quite happened, although growth is strong and steady, hitting a peak in 1983, pausing for breath in 1984. Recently Bob Arum, a promoter with a nose for the action, has been heard to speculate about buying a franchise, and Arum is never far off the scent. At any rate, a grass-roots resurgency of live baseball could not be better timed. The mega-money that now flies routinely around the Golden City has rendered it more remote from real life than ever.

Droves of free agents have made it pitifully clear that teams, cities and fans mean almost as little to them as they do to owners—so why should they mean so much to us? It seems a bad deal to break your heart over some guy who has declared a passionate craving to leave your neighborhood, your very presence, as fast as his lawyer can carry him. And even the dreamer in the outback may begin to wonder why he should plight his troth to any one team when he might declare himself a free agent and choose a new one each year.

For minor league fans, it must be frustrating to lose their best men, but a pleasure to watch the precious few make it, and an unadulterated pleasure to root in a place where you can be heard, where a wisecrack may get a laugh from across the field, and maybe even break up a player or two as well. It is intimate theater, cabaret, and if you don't like the show, you can always thrill to your own performance.

American, no doubt, but not cartoon American. The paint peels in the locker rooms and the shower stalls would wring a complaint from a guerilla leader or a nineteenth-century English schoolboy. All is transcended by the joy of the game. The park

itself is ramshackle, halfway between a sandlot and a super-
dome, a child and a man. The guys hope for better but they've
seen much worse. Baseball below the top is gloriously shabby,
the backside of America that we don't show to the neighbors.

Little League has been much maligned, as being far too organized and parent-dominated. But as a kid I would have given
my Wally Moses and even my Arky Vaughan bubble-gum cards
for such organization. The way it was then, we used to spend
the best part of Saturday trying to scrape together enough players just for one o'cat, and when you finally had them, there was
no place legal to play. The rare diamonds were all booked in
advance by the CYO and the PAL and other goody two-shoes
operations.

Parent-dominated we did know about, but Little League only
flushed these parents out, it didn't invent them. Some of them
were pretty scary at that—fathers who heckled their own kids,
mothers who demanded to know why their Willy wasn't allowed
to pitch every inning—but it was probably good to get even
these creeps out of the house where we could see them.

My son played in Little League, and even the bullies looked
smaller and paler in the sunlight and who knows—maybe the
presence of other grown-ups may have civilized a few of them.

There is a diamond chain running from PONY League
through Little League to Babe Ruth (which gets you through
age fifteen), and after that, American Legion to eighteen or semipro where available, and at last some colleges that teach baseball
as seriously as they teach football; then on to various degrees
of minors and finally the brass ring itself, toward which the
whole chain strains; and blessed are those who follow it all the
way. Or even part of the way. A guy who's played one game
in the pros is like a former state senator, a big man in most
neighborhoods, and any saloon, as long as he lives.

But suppose you just go bumping along the bottom all your
life, playing pick-up softball with fellow physical defectives?
Well, life can be sweet at the bottom, too, and there's always
plenty of room there, with leagues beneath leagues, for infants,
old folk and just plain incompetents. And if you can't stand all

that organization, you can simply organize a *disorganized* game, as we have in my neighborhood. Wherever you wind up, you will find yourself with better equipment and less menacing surfaces than we had as kids.

The only thing we did prove for good in those deprived, pre-Korean glove days was that Americans will stop at nothing to play with a bat and a ball: stickball, stoopball, wallball—every alley and cow pasture dictated how you played there just as imperiously as Fenway Park. For bats, everything from broom handles to rolled magazines (excellent for libraries) was pressed into service; as for balls, the great Paul Waner learned to bat by striking corn cobs, whereas the current National League batting champion, Tony Gwynn, worked out against a soxball, i.e., a sock rolled tight inside a rubber band. In the wartime forties it was a melancholy rite of spring to watch the season's ball start to unravel. You could shore it up for a while with tape, but the tape weighed like lead and could easily break the season's bat. We played on grimly with the remains.

The true zealot wants his baseball with him everywhere he goes, even to bed, where he can play it electronically on the ceiling, or by inventing his own private league (as in Robert Coover's classic book *Universal Baseball Association Inc., J. Henry Waugh, Prop.*) or by phoning a fellow addict for relief. But for the average citizen, simply trotting out onto the spring grass, and maybe backhanding a grounder and flipping it, and bathing one's ears once more in the immemorial chatter—"Only takes one to hit one," " 'S'lookin' 'em over," "No pitcher, no pitcher"—will do.

To such a fan, an American summer without those sounds would be as empty as Rachel Carson's silent spring. Those piping chirps of "A walk's as good as a hit" are like crickets in August. Where do they go in the winter, anyway? Some fly south, others disappear into the closet, where, I suspect, fans mouth them silently as they pound their mitts.

But right now the voice of the umpire is heard once again in the land, the ducks are on the pond and the goose hangs high.

The season isn't over till it's over, but the clichés can already beat you a lot of ways. If the mark of a grand passion is that you can love it even when it's kind of dumb, then baseball wins out by inches, one game at a time. Baseball is pre-eminently the talking man's game and who cares, or even notices, if the conversation is sometimes awesomely dull?

The big-league mystique totters on, because it is existentially necessary, as we used to say at Ebbets Field. Without it, the whole diamond chain breaks. The big time is the vision of heaven that keeps the peasants toiling cheerfully in Waterloo, Iowa, and in your own backyard. And even the nonbeliever bends his knee to the World Series.

But if the simple pleasures of loyalty and team spirit are not to be found at the top—except among winners and on a one-year lease—they must be sought a little lower down. The biggies will always be loved and returned to for their icy perfection. But for everyday comfort and satisfaction, there's a lot to be said for the game next door.

AUTUMN, AND OUT

Why God chose to divide his creation into little baseball fans, football fans, and mystery of mysteries, hockey fans, is not altogether clear. Each of these and other sports comprises a very limited series of actions, or restraints on action—things you can't do and places you can't do them—so that the effect on nonbelievers is not merely indifference but tooth-grinding boredom.

Stripped of its particular grace, each game is reduced to numbing repetitiousness. Batters swing, football teams huddle, strings swish. Over and over and *over*. If you don't like it the first time, you probably never will, because it usually gets worse, not better. Conversions to a sport are consequently rare and frequently superficial, hammered out hastily in the furnace of love. Do not trust them any more than promises to raise the children Catholic [this was written for *Notre Dame* magazine. For *Commentary* or *Christian Century*, I might have phrased it differently]. Sex-inspired enthusiasm is a social disease for which you can pay a lifetime.

Every sport has its own hook and lure designed for the right mouth, and taking its sweet time is a big part of baseball's come-on. The clock has been blasphemously promoted in both football and basketball to the role of leading man. Before the twenty-four-second clock and the two-minute warning, spectators could pass whole minutes at even those games without knowing the time, a blessed condition. There's quite enough time in real life without dragging it with us into our stadiums. Speaking of which, am I alone in noticing a steady shrinkage of functioning public clocks and clocks you can see through store windows? If so, *all* Americans may be on the run from time, racing away from the clock.

In which case there is no better refuge than a ballpark. Because baseball not only has no clock, there are moments when it seems to have no calendar either and time under the blue vault simply stops. Not only does the season seem to take forever, but each game takes its own sweet time joining the season. In fact, the games go on twice as long as they used to in the Age of Leisure, to accommodate the swelling volume of chewing, scratching and good hard thinking, as if all concerned were afraid to wake up. No real fan wants the game speeded up a jot: in fact, the purest of us actually treasure each meaningless mound conference and operatic stalling device. Once again, the futurists fall back baffled.

If every final out is a little death, the end of the Season is the real thing, especially for the young fan who isn't used to it. The long shadows, the sudden cruel bite in the warm air, the newspaper scudding across the infield untended as two teams battle it out for fifth place—that's mortality, that is. And you know it before you're old enough to know what mortality is. It's sad enough when they roll back the baskets in the school gym or uproot the goal posts, but in each case you know there'll be another sport along in five minutes. A kid walking home in the cool early twilight knows only that the earth has died.

"I'd rather be lucky than good" as Lefty Gomez, the whimsical pitcher, used to say. And in the matter of timing, baseball
has been very lucky. The long hot summers of North America
demand a cool, unhurried game to offset the temperature and
baseball just happens to be there, so artfully intertwined with
the season that to the fan they are identical (just ask one where
he was in July '73 or whatever, and he'll work it back from the
World Series of that year. So every October marks the end of
another summer romance).

The game is lucky in other ways.

Even in terms of romance proper, and even when the weather
turns nippy, baseball has a lot going for it. In football and
basketball, affairs come to the boil, or expire much too quickly:
even in the stands you are racing the clock. But everything about
baseball reminds you to take your time; and if it doesn't work
out—well, the game is still there, bobbing along beside you
keeping you company like an old hound dog, or a friend who
knows exactly how to distract you. Each day the standings
undergo a delicious little shudder all along the line—half-game
down, two up in the lost column; a favorite hitter drops six
points, picks up five; Pete Rose extends his hitting streak on a
disputed call. You only have to attend one game to set the scene,
to get the dimensions right and remember how high those flies
are and how long the throws, and you can play the rest in your
head.

We may not like time, but we do like our numbers, because
they jiggle the imagination with every move. Robert Coover's
book *The Universal Baseball Association,* in which an accountant fantasizes a flesh and blood league from rolls of the dice,
was a prophetic text for this generation of the Fan: because we
all fantasize no lesser prodigies every year from numbers in the
sports page. In fact there are sheer numbers fans who care as
little about the game as played as stock-market freaks care about
IBM.

The World Series is the only possible end to all this. In the
crispness of autumn, the game gathers its wooly wits together
and sharpens up like a fall sport. Suddenly it is not the Season

but the game that counts. The judicious juggling of pitchers through the long months, so that you'll always have a left-hander for Yankee Stadium and righties for Fenway is compressed into an inning-by-inning, hitter-by-hitter, pressure-cooking crap-shoot. "We'll have all winter to rest" is the ominous phrase they use, and it strikes a chill in the heart. The World Series even looks elegiac. The sun is low in the fielders' eyes, the hitters peer from the shadows.* Starting pitchers shred their arms in relief, lazy outfielders stir themselves like crocodiles and go hurtling after balls they usually wave at. My first hero, the sainted Pete Reiser, even tried once to disguise a broken leg (and succeeded. He was walked intentionally, and his pinch-runner Eddie Miksis scored, on Lavagetto's famous double). Everything is flung into this last mad fray before the Long Rest.

"Well, it still looks dull to me," say those who have hardened their hearts. But could they possibly be right? After six months of this stuff are you still really interested in seeing one more pitch fouled back into the stands by one more batter? Or are you just being carried along for the last lap by the same electric energy that causes even the glassy-eyed celebrities who swipe the real fans' seats during the Series and keep the noise (and comprehension) level down to seem to enjoy themselves a little? One has a duty to feel excited.

But is that all there is? This brings us at last to the bats and balls, which for some are enough in themselves: like Dr. Johnson kicking the stone, we refute the heretic thus. But even perfection palls, and the unearthly elegance of baseball can take on a red shoes quality, as if the dancers only go on because they can't stop. The trick, as with other temptations, is to keep your mind occupied. One possible line of thought out of many that keeps away *accidie*, the Noonday Devil who whispers "it's only a game," is the vexed matter of guess-hitting.

It seems that the current quality of pitching, especially relief pitching, has driven all but the greatest, the Rod Carews and

---

*In the current reign of night games, these phenomena only still occur at such times as a West Coast game is piped into Eastern prime time. Otherwise you can tell it's autumn by the fact that the fans have on overcoats and the players seem to be freezing.

Ted Williamses who can read the spin all the way, to guess-work [I've since learned that Ted guessed too]. Pitchers have natural patterns, scramble them though they may, and it is up to the hitter to sense his man drifting toward the familiar, inside, outside, fast ball, slider, round and round. The pitcher, being a canny fellow, may even lull the enemy with such fixed sequences in the early season, only to alter them slightly like off-rhythms in verse when the chips are down.

Hitters seem to have great instinctive memories. A pitch they got in May will stick in the mind all season. The pitcher has to be more systematic, forcing variety into his work like a mathematician in search of a random number, and then keeping variety itself from becoming his pattern. A batter's mechanical flaws are subject to endless revision, because he gets so much free practice from pitchers trying to exploit these flaws. His one incurable weakness is the unexpected.

Is any of this true, or is it just the mad accountant at it again? Fans in their aeries must themselves resort to guess-watching. The infield moves at the last second, giving the hitter late-breaking information—but can he trust such information? Meanwhile he takes a fast ball right down the middle, his body still aching for the curve that never came. These lunges, hesitations, loud pulled fouls are the clues a fan must sift through. The true arcanum of the game is sixty feet six inches long; the rest is evidence and explanation. The way a ball is hit describes precisely the way it was pitched, and the fielder's exertions measure how far the pitcher's plan has gone wrong: in a perfect world they would never move at all, like Atari figures. The called third strike is the ultimate mental victory and proof positive of how far a particular hitter is sunk in guess-work.

The longer you watch, the more you fancy yourself entering this holy of holies, where every twitch on the cap tells a tale and every pause is pregnant. Make-believe perhaps, but it's all yours, to holler about as you see fit. You are an initiate-of-one. The true fan knows what he knows. He has gnostic insight into a pitcher's stuff, and needs no mound conference to confirm it. He is two jumps ahead of any manager who ever lived. He is also a heller to argue with, and a bad man to sit next to, unless as often happens he is too proud to talk.

Between such madness and know-nothingism there is much room to gambol: perhaps a little thinking, a pinch of mindless excitement, a stretch of serenity as the white figures move crisply over the gleaming lawn and the sun stands still—you have all season to work on your inner game. And then, of course, all winter to rest.

What Money Hath
(and Hathn't) Wrought

his may be the only baseball piece ever to appear in The Nation. *Hence the emphasis on class struggle, dialectical materialism, economic determinism—and their ultimate subordination to the percentages which rule baseball with the iron whim of a pagan god.*

The 1980 World Series was supposed to feature the spoiled millionaires of Philadelphia versus the enlightened millionaires of New York. I don't know what sort of millionaires they have in Kansas City—this was written before we received the definitive answer in 1989: "overpaid" ones. But money and the modern ballplayer has been the talk all season, even when the lads fall to fighting over beanballs. (Nobody that rich wants to be hit in the head, goes the reasoning.)

Thus the Yankees put up with the bully-boy ravings of George Steinbrenner because they can't afford not to. New York is such a lucrative playground, in TV commercials alone, that Steinbrenner can chew out the help with impunity. Philadelphia apparently does not cast quite the same spell, so there the players chew out the manager instead. The question the World Series was *supposed* to answer was, which is better for you, to chew or be chewed?

The Series we got did suggest that perhaps these are not baseball questions at all, but messy fallout from the gossip culture. The Phillies were supposed to hate their manager so much that they might well lose four straight, or whatever it took, just to spite him. The Kansas City Royals, who, it seems, only mildly dislike their manager, should have cashed in on this quirk of brotherly love handsomely—everybody else has, who's had the good luck to encounter the Phils in October, by which time they must be a ball of seething hate.

Yet when the blather had cleared, one team had made sixty hits and the other fifty-nine; one team (a different one) had outscored the other 4.5 to 3.9 per game—which I believe comes close to the average score of all ball games played anywhere since the beginning of time. In short, the verities triumphed over the froth of the press. Baseball is so finely calibrated that the super teams win three out of five, and the dogs two out of five. It is not the least surprising to find two teams with exactly the same records after *160 games*. So a series between *any* two big-league teams could be close. Yet in a World Series, these percentages fly out the window and everything is supposed to come down to character, as if ballplayers were prisoners of their nerves, like the rest of us. Arnold Palmer once remarked that laymen who talk about "choking" under pressure have no idea how many things can go wrong with your golf game besides fear. However jumpy he may feel, a professional athlete can call on a reserve of sheer skill, as a musician can: e.g., you don't praise an Isaac Stern performance because the house was bigger than usual that night and he didn't trip over his shoelaces in fright.

The salient neurological factor about this year's Series was that *neither* cast had been in one before. That took care of the stage-fright margin, or old Yankee edge. Maidenhood is everything in these matters. Yet while everyone else talked about

money, the players themselves talked about character, as millionaires are wont to do. The word must have a special meaning
for them. Because as soon as a team begins to win it *believes* it
has character. Just let a couple of lucky hits fall in and the guys
will say, "Yeah, we're that kind of team." The rhythm of streak
and slump is so wild and unfathomable that the men riding it
feel compelled to assert some kind of control over it. Contrariwise, in defeat the players "get down on themselves," search
for scapegoats, question their own character. "We *proved* we
had character," said the Phillies. Obviously. To win *is* to have
character.

Morale also is more a function of winning than a cause of it,
but it's a necessary function. It prolongs the streak from six
wins to seven, and picks up the junk game that could go either
way, that magical third game in five.

There are some teams that sin against the Holy Ghost and
reject the energy that victory brings. The Phillies were felt to be
one of these, like the Red Sox. Pampered by country-club own-
ership, went the talk, they could not rise to the myth of team
spirit, the sense that the Collective can somehow coordinate its
private streaks and slumps to squeeze the extra game. Too rich,
not hungry enough, injury prone (injuries strangely are no excuse: character is supposed to thrive on them); teams like the
Phillies are the pouting villains we need for our annual play-in-
the-round.

Yet give one of them a hot hand—the Red Sox in '75, the
Phillies last month—and you'll see who's pouty. Philadelphia
did all the things rich brats are expressly supposed not to do.
They came from behind four times in a row, counting the playoffs. Outfielder Bake McBride, the brat of brats, turned his
orneriness into pure menace, treating the enemy as if they were
his manager. Shortstop Larry Bowa, the team cynic, started
seven double plays (a record) and cried with joy when it was
all over. Pitcher Steve Carlton, who won't even talk to his
friends, popped his fast ball so hard that the catcher's mitt
sounded like a bat. (I've never heard this effect before.)

Perhaps the best symbol was third baseman Mike Schmidt,

because he seemed to personify defeat, almost to anticipate it, *without* being obnoxious, a more evolved mutant. Some dismal playoffs in the past had made him a loser in a Sartrean sense: i.e., *first* you lose, *then* you are a loser, you have defined yourself.

Yet suddenly he had his touch, and he seemed like a different man. And one realized how much one's concept of a team is a problem in perception, or propaganda. Because all the Phillies looked better in victory. For instance, that surliness in the clubhouse—was that really because they were counting their money, or was it because they just don't like reporters, the old-fashioned way? Being civilized to the press is often the only clue we have to these guys' personalities, and it isn't a bad one. But ballplayers from the outback can be unduly disturbed the first time they see themselves misquoted or laughed at in a big newspaper. (And what kind of a man would do that for a living anyway?) A team, like an administration, is as lovable as its press corps makes it.

Baseball is pre-eminently the country game, because it takes up so much space, artificially transposed to the city where strangers boo you; the suspicious, uncommunicative rube has graced every clubhouse since Ring Lardner. In fact, you can probably find Steve Carlton himself somewhere in Lardner, right down to the hideous grimaces.

One of baseball's charming legends has Whitey Ford of New York City playing Henry Higgins to Mickey Mantle of Oklahoma and practically turning him into a boulevardier. Pete Rose struggles to perform the same task for the Phils, but it's tough work Higginsing half a squad. And of course the black styles of resentment practiced by McBride and Garry Maddox were undreamed of in Lardner, and will presumably have to be resolved outside the clubhouse.

As to those miserable objects, "today's kids," who allegedly can't stand discipline from an old-school manager—what about yesterday's kids, the Cleveland crybabies of 1940, or the Dodgers of '43, one of whom (Arky Vaughan) flung his uniform at Leo Durocher's feet? Ballplayers, rich or poor, have always been hard to handle—it is one of the few real tests of great managing—and a flinty-eyed brute like Rogers Hornsby had as little luck with it way back when as he would today.

On second thought, has anything changed as little as a major league ballplayer, unless it be the game he plays? Babe Ruth holds a mirror to the 1920s, and the Gashouse Gang might be said to reflect the Okie spirit of the 1930s. But it's a weak reflection. You might have guessed from the hairdos in the 1960s that *something* was happening in America, but what?

You can't deduce much about an era from its ballplayers. Solitary men in a solitary game, they make their way one by one into the big leagues and out again, always slightly to the side of normal society. The team spirit they invoke so fervently is always ad hoc, always this gang this year. Their teammates while they last are closer than family, but they are always being ripped apart and replaced. No wonder some players are withdrawn, and others full of empty good cheer. A barmaid in Lindells of Detroit told me that ballplayers were the stingiest and least friendly of all the athletes who traipsed through the place. Yet there are the Tug McGraws and Pete Roses who thrive on the change and uncertainty of the gypsy life, and who can briefly ignite the rest—as long as the rest are winning anyway.

Team spirit in baseball follows the percentages, it doesn't cause them, though it can quasi-mystically keep batting rallies going (or is it the rally itself that creates the spirit?). This Series came down to Willie Wilson's strikeouts and Willie Aikens' stone glove, and all the character in the world couldn't have done a thing about that. If Wilson never plays another Series, he will become another Mike Schmidt, a loser; if the wheel spins right, he will become Mr. October II. He will still be the same player, but he will look different and a new type of legend will form around him.

Otherwise, chalk up a small one for the brat who chews, and file this World Series away under "arrestingly average." Nineteen eighty was the year the percentages came back in the guise of melodrama: in other words, it was baseball at its purest.

2

The People

◇

Aristocrats

KING DIMAGGIO

*D*on't look round!" my wife said, and for some reason she didn't have to explain herself. With the same uncanny anticipation that marked my subject's work in center field, I already knew who it was back there and what I had to do; and like a million fans before me, I swiveled my head and gawked through the window at Joe DiMaggio, who seemed to be heading into our restaurant, in company with the regulation blonde. I can only report that he gets out of taxis beautifully.

In the most literal sense, they don't make heroes like that anymore—heroes whose aura you can feel through the back of the neck. The great diminisher in the living room has seen to that. If you compare, say, Don Johnson with Clark Gable, the TV guy looks so small and disposable: you don't have to climb over people's knees to get away from him. And DiMaggio, whom many Americans never got to see at all, was in some ways even more awesome than Gable.

Unlike Gable, he had actually *done* something. After an era of flagpole sitting and dance marathons, his record fifty-six-game hitting streak was a feat of endurance that really meant something, and for a couple of precious months it burst the confines of sport and almost upstaged Hitler himself on the national screen. I remember careening around our village on a June afternoon in 1941 asking strangers, "Did he do it?" Even the ones who didn't speak English knew who *he* was: "Di-Maggio" was one of the first hundred words immigrants heard on arrival.

A Rose by any other name may smell any way it likes, but the DiMaggio mystique would be unthinkable under a different title. In radio days a man's name counted for something—it was, somehow, a bigger part of him—so it helped enormously to have one like DiMaggio that people seemed to like to say, and even sing, for its own sweet sake. The song that year went, "Jolting Joe DiMaggio . . . we want you on our side," and it fit right in with "Mairzy Doats" and "Zip-a-Dee-Doo-Dah" and other mantric songs of the forties that simply made you feel good. Thus, in parts of the country that had never seen a big-league game—everything south or west of St. Louis, and lots else besides—DiMaggio's name *was* his fame.

There was more to it, of course, than just a hitting streak and a pretty name. Something about DiMaggio grabbed the imagination and made you want to tell other people about him right away. In 1936, even before he came east from San Francisco (which was still an event then, like crossing the Atlantic), his aura preceded him, as it did when he entered restaurants. "Wait till you see this kid," was the word everywhere his rookie year. The new Babe Ruth, he was called, so that even the shoes he was expected to fill had an aura.

But I'd swear, if you'd never heard of him at all, his body, with the loping stride and the gracefully swaying shoulders, was still the one you'd notice first as his team hurtled out of the dugout to start proceedings. "The Yankee Clipper," the flag ship. As teammate Red Ruffing put it, "You saw him standing there and you knew you had a pretty damn good chance to win the baseball game"—and by the same token, the enemy knew they had a pretty good chance to lose it. At any rate, DiMaggio was surely the winningest of baseball's legends in terms of big games won and lost, and the reason may simply have been that both teams "saw him standing there."

As a newly arrived refugee, I was lucky enough to see him standing there myself, and by then fame radiated from him. But through the glow it could be discerned by the merest ten-year-old that he swung the bat with a controlled savagery, which contrasted sharply with his usual stillness, like an explosion on a calm day, and that he fielded with a preternatural grace.

During batting practice, he hit several topspin one-bouncers that were almost unfieldable. These must have provided his bread-and-butter hits during the streak. Out in the field, he intercepted a couple of sure singles by fielding just in back of second—then cantered back to steal a couple of doubles near the fence. His kingdom seemed to know no boundaries, and one pictures batters fairly sobbing with frustration by the end of the day. In dreams I can still see him gliding after fly balls as if he were skimming the surface of the moon—although his teammate Tommy Henrich says it sounded more like a cattle stampede from up close.

You had to be there—which may account for a mild hullabaloo caused by his selection as Greatest Living Player by sportswriters and broadcasters in a 1969 poll, even while the superlative Willie Mays was still playing. Future historians may wonder about this choice, the way they may wonder what we ever saw in Ronald Reagan. (You had to be there for him too.)

Seeing DiMaggio was an illumination that left nothing much to argue about. But reading about him could be somewhat murkier. When he first hit New York, several writers reacted as if they had never seen an Italian before. The *New York Times* described him tentatively as "a rather bashful signor of olive complexion," while *Life* congratulated him whimsically for not reeking of garlic or dressing his hair in bear grease, and for being "well adapted to most U.S. mores." All hands fell upon his taciturn family with the glee of a travelogue host alighting on a remote Papuan village. Herculean efforts were made to make the DiMaggios sound colorful, in the teeth of the evidence. Italians *had* to be colorful, dammit—all peasants were colorful—but the DiMaggios didn't make it easy for anyone with their monochrome life and their monosyllables. The strains of the enterprise can be judged from an interoffice memo written by a *Time* magazine reporter in 1939, which grumps (as *Time* used to say) that "the family is curiously closed-mouthed, uninterested and uninteresting." It was small wonder. Americans in general hadn't learned how to open their mouths for the camera yet, and the sight of a bunch of strangers clamoring around the door and through the living room with notebooks out would have knocked the color out of anybody.

Nevertheless, the press did manage to come up with a warm and peasant-smart mother for him, and this and that for his brothers, until they could have passed for cinema immigrants, and the stage was set for whatever he managed to bring to the party himself. Quaint backgrounds were standard issue for celebrities then. (Now it's tormented ones.) And baby Joe stories had him alternately loving pasta and hating it, and either refusing to go crab-fishing or taking to it so avidly that he still did it between seasons. As with frontier days it seemed that you could tell any story you liked about the West Coast and no one would know.

It sounds as if Joe would have been a quiet man whatever happened (it's the one Sicilian custom the vultures missed) but the goofy nature of the press coverage drove him to total lockjaw in the presence of anyone who looked as if he might have a pencil on him. So naturally the press had to make up a voice for him. "I sure have missed the feel of that old apple," said the new, improved DiMaggio after a winter layoff. In a column written in 1944 under the nom de guerre Staff Sergeant Joe DiMaggio, he averred: "Leo Durocher? Quite a jockey was Leo the Lip. I remember an all-star game in particular when he really was in rare form. Yes, quite a jockey."

Insofar as one could deduce anything from this, it would be

that DiMaggio wore a monocle and spats. And oddly enough, this might have suited him. One authentic quote from the period was the tag line: "I've been nonchalantly meandering down the pike," part of the patter he'd picked up from a raffish teammate on the San Francisco Seals, and it suggested that if he ever *did* speak, he would sound more or less like David Niven.

Later on, these aspirations to dandyism would be incorporated into the Grand Manner that he wears today, but back then, his persona was still in the making. We had two versions. There was the *Catholic Almanac* DiMaggio, awarded center field in perpetuity on its all-Catholic team: Joe was happily married to one Dorothy Arnold, a bit-part movie actress; and then he was divorced, but that was all right, because he hadn't remarried and we assumed he was grieving. He looked so solemn, and newspapers hinted at a reconciliation when news was slow. Luckily, he had retired before he married Marilyn Monroe, or the team might have had to make do with his brother Dominic in center.

Marilyn would have been inconceivable in the *Catholic Almanac* version, but she would have been almost expected in the other one. To gossip columnists DiMaggio was a night owl who hung out at Toots Shor's, the great New York sports pub, where he hobnobbed silently with Hemingway and even admitted to a taste for "restrained merriment." (Toots Shor himself once described Joe as one of the three best drinkers he'd ever known— a compliment beyond price in his particular world.) Sportswriters knew this side of DiMaggio, and while they didn't report on it, it is there as flavoring matter in their stories so that when they talked about his innate class they included the way he carried his liquor and himself in nightclubs.

A story I read back in 1941 in the *New York Times* might have put the two DiMaggios together for me if I'd known at that age what the writer was talking about. "Until recently," it said, "he was always getting hurt. Where? In his legs. Something was always going wrong. Perhaps there might have been a little bit more to it than that, but Joe is married now."

Marriage good for the legs? It was one of those unfathomable bits of information that come your way as a small fry. Whether or not there was any truth to it, it didn't help Joe for long, because in a couple of years he was divorced and hobbling again. And so it went for the rest of his career. DiMaggio's injuries were as much a part of his legend as consumption used to be for poets, and one pictures him rising eternally from a bed of pain to smite the latest enemy.

In fact, one of his finest such moments has just been recaptured in David Halberstam's *Summer of '49*. DiMag has taken an eternity to heal from a foot operation, and the black cloud that's been hanging over his career off and on since the war is practically sitting on his head by now; but it seems our hero has one more epic in him, and he makes it to Boston and hits four home runs in three games and turns the season around.

What's notable about this is that without the injury it is just another baseball story. Heroics of that kind get swallowed up in the mill of history, and even the greatest players are lucky to have two or three shots at the kind of grandeur that lasts more than a moment. Kurt Gibson, for instance, could play a hundred years without ever getting another chance to hit a one-legged, game-winning World Series home run. DiMaggio's injuries multiplied his chances of glory, and he can console himself, like Lord Tennyson's Light Brigade, with the thought that if things hadn't gone so badly, there wouldn't have been any poem.

But it wasn't any consolation at the time. Those injuries cast a blight on what should have been a joyful career, and they aged him prematurely as a ballplayer. The opposition scouting report on him for the 1951 World Series read, in part, "He can't run and he won't bunt...his reflexes are very slow." All this at age thirty-six. DiMaggio would soon be accepting congratulations for having the pride to retire from baseball that year; but it couldn't have needed much pride to quit on that note. Even before he had retired, he had become something of a ceremonial player, as can be judged by one simple *New York Times* headline: "Decision to Retire Saddens Japanese." And indeed the crowds that had lined the streets of Tokyo to cheer him a few months earlier had been estimated as twice the size of General MacArthur's best. "You've never seen anything like it," said Marilyn describing the crowds that welcomed her in Korea. "Yes, I have," said Joe, a phrase that reminds me whenever I hear it of the sweet part of the bat connecting with a fast ball and dismissing it from sight.

Back home, he slid briefly in and out of the sort of ramshackle radio and TV shows that they used to run up overnight around famous names, and his voice, which had mesmerized me as a child, might have done particularly well in radio; but radio was deemed to be on the way out, and he probably just felt silly on TV, and DiMaggio cannot abide feeling silly. It may bother his fans slightly that he doesn't seem to feel the same way about doing TV commercials, but he obviously regards that as an honest job with clearly understood rules. And he apparently uses the rest of his time the way one might wish one's ex-presidents to, touring the country being a credit to his old profession, raising money for good causes and, in a haunting phrase he gave to one interviewer, "sharing my gentleness with people." He has discovered the joys of conversation but he doesn't need them. When Columbia gave him a degree in 1990 the place was packed. The magic still works.

But the climax of Joe's celebrityhood had already come and gone, and if *that* were a test, he passed it brilliantly. The story of Joe and Marilyn is that there is no story. Concerning every other inch of Marilyn's life there is endless, scabrous gossip, but this ceases abruptly at the approach of the Yankee Clipper: DiMaggio has imposed his massive, fiery silence over the magpie twittering, and for a moment in that turbulent life and afterlife, you can hear a pin drop.

And you can still hear it. When it became widely known that DiMaggio still put flowers on Miss Monroe's grave every week, he stopped doing it, presumably because to continue would attract attention to him, not her. Thus, as if to show how well he has "adapted to most U.S. mores," the bashful signor has given our slobby times a lesson in how a gentleman behaves that you couldn't learn from an English butler.

But it wouldn't do to make a fuss about it. Let's just call him the greatest living ballplayer and leave it at that.

TED WILLIAMS: ODE ON AN AMERICAN URN

This was written for Memories *magazine—itself a memory by now—for their "nines" issue celebrating 1919, 1939 etc. Hence the peculiar confession in the first sentence.*

To be honest, I didn't actually catch up with Ted Williams until 1941, two years after he had come thumping his way east from California to Boston. Mind you, I had my excuses. For one thing, I had never even heard of baseball back in 1939, but, if memory is to be trusted, I spent most of that summer watching barrage balloons go up over London and cadging cigarette cards featuring pictures of the world's greatest war planes (I could swear the Russian one had three wings); and for another, I was eight years old.

At any rate, what I saw when I finally got around to it in '41 was a scrawny young chap with his pants around his ankles (a style I favored myself that year), who looked as if he had strayed over from the adjoining sandlot. Even when he swung his bat, it was with the crazy abandon of a country boy playing with an imaginary ball—except that he seemed magically to connect every time, the *real* American dream. For a split second, or as long as it took, this impossible-looking kid had become perhaps the greatest hitting maestro the game has ever seen, but *I* didn't know that. I only thought that if *he* can do it, it must be easy: a fallacy that haunts me still.

That was Williams' romantic period, and savants claimed that he could actually see the ball so well that year that he could pluck it right out of the catcher's mitt and jerk it around to furthest right by dint of sheer ferocity. (If I may wax pedantic a moment: twenty years earlier, Babe Ruth had stood baseball on its ear by letting all the slack out of his swing without sacrificing too much accuracy; but Williams seemed to let out more slack yet and, by committing himself so late, to sacrifice nothing. Thus did "the Splendid Splinter" become "the Thumper," a home-run hitter with the body of a singles man.)

When I next saw Williams after World War II, there was a bit less splinter about him and a touch more thump, as if (a largish) Frank Sinatra had grown into (a smallish) John Wayne. His swing seemed if anything deadlier now, but less improvised, less dashing but more majestic. Like Muhammad Ali after his Vietnam War layoff, he was still a genius, but a *different* genius.

So here's how it went.

Everybody remembers his exit at least, if not that gorgeous entrance. The last major league game of Theodore Own Williams was one of the handful of historical events that have evoked works of art precisely worthy of them: which meant, in this case, not exactly major art and not quite a world-shaking event either, but both simply perfect of their kind. Grecian urns with summer days on them, American urns with a bat chasing a ball, forever and ever.

John Updike's "Hub Fans Bid Kid Adieu" also suggests with its title that Ted Williams left baseball pretty much the way he came in. And this is the legend, the folk song version as it were. "The Kid's last spit." In sober fact, however, the droopy-drawered elder statesman who refused down to his very last game to tip his cap after a home run, had come quite some distance in character as well as style from the twitchy hyperactive braggart who hove into view back in 1939.

Now there was a real Kid for you, baseball's Amadeus; no one had ever seen anything quite like it. Insofar as history is defined by the things that hadn't happened yet, the names to bear in mind here would include James Dean, the aforementioned Muhammad Ali, and John McEnroe, along with successive swarms of brats and punks who have taken all the sparkle out of rudeness and the youthful joy out of self-absorption (and whatever became of the word "fresh" anyway?).

By now we might feel quite at home with such a one as Williams—in a world full of "Kids," what's another one more or less? But in a mid-Depression training camp spring, what was anyone to make of a lad who, according to myth at least, ordered the Red Sox regulars (including three Hall of Famers) to stand aside from the batting cage and let a real hitter hit?

The only thing thirtiesish about Williams was the hungry intensity with which he swung the bat, as if life itself depended on it: there would be no early retirements for this Kid, and no detours into pleasure. For him, this was pleasure enough—expectation and performance and reward all in one swipe—and everyone remembers him dancing with delight as he ran out his game-winning home run in the 1941 All-Star game: all the celebration a man needed, or at least all he allowed himself in those days, and he squeezed it to the last mad drop.

Unfortunately the rest of one's day had to be gotten through somehow between trips to the plate, although young Ted did his best to keep these intervals as short as possible, by swinging a phantom bat in the outfield, at the risk of being nailed to the ground by fly balls, and a real one in front of hotel mirrors, at the risk of smashing one. "Boy, what power," Richard Ben Kramer reports him saying as he belted a bedpost one night and totaled the bed with his roommate inside. Ted the Child had actually polished his art playing the game by himself with one friend, and he never really saw the need for more company than that.

Unfortunately that *still* left time, and he filled it with all the jumpy irritability of a man who's been interrupted in the act of love. Having fine-tuned himself as a virtuoso, he never quite got over the idea that people were allowed to scream during his performances, and the crowds at Fenway Park for their part never got over the pleasure of riling the maestro and bringing him purple-faced to the window. Williams, for his part, picked up every voice, as if it were a squeaking bed-spring.

Later on, Williams learned to discipline himself down to one measly spitting incident and one pioneering wave of the finger (now of course everybody does it): altogether a modest output over a twenty-odd-year career. But for baseball fans, and even more so for Boston sportswriters, nothing can compare with an idea whose time has passed, and even after Williams had war-gamed fielding and had actually fractured a shoulder going after a fly ball in another All-Star game; and even after he had war-gamed war itself, as a combat pilot in two wars (most players never actually *fought* in any wars at all), the legend persisted grittily of a rabbit-eared monomaniac who had no life at all outside the batter's box.

It should be added that Williams helped matters mightily by disdaining to dispel any misunderstandings whatsoever. If the writers thought he played only for himself, to hell with them; his answer (and it would not have occurred to the average man) was simply not to talk to them. And if the fans could be won round with a simple tip of the cap, then a tip of the cap they would not get, even if it would silence their yelps forever. Stubbornness was essential to his art, even if it seemed at times to leave a whole city baying for his attention.

And what an art it was. People who think that hitting a baseball is not worthy of a grown man's fullest powers have obviously not heard Ted Williams talk about it. Ballplayers at least know better and still flock to his shrine for one million-dollar tip, some trifle of footwork that will lift them overnight from the slums to the house on the hill. And they always emerge not only refreshed, but almost as stubborn as he is.

From what seeps out of the oracle's cave it seems fair to suggest that a man possessed of that particular vision would *have* to appear to play selfishly. For instance, Williams could not swing at a bad pitch if a pennant depended on it, because his sense of the strike zone was worth more to him (and ultimately the team) than any one hit could ever be. And when opposing managers stacked the fielders over on the right side, he could not hit to the left to save his life, because it would have meant messing with that magic swing. "Just once," howled fans and sportswriters alike (the latter would, for instance, gladly have split infinitives in such a cause). "Pretty please. *Ugly* please. Anything."

To which Williams might have answered, if he ever answered anything, what more can I do for you? The *New York Times* once estimated that had Williams not lost at least five years to warfare and injuries, he would have finished an incredible second in all-time runs *and* runs batted in, and no team player could have done more.

In fact, being a team player for the Red Sox of that era would have been a fool's errand anyway. Their employer, Tom Yawkey, was a singularly infantile man even by baseball owner standards, and it seems that he liked to hire expensive ballplayers just so he could meet them, and if all went well, buy them a drink. As a consequence, the Sox were known as a country club team even when they were good, and they weren't often good during Williams' tenure. So a team player would have stuck out like a sore thumb.

As a consequence, there were very few events in Williams' career, except for such as he chose to create himself. Otherwise he played in a vacuum, and in memory one still sees him swinging away by himself, as he had as a child, alone on his podium. But he did not create this situation; he just played for a very odd team.

In the one World Series that came his way, Williams performed indifferently, and the Boston writers incredibly put it down to selfishness, as if Williams had gone out of his way to lay an egg while the world watched. Indeed, he still refused to hit to left because it still wasn't his game (and because "it isn't that easy," as he once said privately), but his whole gaudy postwar career testifies that in the long run he was right; it just so happens that for those seven games he wasn't. The law of averages can play tricks even on the gods.

Afterward, Ted the Selfish locked himself in his train compartment and cried, and his feud with the writers and their readers was unnecessarily reopened and prolonged for another five years or so. Indeed, in the dancing light of history, it rather looks now as if those writers may have done more harm to the team, to those same good-for-nothing Red Sox, with their genius-baiting than Williams ever did, as the slogan "Ted can't win the big ones" became a more formidable barrier than any shift of fielders.

At any rate, whatever was left of their clownish allegations was put to eternal rest in 1969 when Williams decided to try his own hand at managing for a while. It goes without saying (or at least I wish it would) that superstars make lousy teachers, chiefly because even the most modest of them can't fathom what ails the incompetent.

So what did Williams do but become manager of the year immediately, against stiff competition, precisely by persuading his humpty-dumpties to play over their heads. And when he did come to grief, or at least normality, three years later, it was not from Great Man's Disease, but partly from his old virtue stubbornness, as his *aperçus* hardened into dogmas (as is still their wont), and largely from yet another foolish owner who had traded away all his prize chicks and blithely requested him to incubate a new batch.

Faced with being less than the best at something, Williams repaired double-quick to the privacy of fishing, at which he is said, and not only by himself, to be merely incomparable. His years of solitude have apparently given him, or exaggerated in him, the kind of booming voice that one associates with slight deafness, and in this voice he can sound, from the record, anything from brilliant to oafish, but in either case not the least like anyone else. Wherever Williams gets his thoughts from, it is not from ordinary human interchange, and one assumes some lightning contact between eye, brain and subject that is his alone.

To judge from Richard Ben Kramer's splendid article from *Esquire* cited earlier ("What Do You Think of Ted Williams Now?" June 1986), the aging Kid is still given to explosions of unfathomable rage, pure energy turned inward, which powerfully suggest that his life may never have been self-indulgent after all, but a breathing monument, as his hitting was, to iron self-control. The man who once left his fetish behind with a spring in his step—although he raged inside at the injustice of it—to fight for his country two more years in Korea, at an age (thirty-three) when he still had the record book at his mercy, is not some child of whim, but maybe a regular hard-nosed Depression Kid after all.

And then when it was all over, rather than hang around spluttering and getting mad at things, he made himself scarce— but not preciously scarce, like some of our famous recluses, just scarce enough, a triumph to the end of style over temperament.

JACKIE ROBINSON: SACRIFICIAL LION

It had to happen, and somebody had to get hurt. By 1946 the northern cities were crammed to bursting with black munitions workers, returned veterans and the flotsam of war, and they were in no mood for lily-white baseball. Since these newcomers still had some mad money to throw around and since the sophisticated Negro leagues had already groomed a mouthwatering pool of talent, there was clearly a killing to be made by whoever had the guts to break the color bar.

The man with the guts was Branch Rickey of Brooklyn and he received his reward: besides well-deserved canonization, he found himself with an instant baseball dynasty, one of the most exciting teams ever, which played to full houses whenever blacks and liberals were gathered together. The victim was Jackie Robinson and his rewards were more elusive.

It is hardly too much to say that Jackie gave his life to Mr. Rickey's breakthrough. Enjoined to silence during his rookie years, this articulate U.C.L.A. graduate had to endure enough guttersnipe humiliation to shatter the strongest psyche. Thrown at, stepped on, boycotted and spat upon by the surliest rearguard movement since Reconstruction, Jackie bore the whole burden of the black athlete with Christlike patience; for two years and up, he suffered that a hundred Aarons might bloom; indeed, for those years he *was* the Civil Rights movement, to most of us.

When time, and Rickey, removed the lid, Robinson came out snarling. By now he had plenty of company, and a milder man might have licked his wounds and waited for the scabs to form. But Robinson had bent his nature too far in the direction of saintliness and from now on it seemed he spent a career getting even—not with anyone in particular, there were too many for that, but with anyone who crossed him. He even accused his black teammate Roy Campanella of being an Uncle Tom, not realizing that his own feisty independence had knocked the category practically out of baseball. Thanks to JR, blacks were even free to be nice without shame.

Robinson's smoldering rancor made him perhaps an even more electric ballplayer than nature intended. When he got caught in a run-down one felt sorry for the infielders; when he was on third one feared for the pitcher (I secretly felt that his real sport was soccer). But he always seemed to give a little more fun than he was getting. When the infield dust had settled over his career, he claimed that the Hall of Fame would never accept him because he was a black. In fact they did accept him right away—because he was a black. He didn't understand his own revolution.

For a while after that Jackie dabbled at being a black spokesman, pioneering for a much more mixed breed of cat. The fire in him seemed to die down gradually. And when I met him toward the end he seemed as gentle as a Pullman porter, white-haired and prematurely old. From the moment he had first stepped on a white man's diamond he had accelerated a hair-raising life cycle of ups and downs that could only burn itself out. God knows what would have happened if Rickey hadn't chosen this man expressly for his maturity and balance.

Robinson's reward was and is, of course, his legacy, which he must have enjoyed at least sometimes, perhaps enough to feel he could move on now. As soon as it was chronologically possible, a black man (Aaron) had broken the unbreakable record, Babe Ruth's 714 lifetime home runs, and another (Lou Brock) had scampered past Ty Cobb in stolen bases. Perhaps the most inconsequential by-product of all was the conversion of liberal intellectuals to baseball, as Ali later converted them to boxing. Every little bit helps.

But baseball wasn't the half of it. Under cover of helmets and Tweedledee padding, blacks sneaked into pro football quite quietly (who can remember the first one?)—at least as far as the public was concerned. But the battle of the locker room had

been won for them by Robinson: dressing, showering, celebrating together—suddenly what was the big deal about that?
Seldom has such a big problem dwindled so quickly, although
ugly pockets of resistance remained.

By the time pro basketball—a game which practically looks
and smells like a locker room—got really big, black players
were already so much a part of the scenery that a white guy
who once wouldn't have shared a hotel with a black now
thought little of having one stand on his feet breathing fire,
pouring sweat and stealing his job.

The acceptance of physicality was the real breakthrough. Joe
Louis and Jesse Owens had long since proved that Negroes were
good athletes and in the 1948 Olympics, someone computed
the final scoreboard as something like: Black America 1, Sweden
2, White America 3. But the blacks ran alone. And when they
boxed it was from segregated bastions, to which they immediately withdrew. Team sports were the sticking point. An irrational dread of proximity kept the uni-race locker room the
last redoubt of sporting segregation.

The white southerners who made life hell for Robinson have
mostly died or apologized, wondering perhaps what all the fuss
had been about. Once the physical distaste had been dissipated,
the racist arguments from scripture and cranial capacity looked
mighty frail. One hesitates to claim too much for Sports: Civil
Rights after Robinson still had a long, bloody way to go. But
Americans do spend a lot of growing-up time in gyms and such,
bashing and hugging each other, and this has to flow over into
real life. So the Civil Rights legislation of the fifties and sixties
may owe at least a little something to the relaxation of ancient
terrors on the playing field.

And then there is the figure of Robinson himself. Branch
Rickey was an incomparable talent scout, and he never chose
wiser. By first proving himself a gentleman and then a proud
gentleman, Robinson saved years of aborted experiments. What
he did could simply not have been done better. And when his
hazing was over, one of his teammates paid him the accolade

of complaining about some "nigger" who was trying to take away Jackie's job.

By present lights that may not sound like much of an ending—an "honorary white" was the last thing Robinson wanted to be—but in the temper of the times, which one has to strain to remember, it was a great leap forward. If one man could, by hitting .300, cease being a nigger so could the next one and the one after until .250 would do. The trick of course was how to hit .300 while turning the other cheek. Robinson knew he had to get a hearing within the language of his profession. A stoic who can't hit the curve might as well give up and scream with pain.

Robinson proved, over-proved, under unrepeatable pressure, that he could break your concentration before you could break his, that he could run the bases with a bucket of water on each shoulder if necessary. His final message to his own gang was: be first-rate, then you can argue; and it was picked up by many.

Ironically, Robinson wound up as a Rockefeller Republican, to the bafflement of his liberal spear-carriers. But it was they, not he, who had reduced him to a children's book character, a Mrs. Roosevelt in spikes; and he wasn't going to dance to their tunes any more than to Jim Crow's. Being his own man was his life-work. And you didn't have to be black to be fortified by it.

Hall of Fame

*T*he Baseball Hall of Fame Old-Timers Committee eternally patrols the troubled border between the Great and the Very Good. Every time they permit a Very Good to enter the shrine, the other Very Goods and their fans come yapping around the gate: if him, why not me? If Reese, why not Rizzuto?

The purists usually send up a howl too. If so-and-so wasn't good enough in his eligible years, why sneak him in now? He can't have improved that much. The impurists prefer to take it case by case. If a guy brightened your early summers, or played up a storm every time you went to the park, why, he must be great. Otherwise your life has been wasted.

As a purist with occasional impure thoughts, I have mixed thoughts about this year's immigrants. I never met a serious

126

baseball man who didn't think Arky Vaughan belonged in there all along. On the other hand, if the voting were turned over to the fans, Enos Slaughter would probably edge out Vaughan, because fans place a higher value on pure excitement than experts do, and Slaughter was made of excitement.

Everyone remembers the country boy scoring from first on a single to win the World Series of 1946, but they tend to forget his heroics in 1942, when he helped drag a scruffy Cardinal outfit past maybe the best Dodger team ever, and then past the unbeatable Yankees as well just to prove it wasn't a fluke.

Make no mistake, it was Slaughter we Dodger fans feared. Musial we resigned ourselves to, as we did to DiMaggio: genius deserves that tribute. You're happy to have seen it. But this guttersnipe, running from first to third on everything including his own doubles, seemed to be stealing our very uniforms.

1942 was especially galling because the Cards seemed to have conceded the pennant that winter by trading Johnny Mize to the Giants. Stan Musial was still a year away from mastery (he hit .314) and we were damned if we were going to be beaten by guys called Creepy Crespi and Jimmy Brown. But we were. Aided by an endless supply of young arms, St. Louis came from ten games back in August—and we didn't even fold that year. Bitter, baby. Slaughter led the league in unearned triples, but nothing can convey how he juiced up Branch Rickey's youth camp of a team that year.

What happened next, and it may be enough to tip the scales in his favor, is exactly nothing. Slaughter spent what had to be his three best years in the military. He came out kicking and snarling as usual, and it is well remembered how he tried to relieve Jackie Robinson of his foot en route to first base in Jackie's first year. But as time went by, competitiveness more and more had to do duty for talent, and Slaughter wound up at .302 which is not a Hall of Fame number for an outfielder who doesn't hit the ball over buildings.

Arky Vaughan by contrast was something of a pennant avoider. In 1938, his Pirates lost out to the Cubs at the last minute on Gabby Hartnett's famous "homer in the gloaming," a shot to left field that Vaughan probably had to strain his eyes to see from shortstop.* Then, in 1942, he joined the Dodgers just in time to watch the Cardinals go scampering past. After sitting out or ploughing out two good war years on his farm, he had a last limping hurrah against the Yankees in 1947, getting one double in two trips.

But Vaughan's allergy to pennants is about the only bad thing that can be said of him. His presence at shortstop was positively regal. Built with the military bearing of a Craig Nettles only more so, he seemed to rule the area by fiat, and was even known to poach stuff to the third baseman's *right*. On the bases, he regularly led the league in triples and he had at least some of Slaughter's nuisance value. Once I saw him single a runner from second to third and then calmly take second himself as the fielders stood by, bemused, not quite believing what they were seeing. (Yes, he brightened my afternoons.)

But it was at the plate that Arky really blazed. The kind of year that Robin Yount had just once Vaughan seemed to have every year. From his wide open stance he seemed to learn more about the pitch than is given to most hitters in a lifetime, and he swung with a kind of savage certainty. His best average was .385, and even allowing for some slippage at the end, he wound up with .318 lifetime, which is quite good enough for a Hall of Fame shortstop.

Once, in a fit of childish bravado, I ran up to Vaughan after a game, no doubt to tell him how he had brightened my afternoon and to pat his butt reassuringly. His face when I got up close was stone cold, registering nothing but unused rage, and my hand barely grazed his galloping backside. And I thought, well, that's right, that's exactly how a great man should act. Which proves that kids can adjust to anything.

Anyway, now they're going to make it official and cast him in bronze, his natural element, and no plaque on that whole

*This was intended ironically because when it was written, Wrigley Field *still* had no lights. I'm sorry to say it has them now.

long wall will look more at home there than Floyd "Arky" Vaughan's.

NEAR MISSES: PHIL RIZZUTO AND
A CAST OF DOZENS

You know that if you hit it you're just going to wind up with a sore ear. But every summer the buzzing comes back worse than ever, until it feels like part of your head. And the song the mosquitoes are singing is "Phil Rizzuto . . . Cooperstown." What the hell, you can always listen with the other ear for a few days.

Probably every city has a Rizzuto in its past—an excellent ballplayer who, in the eyes of love, swells just that tiny bit it takes to look like a great one. To an old Cub fan Stan Hack and Ron Santo make an overwhelming entry at third base. *Four* Cub pennant winners, you say? Hack alone played superbly on all of them, and hit .348 in the (inevitably) losing World Series that followed; for Santo you change the subject—no pennants, but oh, what numbers. Home runs, ribbies, and some swell averages for a slugger.

And then for Marty Marion of St. Louis you change the subject once again to "you had to be there." Back in the forties "the Octopus," as they called him, was a presence at shortstop the way the left field wall at Fenway Park is a presence. You couldn't hit a ball through the hole against Marion because there wasn't any hole. In fact, half the time there wasn't even a hole up the middle: like the great dancer Ray Bolger, Marion seemed to cross the whole stage in a single stride. However, his hitting was so indifferent that, alone among today's candidates, his numbers are actually slightly lower than Rizzuto's, and that's nowhere near good enough.

What's interesting is that the Yankees themselves have a Rizzuto in their past—only his name was Joe Gordon. For Gordon, either the numbers *or* being there yourself will do it—or even winning pennants in unlikely places. The fates tested Joe severely in that respect by shipping him to Cleveland in mid-late career;

but thirty-two homers and 123 ribbies later and the deed was done.

That was nice, of course, but no more than one might have expected from any of the Yankees of that golden, pre-war era. But what made Gordon really stand out even among those demigods was his fielding. Everyone named Gordon, be he ever so clumsy and slow of mind and limb, is of course called "Flash," but Joe was rare among Gordons in taking his obligations seriously. His feet flashed, his arm flashed, his glove was a blur. Fans came early to catch fielding practice when Joe was on tap, because he seemed to put a snap into even the routine stuff and tie it with a ribbon; and when he went to Cleveland, connoisseurs consoled themselves with the thought that he would soon be turning double plays with Lou Boudreau, to go straight into the time capsule along with Babe Ruth's swing and Walter Johnson's fast ball.

To be fair—Bill Mazerowski might have made such plays almost as well if teamed with Luis Aparicio; and to be *excruciatingly* fair, Jose Lind of Pittsburgh might have executed most of Joe Gordon's solo plays too. But none of these virtuosi could have carried his bat. And Bobby Doerr, who *is* in the Hall of Fame, couldn't have carried any part of his equipment.

Or at least so it was felt at the time. For my last witness, I call upon the buzz I heard as a kid in Shibe Park, Philadelphia, where we didn't give a damn who was better, just so long as they'd just get off our backs for a minute. From where we sat, it was simply no contest. Bobby Doerr was some kind of journeyman second baseman toiling in the shadow of Ted Williams. Gordon was a genius in his own right, and even the great DiMaggio playing a few feet away in short center field—a position he invented for himself—couldn't throw a shadow that reached him.

To give Rizzuto his due, you noticed him too, if only to wonder what he was doing out there. It wasn't just that he was five feet six—he was a small five feet six. He not only didn't hit home runs, he didn't even hit that many doubles, which are a small man's home runs. In fact he didn't hit enough of anything to bat higher than seventh or eighth for eight of his thirteen years in the bigs.

It's an unjust world, but kittens like Rizzuto and Bud Harrelson have to face what amounts to an eight-man infield every time up (even the pitcher plays in against them) and Phil the Scooter's .273 lifetime does him a heap of credit. To get there, he needed to make twice as much good contact as Mickey Mantle and maybe forty-three times as much as Dave Kingman. And who knows, maybe a few years lifting weights and eating whatever it is Jose Canseco eats might have turned him into a regular Lenny Dykstra.

But he didn't, and his admirers are reduced to foraging for scraps. For instance. He had a great year in 1950—and indeed he did; but you should see the others. In the good book of baseball, that year looks almost as if it belonged to some other guy. 1950 was only one of two seasons in which he scored over ninety runs—for that team!

Scrap two. He was a great bunter—true again, but bunting for the Yankees of that era was the equivalent of a party trick, like Ron Hunt's gift for getting hit by pitchers. The team didn't strictly need bunts, but any old way you could arrange to get driven in by Keller or Henrich or Mantle or Yogi was fine with it.

Three. He had great anticipation in the field. Most big-league shortstops do. But Rizzuto really needed it, because he had an arm that reminded me of the early days of plane flight. You held your breath till the throws arrived.

Again, more power to him—he was a hell of an athlete, and he made himself into a fine shortstop. But right now, we're talking about the immortals—guys who made no mistakes at all, like Eddie Miller of the Reds and the Boston Bees, or who could cover for a paraplegic shortstop from third if necessary, like New York's own Clete Boyer. (Incidentally, these guys didn't make the Hall either: there's some great company on the outside.)

Four—and you really have to get down on your knees for this one: the old-timers committee is prejudiced against Yankees, or Italians, or *something*. In an Al Sharpton era, people seem to have a terrible time coping with the concept of an impartial jury as such. What's their angle, where are they coming from? But the answer in this case is simple—members are coming from the Hall of Fame themselves, and if they cheapen the place with cheap, petty-minded selections they're only devaluing the glory for themselves and all the other titans in there. If you insist on self-interested explanations, they've got a great one.

But who needs one? The fact that it's called an old-timers committee should also tell you something. It should tell you that the cases that come to it for review have already flunked the normal entrance exam, and are not precisely *entitled* to anything at all. For fifteen years, while their memory was still at its freshest, they failed to convince the nation's sportswriters that they belong in the Hall of Fame, so if they get in now, it's a gift.

None of this will, however, deter the Rizzuto-ites, who seem to feel that every rejection strengthens their case. "For twenty-five years, this man has been spurned . . . isn't it about time? Wake up, Baseball!" I can only say that Phil is lucky to have such a large city behind him.

For a case where the player is less fortunate—where, in fact, he has no city behind him at all, to push his cause or even remember his name, I would like to present my own private candidate—one Cecil Travis of the old Washington Senators.

Travis had a comparatively short career: eight good years, and two and a bit quite excusable bad ones. But for the eight good ones, he blazed, playing short and third and hitting .327—which was, unless I've overlooked someone, a few points higher than any shortstop *or* third baseman between Hans Wagner and Wade Boggs.

And he was getting better. In 1941, the last of the magic eight, Joe DiMaggio hit safely in fifty-six straight games, but Travis, at .359, came in two points ahead of him; Ted Williams hit .406—but Travis got *thirty-three* more hits than Ted.

But what was truly astounding about that year was that Travis also managed to score 106 runs and drive in 101 for the *Washington Senators*! All the punctuation in the world cannot do justice to this feat. The Senators had an average sort of year in '41, finishing in a—no other word for it—flatfooted tie for sixth with the St. Louis Browns (there was no question of finishing underneath Connie Mack's Athletics in those days). So where the runs came from, I'll never know.

Anyway, come they did in that gorgeous sunset of a peacetime season. Baseball itself would eke out one more good year before the War moved in seriously, to reduce the big leagues to temporary triple-A status, but Travis wouldn't. He was one of a tiny handful of ballplayers who were drafted that winter—such a small number that they got some special ink for their heroism and sacrifice, which I hope they appreciated because most of them would never see any ink again.

Cecil Travis, in particular, packed up his great year in his kit bag and marched off, to a roll of drums, into oblivion. Both Rizzuto and Gordon would miss three baseball years in the War too, but I haven't stressed it because things were tough all over and you just subtract quietly. But Travis' three and a half years were different, because Travis actually *fought* in the War. He was again one of a small handful of big-league ballplayers (he got on all the wrong lists) who saw live combat and who had something to show for it—namely, a case of frostbite contracted at the Battle of the Bulge, which was apparently bad enough to knock a good thirteen points off his lifetime average before he disappeared for good a couple of years later.

And from that day to this, with no constituency like Rizzuto's to talk him up, Cecil Travis' obscurity has remained so impenetrable that even the omniscient Bill James forgot to mention him in his *Historical Baseball Abstract*, while storytellers in search of good martyr stories skip over him every time in favor of Shoeless Joe Jackson whose baseball career ended after *thirteen* good seasons, because he dodged the draft in 1918 and decided to stay home and make a little money instead.

However I'm not even suggesting that Travis belongs for sure in the Hall of Fame—only that Rizzuto supporters should realize that he is part of the competition they expect their guy to be swept regally past.

New Yorkers, and most especially Yankee fans, always used to be proud of not being provincial, of not needing a chamber of commerce to tell the world the obvious about their city and its various stars; and contrariwise, great ballplayers from the outback, such as Stan Musial and Bobby Feller, could always count on getting their due in New York even when they were beating the socks off the local heroes (Stan Musial could have run for office in Brooklyn). Class was the test, and New Yorkers didn't lower the bar so much as a quarter inch for hometown favorites.

But if you're still in any doubt about how New Yorkers, and most especially Yankee fans, used to behave, just ask yourself what George Steinbrenner would have done and you'll know. For years, Herr Direkter George used to boycott Cooperstown because they wouldn't let Rizzuto in, never understanding that if you have to push that hard for something, it probably isn't worth having; or that if no one outside of immediate family has ever said "I hear Rizzuto's in town next week—who do we kill to get tickets?" you've probably got the wrong man to begin with.

Anyway, all may not be lost. I believe the Hall must have an opening for an announcer right now—else how does one explain their invitation to Harry Caray of Chicago last year? Rizzuto, for all his cow-worship and his wedding announcements, is at least likeable, a genuine pleasure to have around for a few minutes, every now and again. And he doesn't try to sing. Isn't that enough?

Whatever you may think of this suggestion—and it's really meant more as a peace offer—believe me, it makes more sense than trying to get him into the Hall of Fame as a shortstop.

Heroes with Asterisks

PETE ROSE, BEFORE (1980)

*T*his may be the only even mildly prophetic piece
I ever wrote. But it turns out I wasn't just
prophesying about Rose. Today's ballplayers
have so easily surpassed Pete's record for rapacity and disloyalty
that any suggestion that he might rub along on $400,000 a year
seems almost touching.

There is nothing in a fan's contract that says he has to be fair-
minded. So I'll allow that a Rose on any other team would smell
at least different. If Pete hadn't once gone barreling into our
mascot Bud Harrelson of the Mets, well-nigh totaling the little
fellow, I might take a kindlier view of his greedy ways today.

As it is, Rose's hustling on the field and off seem to blend
into a single act of pointless aggression. Racing from city to city
this winter, sliding into tax shelters and beer distributorships as
if they were so many potbellied catchers, one had to wonder

what he hustles for, and whom.

Baseball has always had a soft spot for guys who bustle about knocking people down. So Rose has always been a model of sorts: running out his walks and pop flies and tearing out to his position as if baseball were actually an activity rather than a cud-chewing rumination. Even those of us who prefer the grace of a DiMaggio or Clemente enjoy these baggy-pants guys for contrast, like a burlesque team of Smooth & Dirty, Abbot & Costello. After all, we could never be a Clemente, but we could run out our pop flies, and, by George, we probably would.

What was unspoken, perhaps even unthought, was one's gut belief that the superstars probably played for themselves but that the hustlers played for us. So when Reggie Jackson reached for the Rolls-Royces, it hit our mythology just right; it's what we expected of him, and the dude in all of us silently applauded.

But Rose . . . with his all-American face, born in Cincinnati and owing that city at least as much as Socrates owed Athens; leaving a squad that had shared as rich a life together as an infantry platoon; and leaving it just for money . . . well, it was a shock to the system.

Our mistake, of course. Rose's prototypes, such as Ty Cobb and Country Slaughter, were very private players, for whom an extra base was always more real than any human flesh in front of it. All the jokes about spiking one's own grandmother were not jokes to Cobb (there were no jokes to Cobb): in fact, this kind of player, often hailed as the very essence of the game, sometimes seems to verge on the psychotic.

Pete Rose is, of course, a far cry from that. He is an affable fellow with a relatively low body count. But he plays with the same narrow monomania as Cobb did, and it shows in his banking habits. Exhibition game, World Series, Reds, Phillies, it's all the same to him; he would do his same spastic number in an empty parking lot. There is no more reason to praise him for hustle than to praise a hyperactive kid for tapping his foot. He can't help it. If one wants to throw in a little psychodrama, it turns out that Rose's father had only one comment after his young son's performances, to wit: "You didn't hustle enough."

Rose's desire for the most money in baseball is an extension of the same single track. Between that and breaking Stan Musial's National League record for hits, there seems no significant difference. You simply fling yourself on your belly and slide for what you're worth. Since the hits and the cash *are* dimly connected, Rose has actually taken a pinch less money than he might to go to a club whose park and line-up should suit his lonely record obsessions to perfection. And he can easily recoup as an Aqua Velva man and whatever he is in Tokyo (yes, he even squeezed in some commercials there). Of course, in none of this is he really unusual, but drearily typical. Where you play, what product you hold up, it's all the same, just put the money on the track and he'll follow it anywhere.

We've obviously come a long way since Babe Ruth was admonished for being a bad example to kids and cried his great eyes out in atonement. Just because Pete Rose plays like something out of the Gay Nineties does not mean he has to have a soul to match. What is interesting is that he either doesn't know or doesn't care how much simple admiration his gold fever is costing him. Fans pinned to the floor by inflation can't see why old Pete can't rub along on, say, $400,000 a year. It's nice that his family is secure, but does it have to be eighty times as secure as everyone else's?

It is true that Rose fills the stadium at any price and earns his pay fairly. By the same token, there must be players who don't bring in a single spectator and who shouldn't be paid at all. This way of grading players by box-office appeal was inevitable the day the agents arrived, and it puts an end to any silly notion that one went to watch a whole team, or even a good game. The feeling of camaraderie engendered at the meat counter, or rather locker room as the players stare at each other's price tags may explain why nobody has yet quite succeeded in buying a pennant.

Thus ballplayers join the solitary adventurers who play tennis and golf, and perhaps it suits them in some intrinsic way. At least, there has been no voluble protest from Rose's colleagues about the goofy market they now work in. A ballplayer who didn't dream of making *more* than Rose would lack the necessary fire, the baseball virility, the edginess that managers like to see. A team that voted to share the wealth evenly or to plough some of it back into the minor leagues or even into old-timers' pensions would be the laughingstock of baseball.

Such a team would also do wonders for the game, which is beginning to suffer slightly from circulatory problems as the supply of good, average players dwindles and the superstars find themselves with no one to play with. I remember taking my father to see Willie Mays for the first time. Willie went hitless in four trips, and not one ball was hit his way. So much for the star system. In no other sport can a great player show so little on a given day.

To lapse grudgingly into fairness: Rose nearly always shows you something. And it is not his fault that the sports section reads during the winter like the Financial Times. Publicity has turned salary negotiation into a sport in its own right, with its own long season, and maybe it's too much to ask a competitive man not to try to win. If one hoped for more from Rose, chalk it up to the twelve-year-old in every fan: a kid who has taken some brutal beatings lately and may not recover.

Besides, Rose has gone to a team I like, the Phillies, and that automatically improves his character. It will be instructive to see whether he brings that team to life or whether that team does what it usually does and puts him to sleep for good. If he brings a championship to Philadelphia, I for one will refuse to listen to a single bad word against that finest of men, Pete Rose. The twelve-year-old fan in us is not all heart. He likes a winner. He is as American as Pete Rose.

PETE ROSE, AFTER

(Written just one week before Bart Giamatti lowered the boom and expelled Rose from baseball forever)

Usually when someone sits in the public stocks as long as Pete Rose has, the world will have reached its verdict about him long before this: if he's Richard Nixon they'll vote to hang, if he's

Ronald Reagan, they might prefer a standing ovation.

But people remain in two minds about Pete Rose. Just as a personality (his talent is something else), there seems to be something about him they like, and something they don't. He is a charmer with a piece missing. Sportswriters have no trouble with him because they want precisely what he wants: great stories about Pete Rose. But observers who don't need him for anything seem to wonder why they don't like him more.

Watching his sassy press conferences, one feels torn the same way one feels at certain movies: half of you wants to see the rascal get away with it, while the other half wants to see that smile, or smirk, wiped off his face once and for all—maybe because he's so sure he's charming us and that he has us in his pocket; maybe because the style of con is kind of shabby.

And speaking of movies: the character and set-up he puts me in mind of most right now is Leo Gorcy of the Dead End Kids with the law closing in. But the atmosphere Rose thrives in is actually woven of somewhat softer movies than that. In numerous contemporary films, but let me single out just two, *Fletch* and *Good Morning, Vietnam* (if only because Robin Williams would play the part so well), the hero sails wisecracking through a sea of make-believe troubles without ever once meeting significant opposition; the authority figures, or the squares, or whatever, are not only ridiculous, but weak and resourceless. And a viewer old enough to have been touched even slightly by war or hard times can only marvel to himself: where's the tension in this? when is someone really going to sock it to this guy, the way life socks it to all of us?

Sympathy with Rose depends on pretty much the same act of imagination one brings to these movies: you have to pretend that Commissioner Giamatti is a real enemy, and not just a koala bear in disguise, and you have to believe for a wild moment that Pete is in a real predicament, remotely comparable to things like sickness and poverty—but the very words seem jarring in the context. Rose will never have to work as a night watchman, the way old ballplayers once did, or eat in automats with a brown bag on his lap. His money is safe from everyone but himself, and even when he blows it again, he can always make it back signing autographs (which will soon be worth a fortune) or playing a little celebrity golf for casinos.

And of course he won't have to wait seventy years to become a movie hero. Before Shoeless Joe Jackson, the prototype baseball layabout, was finally rehabilitated and canonized in *Field of Dreams*, he had some lean years. Stripped of his tiny income (Pete Rose bets more than that on one race), he was not, no doubt to his mounting astonishment, besieged by publishers who wanted to hear his side of the Black Sox scandal, or asked to do sock commercials, or even given his own talk show.

On the minus side, Jackson was hounded for the best part of his life by a real villain, a beady-eyed fanatic called Judge Landis, who kept an all-stations alarm out to make sure he didn't turn up in some stickball game—and on top of that reviled by an American public which thought that the judge was right. On the plus side, though, baseball didn't take away his pension, because he didn't have a pension, and no one ever embarrassed the illiterate Joe by asking him to sign his name.

Now *that* was a predicament, but it was felt to be only commensurate with Jackson's sin, which was in fact a rather peculiar one: he took money to throw a World Series and then didn't throw it*—essentially a sin against gambling, not baseball. Never mind. His teammate Buck Weaver actually received the same punishment for not doing either, but simply for not informing on his teammates. The message was simple: don't let gambling so much as touch your skin, or we're both in trouble—but you first.

Baseball, like the Garden of Eden, has only one sin proper to it, because only one sin affects its survival: all the rest, including drug addiction, is police work. And the sin is printed up loud and clear in every big-league locker room, like a giant scarlet letter G. And it is this sin that Pete Rose has allegedly chosen to defy, because defiance is his essence, the thing that makes it all work.

---

*At least he didn't throw much of it: see next chapter.

So how can we still be in two minds about him? Well, partly because he played the game the same way, and we admired that, even when he stuck his face in the umpire's the way he's doing now, fairly daring the man to throw him out of the park. Hustle in baseball is revered the way competitiveness is in business, and we tend to think of both as kind of apple-cheeked and American. But they can lose some of their shine up close, and we shouldn't be too surprised to learn that both Pete Rose and his model Ty Cobb doubled on the side as ferocious financial games-players who occasionally forgot which game they were playing and tended to slide around rules as if they were tags.

Compared to Cobb, who carried competitiveness over the brink into madness, Rose seems benign, almost slaphappy in fact: a blessedly inept gambler who bet more for kicks than profit, and who actually *lost* money on ball games; in short, an essentially silly man in a silly time. And then again, compared with the big boys who make the cable deals that wall off the game from the fans, Rose is definitely our kind of sinner. (And isn't the commissioner ultimately one of *them*, a hired hand of the owners who blinks at the larger corruptions while cracking down on the likes of Rose?)

Besides which, say Pete's apologists, everybody gambles these days, so how can you blame him? But that of course is precisely why something has to be done about him—to teach people to make distinctions. It's often forgotten that the Black Sox scandal was not a lonely aberration but the culmination of two decades of growing suspicions. Gamblers and fast-money guys swarmed around the clubhouse the way agents and advertisers do today; and if baseball was to expand in time for a possible postwar boom, it had to fling up the windows fast to let the stench out; and I don't see how that need has changed, except to intensify, in our own gambling-soaked era.

But Pete would be lost without baseball, say his friends, in a final attempt to keep his predicament from *ever* becoming real. But lots of dedicated ballplayers, especially black ones, it's said, have to make do without jobs in organized baseball. And I'm sure big bad Bart Giamatti would still allow him to teach the game in the inner city, or make himself useful in a hundred different ways. It would be impudent to say that the experience would be good for him, but it would surely be good for a lot of other people, who've never seen a live spanking.

As it stands, many kids today have reason to believe that after you've sinned your heart out in the direction of your choice, you go into something magical called rehab from which after a mere thirty days you emerge feeling wonderful and giving lectures about it. Okay, I guess—one doesn't want them knowing how excruciating and uncertain rehab really is or they'll never try it. But there's one hard fact about it that it couldn't hurt them to learn right away, which is that the first law of rehab says you have to pay your back dues before you can complete the course.

And Pete Rose's dues are crystal clear: the rule says plain as a pikestaff that if you bet your own team to win, lose, draw or not show up at all, you're out of baseball for life. And Pete's own contracts, the ones he's been agreeing to without objection for the last quarter-century or so, state that the commissioner is to be the judge of this, and not some hack judge in Cincinnati. Rose still has a shot at the kind of greatness you can't get from running around in your knickers if he plays this right. But somehow I'm not betting on it.

P.S. Even if, though, he passes up this chance to be teacher to a generation, Pete Rose still belongs in the Hall of Fame, as indeed does Shoeless Joe. What a guy does on the diamond is also a fact, as stubborn and inalienable as a Shakespeare play or a Stanford White building; and to take *that* away from a ballplayer is to lie about him, and to punish him more cruelly than the rest of us will ever know. So while we're teaching lessons around here, this might be a good one to end with. If baseball has its sin, it also has its specific virtues, and Pete had enough of them to slide past his patron saint and join the immortals.

But first, Purgatory.

*   *   *

And Purgatory it has been. A few months after the Giamatti ruling, Rose hired a public relations adviser and whether because the latter convinced him that repentance is the best PR policy or through some impulse of his own, he has decided to go for it with his usual awesome gusto, owning up to his tax sins and becoming from all accounts the prisoner of the year and more impressively or cunningly (depending on your reading) yet, putting his appeals for reinstatement on the back burner. Even if he is just going through the motions (which I'm beginning to doubt) of repentance, baseball begins to look like a hanging judge if it doesn't at least acknowledge the effort halfway and give the man his plaque. Otherwise the next Palooka may not even bother to try.

THE LEGEND OF SHOELESS JOE

When I wrote about Rose I thought Joe Jackson had it tough. But then I read about Jackson.

Probably the smartest move that Joseph Jefferson Jackson ever made—and it was a long time between smart moves for Joseph Jefferson—came on the day he decided to give his blisters a rest and play a game of baseball in his stocking feet. According to *Eight Men Out*, Eliot Asinof's definitive book on the subject (on which is based the definitive movie of the same name), an anonymous bleacher bum did the rest. "You shoeless bastard, you," he howled and no PR firm working round the clock could have done more.

A man equipped with a name like "Shoeless Joe" has nothing to fear from the verdict of history. It is like a talisman, ready for immediate use in ballads ("Ole Shoeless Joe came callin', one dark and dirty night" . . .), tall tales and silly movies. Whatever mischief may befall the bearer of this name is utterly alchemized by its magic. "We ain't heard Shoeless Joe's side of it yet . . . let's wait till Shoeless Joe gets here." (Who knows, maybe our history would have been altogether different—and a lot less embarrassing—if little Dicky Nixon had gone to school just once in his socks; but of course he would rather have died.)

Unfortunately, looking good in ballads and making out in life are two different things, and it is perfectly in keeping for a Shoeless Joe to get hung by mistake or fall down a well and get lost for years—and that, in baseball terms, is pretty much what his admirers believe happened to Joseph Jefferson Jackson; accused of throwing a World Series in which he hit .375, and condemned on the strength of a confession he couldn't even read to live out his life in baseball-less obscurity—never mind, we'll make it up to him in the ballad. We'll call it "The Return of Sleepy Joe" (" 'you didn't think I wuz dead?' sez he") and somewhere old Joe will be smiling that crooked grin of his and pounding a pocket in his cardboard mitt, or maybe in his bare hand.

At the moment, "making it up" to Joe Jackson consists mostly of trying, or talking about trying, to get him into the baseball Hall of Fame at Cooperstown—but in a sense, this would be superogatory. Insofar as the Hall of Fame has anything to do with actual fame, our hero already has more of it than four-fifths of the current membership.

In the movie *Field of Dreams*, not one of Joe's gifted contemporaries rates an invitation to the dream game at the end—not Tris Speaker, not Honus Wagner, not even Ty Cobb, although Cobb is still famous enough to merit a small joke. What we find instead are Gil Hodges and Mel Ott, obviously the most recently deceased baseball stars the earnestly trendy movie-makers could come up with (maybe they didn't know if Joe, a South Carolinean, would have even agreed to play with Roberto Clemente or Jackie Robinson, dead or alive). Americans love an underdog, but the underdog had better be bankable, a celebrity underdog, if he hopes to get in the movies.

However, the Hall of Fame is not just about fame, any more than a Distinguished Service Medal or a seat in the French Academy is; it's about the kind of recognition you can't get for a catchy name or a tragic story, a recognition of pure baseball skill. And it must have come as just one more vexation for this sorely tried man to find himself blackballed from an institution that didn't even exist at the time he was playing. Unlike Pete Rose, who is currently down on his hands and knees trying to wriggle into the Hall of Fame that way, Joe Jackson didn't even know that there was any such place to qualify for. If the morals clause that attaches to Hall membership was intended as a deterrent to gambling, the warning came just too late, as usual, to help Shoeless Joe.

For this reason, and for another that I'll get to in a moment, and for a third, which is simply to spare his ghost from any more feeble-minded sympathy and grant him a little decent obscurity alongside Nap Lajoie and Freddy Lindstrom, I too would like to see Joe Jackson in the Hall of Fame. But first we should probably try to get straight who we're voting for around here— whether it's a mythical creature, or just a lout with a pretty name and a swing made in Heaven.

There's no doubt about the swing, anyway. The numbers alone tell you that Jackson was a great hitter: .408 in his first full season and a staggering .356 lifetime—after which it's hard to translate, because one era's records are the next one's chopped liver. More to the point is the awe you can still hear in the voices of his contemporaries when they spoke of him. "There was only one Joe Jackson," said Connie Mack. "There was only one Babe Ruth . . . why compare them?" No one else even makes it into the same sentence.

But Jackson was more than just great; he was also a landmark. Look at a picture of Ty Cobb, with his hands spread on the bat, ready to chop suspiciously at anything that moved. What with the pitchers smearing, scuffing and otherwise denaturing the ball with every substance known to witchcraft, you were dead if you took a full cut in those days. You just slapped at the dancing ball and ran like the wind.

Then turn for contrast to those immortal films of Babe Ruth swinging into the Jazz Age with the throttle out and no more spitballs to worry about (they'd just been banned)—and you're looking at Joe Jackson, or the closest thing we've got to him. "I decided," said Ruth, "to pick out the greatest hitter to watch and study and Jackson was good enough for me," and he modeled his very stance and swing on what he saw.

So there you have him, baseball's missing link, a specimen that had come of age jousting on even terms with Cobb (whom Ruth did *not* bother to study), only to wind up bequeathing his style to the next generation and the next. Leaving him out of the Hall of Fame is a bit like omitting the *Tyrannosaurus rex* from the Museum of Natural History—it hurts us more than it hurts him by now, and it leaves an awful hole in the historical record.

So there are two questions to be asked here, the first being of course whether he actually did throw the World Series, even a little bit; but the second being whether the Hall itself is the better or worse for his thundering absence.

On the first, the case against Jackson may be just a smidgen stronger than his proponents care to admit. He had, for one thing, motive to burn: a skinflint owner, a failed business in Savannah, expensive tastes (suits, hats and shoes—for which he was a regular Imelda—and even a chorus girl) and a generalized paranoia toward owners, reporters and even his fellow players: in his grand jury testimony, he took it for granted that even his one friend on the team, Claude Williams, had sold him out as much as the others had. In a word, he was not too happy up north.

It was more than enough to make a man grunt and take the money. But whether, having done both, he decided to screw the gamblers and play his best anyway is a matter that maybe only the Gambling Hall of Fame can determine. Because on the other side of the ledger, we have just two other things that we know for sure: that he loved baseball and that he hit .375, including hitting the Series' only homer—and perhaps a third that we don't know. He may have been, as his first defenders insisted, simply too dumb to know what he was doing.

There is no enigma like stupidity (what does your cat know and how long has he known it?) and the enigma only gets worse with time, because by now we can't even tell for sure if Jackson *was* that stupid. We know that his dumbness wasn't just a

northern invention, because the neighbors back home had noticed it too. But was it merely verbal? Who can say? Harry
Grabiner, the Chicago club secretary, thought that "he seemed
at times like a dumb dog; at other times, more like a fox." But
the fox has disappeared from the current version.

In fact, some of his champions have tended to lay his stupidity
on with a shovel, to the point where it seems like a miracle that
he was able to find left field every day, let alone play it like an
angel. Americans love nothing better than stories of innocence
betrayed (at the same time, if you recall, Woodrow Wilson was
being led astray by Clemenccau and Lloyd George, uptown
versions of Gandil and Swede Risberg) and such evidence as
exists that Jackson may have known what he was doing has
vanished from the collective memory.

But athletic intelligence is always something of a puzzle to
laypeople. How for instance can anyone who plays football so
mega-intelligently as Joe Montana give such dumb interviews?
Suffice it to say that no memories come down to us of Jackson
throwing to the wrong base or making an ass of himself on the
base paths—quite the reverse; he had a brilliant baseball mind;
so he would certainly have known how to throw a ball game
without its showing.

And if he forgot, there were seven other perfectly intelligent
confederates on hand to remind him. At the very outset Gandil
told him, if he didn't already know it, how he could even look
good in the act of dumping. It takes so little: all you need do
is "short leg" a fly ball here, and swing a fraction late there,
and you have the rest of the afternoon to show off. A dumb
old fox like Jackson might even have enjoyed the challenge.

In the end, he denied he had taken the challenge, though, and
there's no firm reason to disbelieve him. In the first game pitcher
Ed Cicotte, a truly tragic figure, suddenly realized that *none* of
his co-conspirators wanted to be the one to throw the game;
they all preferred to leave the whole thing to him.

Honor among thieves. Fortunately for these weasels, the one
player who really looked as if he was trying to throw the game
was Eddie Collins, and he wasn't. But this is all part of the

murk that will probably enshroud that Series forever, long after the last revisionist is hung. Outside of that first game (in which Jackson, incidentally, went hitless), it is not clear that any of the Series was *completely* thrown.

Abe Attell, the ex-prizefighter in charge of disbursements, was one of those sublimely crooked characters out of Runyon or Breslin, who couldn't take a quart of milk home to his mother without selling the cream first, and he began to shortchange the players way too soon, so that from the second game on, compliance became spotty, literally a matter of hit or miss, with the players who were paid the most presumably complying the most.

Jackson himself received five thousand dollars out of a promised twenty, which would seem like barely enough to pay for his silence once he realized he was getting the shaft; but it's possible that he gave just a little bit more. Checking Asinof's timetable of payments against box scores and records of the games, one finds that the day after Williams dumped the payola on his bed, Joe, by chance, went hitless again and may not have distinguished himself in the field either. In the big Cincinnati inning, the sixth, at least two balls were hit to left field and one was a double and the other a scoring fly—and who knows how they were fielded by this time? Left field in the reign of Jackson was known as the place "where triples went to die" but maybe they had a slightly better chance of life that day. Or maybe not.

On the face of it, the best piece of evidence that Jackson did at least *something* for his money would seem to be his own insistence to the grand jury that he'd had a lousy Series whatever the numbers said. But nothing is that clear in the Bertolt Brecht world of Chicago justice circa 1920. Faced with a politically appointed judge of that era, a more sophisticated man than Jackson might have had trouble deciding whether he was looking at a real judge or a gangster in drag; or, in either case, figuring out who was paying for hizzoner's services today. So Joe may have preferred not to get in deeper than he already was by admitting that he took five thousand dollars for absolutely nothing. He batted well, yes sir, and he fielded well too—these were things he couldn't deny under torture. But he had a lousy Series anyway, so there.

And there the matter sits to this day. Unfortunately for Jackson, the least of the above suspicions would have been enough to sink him without trace in the view of the original Hall of Fame charter (1938), a curious document that seems almost to have been directed expressly at *him*. Of the six qualifications recommended for membership, no fewer than four could be called morals clauses: a player is to be judged on "integrity, sportsmanship, character"—three ways of saying the same thing (the Hall has always had a way with words)—and finally "contribution to the team," and on this one, Joe and the others don't fare well at all. The White Sox went in one year from being one of the proudest outfits in baseball to being the team that dare not speak its name, for fear the nation fall asleep. (And hats off here to the late Jean Shepherd for at least making them seem funny. They weren't.)

However, despite the Hall's strictures, a number of voters voted for Joe in the first election anyway; and the heavens didn't fall. Cooperstown is a sunny sort of place that can't hold a frown for long, and the powers that be there were quite happy to leave it to the writers. Yet, curiously enough, the case against Jackson seems to harden each year, the louder his supporters holler and the further we get from the original scandal. And the Pete Rose affair may harden it even more. It appears, incredibly, that the one or two lessons that *everybody* should have learned once and for all from the Black Sox caper—that you can't trust gamblers, that you can't hide big money—have to be taught all over again. So maybe this isn't the greatest moment to salute baseball's most famous sinner, who, alas, can't be slipped in quietly by the back door any more.

On the other hand, if Pete gets in, maybe Jackson could ride in on his coattails. There would be something ironic about this, with one gambler helping another to sneak past the authorities, but something wrong too—maybe almost as wrong as letting Joe into the Hall on grounds of stupidity.

Jackson's case should not be linked for more than a moment with that of the bubble-headed Rose, who gambled mainly for kicks and knew exactly what he was doing—and if it's argued that at least Pete didn't throw any games, who knows what he might have done if he'd gotten in a hole? And who knows what signals the gambling world picked up from Rose's choice of games? Jackson did what he did (or didn't) for money which, in his far from stupid opinion, he deserved. And if he wanted to use the Nixonian defense that everybody else was doing it too, he wouldn't have been that far wrong.

Bill James, in his *Historical Baseball Abstract*, entitles the 1910s "a Decade Wrapped in Greed," while historian David Voigt uses the phrase "the Myth of Baseball's Single Sin" in reference to the Black Sox scandal. By 1919, baseball was rife and running over with gambling, with even the mighty Ty Cobb and Tris Speaker apparently taking a dive in one game, and that pillar of the game John McGraw being openly accused of bribing opponents to lose another. Indeed, there were so many rumors abroad that when baseball finally hired Judge Landis to bring order to the classroom, his first years in office were fully occupied sweeping them all, conceivably including a World Series or two, under the rug. All except this one.

Some of the sinners were "sports," like the incorrigible Hal Chase, who would have been a handful in any era, but almost all of them needed the money. As Bill James describes it, baseball had just gone through a boom and bust cycle, and the players were hurting. But there was absolutely nothing legitimate they could do about it. The famous "slave labor" clause in their contract, which bound them to a single team for life and even thereafter (someone whimsically raised the question in the forties and it seems that the clause covers resurrections too), left the players no room for maneuver, no bargaining power whatever. They could play or stay home.

In the circumstances, their only recourse was to the kindness of owners, which, with honorable exceptions, was somewhat akin to seeking refuge from a snowstorm in the icebox. The Chicago White Sox were trapped in a particularly grizzly corner of this Dickensian nightmare and, to cut a long story short, eight of them decided they'd better find *someone* they could bargain with—things couldn't get any worse—and they went looking for gamblers.

Things did get worse, of course, and in the courtroom the players learned that Arnold Rothstein, the fixer, had more in common (money) with Chuck Comiskey, their villainous owner, than either man had with them. In the criminal case, the two crooks actually joined forces to protect the players—and their own backsides—and this being Chicago, not only were the players acquitted but Rothstein almost got a round of applause for just showing up. But Comiskey made no such effort to save them later from Landis, preferring at that point to play the King Lear figure, and cut them off without a penny. So the players were broken and have lived in well-lighted obloquy ever since.

Throwing a World Series remains too bad a thing, too great a breach of faith with children, if nothing else, for anything very good to be said about any of them. But this much *can* be said: first, throwing games was the only form of protest available at the time—a primitive kind of do-it-all-yourself strike, in which you used the only thing you had, your baseball skill, to subvert the people who were using *you*. And second, the reserve clause that drove them to it has since been struck from the books forever, leaving the eight conspirators in the twilight zone of outlaws who have defied rotten laws—nothing as acceptable as those who helped slaves escape, but maybe not much worse than rumrunners and speakeasy operators. There is no danger of Joe Jackson, or any of them, being a bad example to anyone anymore because the circumstances that gave rise to their actions are as dead as the Dred Scott Decision.

However it turns out with the Hall of Fame, shed no tears for Shoeless Joe. By 1920, he was not, as usually depicted, a fresh-faced youth who never found out what he could do, but a well-worn thirty-three—no doubt worn down further from listening to thirteen years of jokes about his illiteracy (the journalists just wouldn't quit)—and had proved everything he'd ever need to.

As Donald Gropman tells it in his useful, if star-struck, biography *Say It Ain't So, Joe*, Jackson's last years don't sound
all that bad, as old ballplayers' last years go. He had never liked
those pesty northern cities much anyway, but he was home now,
among friends, with enough pizzazz left to tear the hide off the
ball in the South Georgia semipro league for many more years,
and to grow gracefully in his role as baseball's Bonnie Prince
Charlie, the hero in exile who could have done it all if he'd only
had the chance.

Like the other Black Sox, Jackson grew more saintly—and
talented—in his own mind with each passing year, eventually
releasing his own dry-cleaned (he was in the cleaning business
by then) version of the scandal in bits and pieces. It was a version
that jibes with absolutely nobody else's and clashes with his
own confession of twenty-five years earlier, but who wants to
split hairs with a legend?

Indeed, it seems almost a pity by now, but I guess it has to
be done, to cut him down to size and put him in the Hall of
Fame, which is being made to seem like the heavy in a drama
that doesn't suit it in the least. The Hall is not a court of law,
magically capable of adjudicating matters that could not be
adjudicated at the time. What it can do better than anything
else is simply to judge and reward baseball talent, but it is not
being allowed to do so now in deference to a regulation that
might have been written by Jesse Helms himself. And meanwhile, the museum is missing a Rembrandt.

What is particularly confusing about the Jackson case is that
even inside the baseball beltway nobody seems quite clear as to
who is supposed to "forgive" Joe anyway. Is it the commissioner
or the sportswriters, or maybe the directors of the Hall of Fame?
Just what *is* the relation of Cooperstown and organized baseball
at this point?

The situation seems almost Britishly vague, which means that
it is also blessedly ripe for compromise and readjustment. Perhaps the best solution would be for the whole mishmash known
as baseball to declare a separation of powers, in which the
commissioner punishes your sins while the Hall of Fame ac-

knowledges your achievements, the way having your face on a
stamp does. Being banished for life is a pretty good punishment;
you really don't have to add anything to it. Being banished for
eternity is a bit bloody much, the kind of piling on guaranteed
to turn two-bit chiselers into martyrs. Especially chiselers (if
that's what he was) named Shoeless Joe.

But however it turns out, I like to think that somewhere a
famous southerner will spit on his bat, pound the dirt out of
his socks and mutter "Frankly, by this time, I don't give a
damn."

Outtakes: Field of Dreams,
Fields of Do-Do

*I*t seems fairly clear right off that the Kevin Costner character in *Field of Dreams* wouldn't have liked the original Joe Jackson very much. If you'll recall, there is a sequence in which Costner visits the general store in Nowhere, Iowa, and is completely unnerved by the silent stares of the local farmers, whose faces and bodies are made to appear extra large and menacing, as they would to a frightened child.

But this is a warm scene next to the reception he could have expected in Brandon Mill, South Carolina. Here is Eliot Asinof describing how Harry Grabiner, the White Sox club secretary, felt about visiting Joe in his hometown. "He [Grabiner] had never liked Jackson much. The southerner would stare at him with those dark brooding eyes, never letting go of him, following every move he made." And in Brandon Mills, Joe was considered one of the lively ones.

So maybe Iowa is the right place for Jackson after all. Of course, Joe didn't have the farmers' advantages, he had never learned to read and write. But maybe that was for the best, because in the only other scene involving the local Iowans, we find that their literacy has merely turned them into book-burning fascists, whom Costner's wife Amy Madigan easily routs with a few high-spirited clichés about books and the human spirit that astoundingly haven't reached this part of the country yet (how did they *find* this place?). Obviously the Costner-man subscribes to the Mark Twain ruling "Heaven for scenery, Hell for company," because the human inhabitants of his earthly paradise seem to have barely made it out of the swamp. If I was Iowa, I'd sue.

The movie version of Shoeless Joe who metamorphoses from the cornfields seems on sight to be made of finer stuff than the local mud farmers; this looks like the kind of kid who'd know *exactly* what to do with an education. A diffident hunk of vaguely Italianate appearance, Rousseau's Noble Savage as painted by Raphael—you can make book he'd be writing his own haikus within a week and telling you about this great writer he's just discovered—J. D. Salinger! If he'd only had a chance . . .

But right there, we may have a problem. Because the original Joe Jackson did have a chance. His first big-league manager, Connie Mack, the most patient of men, actually offered to hire him a companion to teach him the ABCs, but Jackson was pig-headed all the way down to his shoes and preferred to play the hand he was dealt, and Mack finally gave up on him. This same Mack, mind you, had gotten along fine with Rube Waddell, an idiot child who chased after fire trucks, and he worshiped talent in anybody, but he found himself no match for Brandon Mill and the towns around it. "It was a county of corn whiskey and ignorance. If a man learned to read and write, he was looked on as a freak" (Asinof). And Jackson didn't want to become one of *those* at any cost—even at the cost of a merciless ribbing everywhere else he went in life.

Although the folks of Brandon Mill hadn't even reached the stage of evolution where you start *burning* books, they were his people, and Joe never quite got over his homesickness for them. His first response to the northern cities where big-league baseball is played was simply to run away from them and head for home.

But eventually he came to his own kind of terms with the action, even more so than I indicated in my previous piece. According to Asinof, Joe "became a slick dresser, very conscious of his clothes. He liked the feel of shiny new shoes and bought more than he needed" ("and hats," Asinof added when I called him— hats being *the* men's fashion statement back then). And that fling he had with the chorus girl almost earned him a South Carolina divorce at the end of his wife's shotgun. "Hungry for more money, he tried to set up businesses over the winter," but like many amateurs he got burned by these, so that he needed more money still.

Catching up with the haberdashery was one thing, making friends was another, and here it might help if we turned the image in *Field of Dreams* around for a moment so that we have one silent staring farmboy entering a store full of Costners. In Jackson's part of the world, when you talked at all you talked *slo-o-ow*, so that he would have needed subtitles just to know what these smarties were talking about. And if cracker memories of northerners were anything to go by, it wasn't anything good.

In his grand jury testimony Jackson spoke of an "inner circle" in the White Sox that he never cracked, but in fact he never seems to have cracked any circles at all. His one friend on the team, his fellow southerner Claude "Lefty" Williams, serves in the story mostly as a go-between with the inner circle, bringing Joe the money and telling him how the conspiracy is going. Lefty speaks Joe's language, but he is still one of "them," still a little too swift for Brandon Mills. It speaks volumes I think that he never seems to have hooked up with Williams again even after they'd been through the fire together but went snarling off alone to his own corner.

When he was through testifying that day, his tongue, which had finally been tripped into action, apparently wouldn't quit on him, and he gave anyone who would listen a paranoid earful about how "they"—the law, the press, the owners, everyone— were all out to screw him. "It was like a little boy hitting back wildly at the big adult world," says Asinof, but this I think is the view from the sixties, when everything in the whole universe was seen as kids versus grown-ups. My own thoughts stray again (and maybe I should look into this) to Richard "Black Shoes" Nixon, and his famous "final" press conference when he, too, gave "them" a piece of his mind.

"They've hung it on me," said Jackson that day. "But I don't care what happens now. I guess I'm through with baseball. I wasn't wise enough, like Chick [Gandil, instigator of the fix and King of the Smarties], to beat them to it. But some of them will sweat before the show is over." Substitute "Jack," as in Kennedy, for "Chick," and throw in the word hardball someplace, and the comparison is complete. The voice of the classic outsider, the eternal cracker, hasn't changed a note in seventy years.

So now we know what Shoeless Jackson *really* said to the small boy who asked him to "say it ain't so, Joe." Obviously he snarled back, "you won't have Joe Jackson to kick around anymore." And we also know that he had motive to burn for listening to Chick Gandil, a southerner who knew the ropes up here, when Chick chirped his siren song of money and vengeance.

One edge he did have over Mr. Nixon, though—and it's the difference between tragedy and comedy—is that he had a real home to go to after the deed was done, where he became quite normal again and just another example of the terrible things that happen to you when you go up north.

Angels with Dirty Faces

CONNIE MACK

*B*aseball fans make a number of strange sounds, but the only one that has been isolated and genetically identified with the game is the sound "boo." And the home of the boo, its very Cooperstown, is Philadelphia, which also by chance gave us Connie Mack, Mr. Baseball for half a century.

Philadelphians have always had a lot to boo about—besides Philadelphia itself (an enchanting city, but infinitely booable). They have had more losing teams than any three cities should be asked to endure. And many of these were provided by Mack, the somewhat different genius.

Mack served up only two kinds of teams: unbeatable and lousy. When I was a boy, he was going through one of his lean periods, which tended to linger a bit, like biblical plagues. The sun shone and the infield sparkled like a dress shirt in that comeliest of stadiums, the old Shibe Park, but something was wrong. The players moved neither to right nor left; they hit not the curve nor the fast ball, nor even the lowly change of pace. If they held the Yankees or Red Sox to single figures we lit bonfires—or rather, being what we were, we booed.

The soul of a fan in a losing city is warped by inches (it being a game of inches anyway, as my cliché adviser avers). At first, age nine in my case, you simply overrate the local heroes like everyone else and are baffled by their consistent inadequacy. By ten, you still believe the training camp reports swearing that everything will be different this year; by eleven, you clutch like the local infielders at rays of hope—fairly good Aprils, split doubleheaders, two-game winning streaks; by twelve, you believe nothing. You are marinated like Nolan Ryan's blister. You take to booing. Also, in those days, to running dementedly round the bases after the game and hook-sliding into home with three other fellows.

I don't know what happens after that, because I left Philadelphia the next year to start a new life as a Dodger fan. But many people went through whole adolescences of this, until the team itself left town out of kindness. By then, the thing had become self-perpetuating. The fans booed the players one by one into nervous breakdowns, until they became even more useless than before. Unless memory plays tricks, visitors were frequently spared, except from the eighth-inning beer cans, which rained indifferently on whoever was standing in left field. The fans saved their fury for their own, and the bigger the better: Dick Allen of the Phils being the consummation, the best player, best booed.

Curiously, though, they never blamed the founder of much of this Beckett situation, the long-faced Irishman in the black suit who had not once but twice led them out of the Promised Land and into the desert: Mr. Mack, who only left the cellar in order to win occasional pennants; also, Mack the Knife, who dismembered two of the greatest teams of all time, in 1915 and again in '33, on the stated grounds that the fans were bored with success! As if they weren't bored with what they got in its place. Jehovah Himself never thought up a prettier punishment for smugness. Nine pennants were paid for with sixteen last places.

Yet no one minded Mack. He was, at first glance, a funny sort of saint. In the "City of Undertakers," he dressed the part to the nines. Connie always seemed to be wearing black, or perhaps one of his festive dark grays, and his cadaverous length was usually stretched further by a derby or straw boater. In this mournful regalia he couldn't very well go out on the field, so he ran things from the dugout shadows, like an Irish city boss or, as I prefer to think, a Renaissance cardinal. He wagged his scorecard as if it were a papal bull, and lesser men went running.

In short, he was a Presence. While other managers bounced around like monkeys in bloomers, or waddled to the mound with arthritic dignity, or even, as in the case of George Stallings of the Braves, offered to bust a puzzled Connie in the snoot, Mack himself sat stiff on his plank-wood throne, a man of respect, a figure from the past, but not one you laughed at— unless you craved a broken nose from one of his employees. He had, I'm told, an inner merriment (at least one got mortally tired of his "twinkling blue eyes" that lit up the *Evening Bulletin*) which must have made you wonder who was laughing at whom. But most of all, he embodied the Game; he was a one-man shrine who preserved himself like a committee, and gave you a glimpse of what it must have been like in a sweeter time.

Only baseball with its layers of history could have produced such a figure. Connie was a good name for him. He had the look of a cheating minister or funereal card-sharp. When he set out in the eighties and nineties, ballplayers were considered lower even than actors, and Mack was the type who could get them into the hotel and assure you they were all good boys and get them out by moonlight. He boasted in later years of how he used to "tip the bat" when he was a catcher, and he was also known to freeze baseballs overnight and to call for quick pitches while fixing his equipment—all devices necessary for keeping his scrawny frame in the big leagues, or what passed for them, for ten years or so.

Later, he had a special weakness for dim-witted roustabouts

like Rube Waddell, the fire truck chaser, who were the very essence of baseball in those days, if you could get them to show up. His great team of 1929 was so foul-mouthed that the boys singed Judge Landis' ears in the commissioner's box and brought down an unprecedented edict to cease and shut up. The test of a manager was and is how much of this animal energy he can hold under rein, and Mack took the limit.

Baseball needed class, but it couldn't have handled a real saint. Mack was the perfect compromise. When he walked onto the field in 1905 to battle Muggsy McGraw's Giants, the two men represented baseball's two faces, dignity versus the low life, pinstripe versus bum, the world versus Durocher, but in odd proportions. McGraw had class, too, of the old New York school of Dinty Moore's and Delmonico's, and he kept it under his hat; Mack wore his on his sleeve. But they were well-matched: McGraw never put one over on Mack and Mack never lorded it over McGraw. A beautiful pair of Irish actors, they could have made a great comedy team or political rivalry, with a twist of circumstance.

Judging from the amount written about the 1905 Series and its re-runs in 1911 and '13, this rivalry captured the nation's imagination more than any other and gave it something to play with, a new kind of drama. Despite the manager's unearthly dignity, Mack's Athletics had been dubbed by McGraw himself the White Elephants, the dregs of the upstart American League, which McGraw's swaggering Giants would shortly put out of business for good. In fact, no five-game series was ever closer than the 1905 set. The difference was two men: Christy Mathewson, who won three, and Waddell, who didn't show up at all (he'd hurt his shoulder wrestling over a straw hat), and such small differences can be adjusted by time. When the teams met again in '11 and '13, the Athletics got even twice. Eddie Plank and Chief Bender were the executioners, and Mack issued his famous edict that "pitching is 75 percent of baseball" or 80 or 90—the number has floated free ever since, and oddly enough is never disputed, at whatever quotation. In 1911, Home Run Baker, who hit two of his namesakes, and six days of rain, made up the remaining percent. Mathewson's arm cooled off in the rain, and Mr. Mack had his first of five championships.

Suddenly he also had the first of his perfect teams. The hundred-thousand-dollar infield of Stuffy McInnis, Eddie Collins, Jack Barry and Frank Baker was the featured attraction, and the word was that they were almost too good for baseball. Mack acquired a reputation as the greatest teacher of fundamentals ever, and perhaps this gave him a Pygmalion or Henry Higgins complex, and he came to believe he could pass *anyone* off as a ballplayer. Because in 1914, he broke up his perfect team as a man might smash a gold watch in a fit of temper. The As had just contrived to lose four games out of four to the Miracle Boston Braves; and while the Braves had amazing momentum, there is hearsay reason to believe that Mack suspected his heroes of dumping the Series. After his ace Chief Bender was strafed in the first game, Bender did not appear again, although Mack always called the Chief his greatest clutch pitcher. Remember we are just five years away from the Black Sox scandal, and the notorious Hal Chase would continue to throw games all over the place almost into the twenties. In fact, rumors of tank jobs filled the air in those pre-Landis years, and an upset on this scale had to worry the manager somewhat. Mack was fussy about his integrity, to such good effect that in 1927 he was able to refute Dutch Leonard's charges that Tris Speaker and Ty Cobb had thrown games back in 1918 (they had) simply by retaining them. And perhaps this legend of integrity began with the break-up of the 1914 team, not for excellence but for naughtiness.

They were easily raffish enough to throw a Series. That year, six of them were summoned by the IRS for failure to report their Series shares. And maybe half of them were playing footsie with the new Federal League, which was offering real money as opposed to Mack's wooden nickels. Connie's hold over his players should not be exaggerated. When Lefty Grove was later asked what it was like being managed by Mack, he said he didn't know, because he never paid any attention to him.

Which was a fair turnabout, because Mack never paid Grove

or anyone else what *they* wanted, namely top dollar. Grove was reported at one time to be getting thirty thousand dollars a year, but he later told a writer that he'd never seen anything like that much. Mack groaned mightily over his payroll, but like that other saint, Branch Rickey, he would have traded his mother to keep it down to size. He deplored the practice of buying teams and stocking them with pricey players (as if stinginess were a badge of integrity), but he had nothing against selling teams and fielding bargain basement ones in their place. His 1916 team, which lost 117 games, is widely believed to be the worst team that has ever played the game, and I'll go along with that, because I can't see Connie settling for anything less. But I'll also bet that it had the smallest payroll.

Mysteriously, the pennant winners of '14 had contrived to lose sixty-five thousand dollars, with a huge drop in reported attendance, and Mack got it back the quick way, by peddling star flesh, most notably Eddie Collins for a cool fifty thousand dollars. Even thus refreshed, he was not able to meet the price tag of twenty-five thousand dollars that Baltimore owner Jack Dunn had put on Babe Ruth and Ernie Shore, a couple of promising young pitchers who might have helped a bit in the coming plague years.

Thus pain entered Philadelphia, and the As became white elephants after all. They proceeded for the next few years to match their manager's eerie detachment, looking either up at the league or down at it, but seldom being precisely in it. In 1915, the Phillies with Grover Cleveland Alexander won one of their rare National League pennants, but there was no trolley series, because the As were nowhere to be found. And in '17 and '19, As fans had to sit by slack-jawed as the great Eddie Collins helped the White Sox to two pennants, and ironically turned out to be one of the clean Sox when that team changed color.

It has always been hard to swallow that the 1914 As were really too perfect to get a decent game from anyone. The Red Sox boasted the immortal outfield of Tris Speaker, Harry Hooper and Duffy Lewis. Detroit had Ty Cobb and Sam Crawford; Chicago, Buck Weaver; Cleveland, Joe Jackson: in fact, an All-Star American League team of that year would have matched the best of any era without needing a single Athletic. Yet the fable endured of perfection blighted and came in very handy when Mack did the exact same thing in the thirties: sold a super team for straight cash because they were too good for this world.

It certainly wasn't the high price of black suits that made him do it. Unlike Clark Griffith, the Scrooge of Washington, Mack wasn't consistent enough to be called a miser. He did home-grow another great team in the 1920s, in his little victory garden, but what made it great was the purchase of the aforementioned Grove from Baltimore in the International League for the record amount of $100,600. The obtainment of Cobb and Speaker, on the other hand, was probably for straight gate-appeal—a penny-wise move tantamount to hiring Buffalo Bill, which may have cost him the pennant in 1928. For once his policy of developing cheap young players was suspended, and Bing Miller and Mule Haas had to watch the two old gentlemen creaking around the outfield a few times too many.

The passing through of Cobb may have had another subtle effect on Mack's fortunes, because in '28, Ty introduced the players, and perhaps the manager, to the pleasures of the stock market, just in time for the Crash. This must have given Mack's payroll fits, as he proceeded to win three pennants in a row with a team of busted investors.

Those years, 1929–31, are the glories of Mack's career: without them, he would belong squarely in the limbo of Hughie Jennings and Fred Clarke and other minor divinities of the first quarter century. But to challenge the lordly Yankees of Ruth and Gehrig and take them three in a row—what manner of strange old man was this? A mere two years before, the Yankees had fielded their greatest side ever, and if Ruth had slipped a hair since then, Gehrig certainly hadn't, and now the great Bill Dickey was on hand to announce a whole fresh dynasty. Yet the As beat them without breaking a sweat. They were not only good but ferocious: "Bucketfoot" Al Simmons, who worked himself into a homicidal rage against pitchers before going up to bat; Jimmie Foxx with his sleeves cut off so that his very muscles might subdue you ("how much air do they hold, Jimmie?" asked Ted Lyons; "thirty-five pounds," answered Foxx); Black Mike Cochrane, perhaps the fastest *running* catcher who ever played and the most competitive, and the best; and the towering, glowering Grove, so unfathomably angry in defeat that his teammates couldn't go near him. Luckily, defeat seldom happened: in 1931 Grove went 31–4, but ripped his shirt and three lockers to pieces after one of the four losses—a 1–0 fluke that ended a sixteen-game winning streak. And these were just the Hall of Famers. The rest of the squad included such names as George Earnshaw and Rube Walberg (pitchers) and Jimmy Dykes (third baseman) that were still magic in the sour-apple forties, and was strong at every position. Yet again, it was not really in a class by itself. The Yankees beat it at almost full strength in 1932, and Mack didn't dismantle it for good until that winter.

"Philadelphia bankers force Mack to sell," said the headlines. A loan of four-hundred thousand dollars had apparently been called in abruptly. What had gone wrong this time? The '32 team claimed a loss of five-hundred thousand dollars, and Mack chattered about the payroll and the cost of stadium renovation—although few fans would have traded Jimmie Foxx et al. for a paint job. Rumor inevitably started in Philadelphia that Mack and/or his sons Roy and Earle had taken a bath in the market and in real estate and that "someone" in the front office (*Baseball Digest*, 1943) was investing the petty cash; and the question was raised whether Mack would dare to show his face on opening day, 1933.

He not only did, but he marched all the way to the flagpole, eyes front and shoulders straight like a Sinn Fein leader defying British bullets. It was enough. He never had to appear again. Whatever else we booed in Philadelphia, which included even each other at times, we never booed the man who had made the long march to the flagpole and back.

The long Mack twilight had begun. His vaunted gift for spot-

ting talent proved to be nothing special. Doc Cramer, Bob Johnson and Wally Moses were fine hitters, but his infields never
came anywhere near his famous hundred-thousand-dollar one
of 1910–14, even with inflated dollars, and he couldn't seem to
spot pitchers at all. Unlike Branch Rickey, who could grow a
cheap star under an expensive one any day, Mack could no
longer either buy them or develop them the old way. He never
got much of a grip on the farm system idea, which Rickey had
invented in the twenties, and his shavetails from Toronto and
elsewhere were just ballplayers, the kind you see all over—
replaceable, anonymous, forgettable.

But still he hung on, like some old chieftain who knows he
will die if he quits. By the late 1940s, fresh rumors began to
float that he was losing his finer marbles, that he couldn't remember his players' names, that Al Simmons really ran the team
from the third-base coaching box. It was hard to tell, because
the game-to-game management was so wooden and featureless
that it could have been coming from anywhere. Only the occasional rank mistake suggested that our leader was dozing.

Yet those were the years when the legend grew the most. The
surprise starting of the aged Howard Ehmke in the '29 Series
was exhumed and seen as pure genius; the ten-run inning in the
same Series was all Mack's doing now. The inability of his
pitchers to hold Cardinals on base in '31 was no affair of his.
All was Ehmke and Bender and the infield of 1914. The modest
achievements any man might rack up in fifty years sparkled
brightly in the dung heap of Philadelphia baseball.

Mack is also a chapter in the history of the sporting press.
Reporters were kindly in those days, as well they might be since
the club frequently picked up all their tabs; and Mack was the
most obliging man in the business. Writers' interests are not
necessarily fans' interests, and last place teams are quite en-
durable for them if the copy keeps coming. In return, writers
would cover up whatever there was to cover up. If they could
throw a blanket over Ruth's excesses, they could hide anything.
I have it on good authority that when Jackie Robinson's Dodgers
were due to play an exhibition with the As, old Mack was less

than enthusiastic about having "the nigger" along. But the writers were off doing pieces about Ehmke and the ten-run inning.

As for the financial structure which had forced Mack to gut his team yet later left a handsome trust fund for his five daughters—that was Mr. Mack's business. You don't examine a saint's books. He was free to give whatever reasons he chose for breaking up his teams, until Mack's excuses became official history. Outside of his shadowy partner Ben Shibe (and presumably his sons) nobody knew *what* the rigid Mack was sitting on all those years. No reporter of the period seriously probed him, because he was famous for his integrity. And why was he famous for it? Because they said so.

Baseball is, of course, whatever the public thinks it is. For instance, when Branch Rickey brought Robinson into baseball, he too was canonized. Yet he had a number of most practical reasons as noted in the Robinson chapter.

It still took courage for Rickey to do it, and Rickey could make anything he did seem like a branch of religion, but what one savors about Rickey is still the slight whiff of hypocrisy, the sense of the pious rogue who does well by doing good, and that's what one liked about Connie Mack. Because he did it on even fewer actual good works than Rickey. *Why* did he have such a reputation for integrity? Because he looked as if he should. Because the closest he got to swearing was when he said to Jimmy Dykes "and nuts to you too, Mr. Dykes." (Not swearing is the pinnacle of virtue in baseball.) Because the sport, having rashly proposed itself as the national pastime, has always clutched at anything that could pass for statesmanlike. Because the players worshiped him.

At the end, as he sat senile and glassy-eyed through a 1954 old-timers' game, the players introduced themselves to him with an appearance of reverence that only stopped short at kissing his ring. He didn't recognize any of them, but it didn't matter. They thought they were shaking hands with Baseball.

Mack had long since ceased influencing the game in any practical way. Some said that he was a prisoner of his sons Roy and Earle, who kept him there for dynastic purposes (since no one would ever bad-mouth Mack himself, his sons came in for a lot of this and came to seem like very dubious fellows. Rightly or wrongly, someone has to redress the balance of virtue in a family). But it was nice to have him there on any terms because he tickled the imagination. Born in the Lincoln Administration, and still staggering through Eisenhower—he was like a tree with initials on it from the Garden of Eden.

As a feisty young catcher, Mack had been active in what passed for a players' association and had even taken part in a species of players' strike in the 1880s. After his death, his team with its strange history ran afoul of a more streamlined Players Association. Charlie Finley, the professional bad boy whose horns had replaced Mack's halo as the As' symbol, found the new free-agent rule posing the same kind of threat that the Federal League had in 1914. And he reacted exactly the same way.

In a ghostly re-run, he broke up the team—because of low attendance, putative stinginess, restless players and the owner's conviction that he could build a great new team anytime he wanted to. And as in '14, the players made their own deals where possible, and the As did not get their money's worth.

It is to be supposed that Mack would not have cared for Finley's vulgarity and carny approach to baseball, but I wouldn't bet on much more than that. Baseball is a game of appearances, of slyness and bluff, and Connie's blue eyes might have twinkled in his mortician's face to see a new kind of actor go through the old motions. The man who brought gloom to Philadelphia and the one who broke hearts in Kansas City and Oakland are brothers under the skin and form a weird continuity of their own. The main difference, and let old-timers shed a tear over this if they choose, was that Cornelius McGillicuddy was always a gentleman about it.

BRANCH RICKEY

Outside of the works of Mark Twain, you have never met anyone like him. Branch Rickey was variously known as "the

preacher," "the Mahatma" (after Gandhi) and, more infor-
mally, as "the pious fraud."

Although he, like Connie Mack, looked like a minister who
would cheat his own flock at bingo, Rickey was not *exactly* a
fraud. He was genuinely pious enough not to play ball himself
on Sundays, thus shortening his only so-so catching career; but
he was also hustler enough to make thousands out of the concept
of the Sunday doubleheader. He had the genuine moral courage
to break the color line by bringing Jackie Robinson into baseball,
but he also had the showmanship to see a fortune to be made
out of black players and inner-city fans. And finally, this man
of God had a special soft spot for sinners like Leo Durocher
and the famous Gashouse Gang and even did his bit to pass on
stories about their devilment.

Rickey is probably best remembered today for the Great
Robinson Breakthrough, but it wasn't the first time that the
Preacher had revolutionized baseball. Besides such minor in-
novations as the batting cage, the sliding pit and the mechanical
batting practice pitcher, he introduced a little something called
the farm system, which changed the whole structure of the game
overnight back in the twenties.

It was Rickey's novel notion to start buying up whole teams
in the minor leagues rather than one player at a time, thus
guaranteeing a huge pool of young talent to call upon at will.
The result was immediately dubbed "Rickey's chain gang," and
the people in it were called "Rickey's slaves," but, for better or
worse, it brought the indigent St. Louis Cardinals an on-again
off-again dynasty for a good twenty years, from 1926 to 1946,
and it soon had all the other big-league teams scrambling to
acquire their very own slaves and chain gangs.

What made Rickey's version work better than anyone else's,
in St. Louis and later Brooklyn, was his freakish and unparalleled eye for talent. In the course of a summer he would per-
sonally scout every team in his system, patiently standing for
hours behind the batting cage, registering nuances of promise
invisible to the normal eye; and anything he missed was probably picked up by the great George Sisler, his third pair of eyes

and lifetime crony. (It takes a very great man indeed to have and keep great associates).

As a youth, Rickey had coached both baseball and football at the high school and college levels and he knew kids inside out. In fact, it was his knowledge of the inside—the guts, the heart—that made his choice of Jack Robinson such a perfect one. With a lesser pioneer than Jack, the whole experiment might have fizzled.

In that hyperactive youth of his (actually, he was hyper till the day he died), Rickey also taught Latin and studied law, and he later used both languages to confuse his players, particularly at contract time. One pictures many a country boy reeling from the Mahatma's office, not exactly sure what he has just signed his name to, after a half-hour of Rickey's inspirational gibberish.

Most of his life Branch spent working for others, so his stinginess was nothing personal. However, he did collect a percentage of every trade his teams made, and so by chance (and, no doubt, God's will) he became one of the greatest traders in baseball history.

He became known for an almost mystical intuition into the precise moment when a player was about to go downhill, although he tended to tip his hand about this by singing that particular player's praises just a little too loudly. ("That means you're trading him, right?" said his knowing son Branch Jr., alias "the Twig.") At any rate, I must have heard Rickey's immortal phrase "better a year too soon than a year too late" at least twice every year since he uttered it.

Although most of his wheeling and dealing was inspired, Rickey's compulsion to tinker may have helped to account for the stop-start nature of the Cardinal dynasty. It must also have driven his employers half insane. In 1941, for instance, he traded the great John Mize, still very much in his prime, and it looked as if he was conceding the 1942 season to Brooklyn then and there.

What actually happened was that St. Louis went on to win four pennants in the next five years, courtesy of Rickey's latest crop of rabbits (he worshipped speed); but Rickey wasn't around to see most of it. Owner Sam Breadon's nerves had presumably snapped over the Mize deal and he didn't renew the great one's contract after 1942.

Interestingly enough, a similar fate awaited him eventually in Brooklyn, his next port of call. After putting together one of the greatest teams of all time, he found, part way through that team's prime, that the fiendish Walter O'Malley had finagled him out of the saddle, as he would later finagle the whole Dodger franchise out of Brooklyn.

Once again, Rickey had built so well that he wasn't needed any more. His immediate legacy, his own hand-picked dream team of Newcombe, Campanella, Hodges, Snider, et al.—a little less rabbitty, except for Robinson, and more powerful than his Cardinal ones to suit the Brooklyn ballpark—continued to scourge the rest of the league; and then, before we knew it, his league began to scourge the *other* league. National League all-star ascendancy may well have been born in Brooklyn the day that Rickey lowered the color bar and added several million new names to the player pool.

But that wasn't the half of what he left behind. When Rickey's own *wunderkinds* finally faded, as *wunderkinds* must, his trusty old farm system magically replaced them, not just once but again and again, so that the Dodgers would proceed to generate contenders in every decade, while other teams rose and fell around them. Even today, the Dodger farm system is still rated by many the best in the business—and the St. Louis Cardinals still run the bases as if the Mahatma was looking on with a stopwatch in one hand and a contract in the other.

In its way, Rickey's last tour of duty, in Pittsburgh, proved to be darn (Rickey was Mack's match at non-swearing, never going further than "criminen-tilies") near as successful as the others; but his part in the success is considerably more cloudy. The Pirates were a terrible team when he arrived and a terrible team when he left and there's no doubt that he'd lost at least some of his touch; but they did burst into flower right afterward, and the championship clubs of 1960 and 1970 had a recognizably Rickey stamp on them—especially in right field, where the great Roberto Clemente testified nightly to the old man's un-wavering eye for talent, and his undiminished slyness; Clemente had started life with the Dodgers, but Rickey still knew that organization better than it knew itself and he used his old skel-eton key to pry loose this quintessential Rickey ballplayer: fast, versatile, and "hungry."

Otherwise, the bumbling Pittsburgh years live on mostly as a straight man in Joe Garagiola's memoirs and in the New York Mets broadcasting booth, where Ralph Kiner likes to reminisce mellowly about Rickey's unremitting effort to trade him, as a last ditch gesture against slow-footed sluggers.

But the best part of Rickey's legacy may be yet to come. Ever since the free agency boom and (comparative) bust, owners have been gradually rediscovering the blessings of the farm system and of the young, *cheap* home-grown player. You actually get better teams that way, as Rickey could have told them. In fact, if Branch returned to the game today, chances are he would still be a good two steps ahead of everybody else and we would be wondering once again, with remembered pleasure, what the old buzzard was about to think up next. So he lives on in his can-tankerous way. Sly, sentimental, opportunistic, and more honest than he looked—Branch Rickey was one of those gargantuan figures they name eras after. Indeed, if you needed one phrase to summarize the years between Mack-McGraw and the reign of the mad millionaires, "the Babe Ruth proposition and the Branch Rickey alternative" would cover all of the major themes and a couple of minor ones as well.

3

Sports Talk

◇

What Are Sportswriters *For*?

*I*t looked like fun when Spencer Tracy did it. Perched eternally in the best seat in the house, batting out his hard-boiled (but sensitive) copy in nothing flat, between wisecracks; then a few minutes with the superstar (who seemed overjoyed to see him) and off to Toots Shor's to collect his anecdotes. Sportswriting seemed like a neat way to make a living.

Its heyday was the teens, twenties, thirties—any time before television. Sportswriters were lords, if not of the earth, at least of the afternoon editions. Some snob once started a rumor that the best prose was to be found in the sports pages, and in certain circles newspapers were rated by who they employed there. Well, why not? Ring Lardner, Damon Runyon, and Heywood Broun wrote about as well as any three journalists I can think of from that day to this.

Nowadays, to watch the heirs of those titans traipsing across the tarmac hauling their dry cleaning from a fight in Cleveland to a basketball game in Detroit is to witness a fall of empire.

Crowds form around Howard Cosell while a TV truck stands arrogantly by, its day's work done. Meanwhile the men with the dry cleaning board commercial flight 000 as anonymously as mailmen. No matter how they scurry, they will never catch up with the news, which went blinking out of town some time ago.

So what do they do, exactly? Heralds without news, eyewitnesses in a world of eyewitnesses—what remains to be said?

"The real object of sportswriting," says a friend of mine who does it, "is to keep readers away from the horrors in the rest of the paper." Thus sports continues its rounds as the Magnificent Evasion, since it also keeps us away from the bad news at home and in one's own psyche. Many men, and a spattering of women, talk about sports from morning to night for fear something else might get in. And strangers reach for it gratefully as a *lingua franca*, something to keep the chatter going while revealing nothing. As a form of cover one invents a sort of "play" self as, say, a Red Sox fan, which one pushes energetically around the board in place of the real thing. It is no accident, I think, that this particular sport within a sport was invented in England, the home of fine acting and the very best spies.

Hence, the sportswriter's task would seem to be simply stoking up the nation's biggest conversation every day and throwing new items onto it from time to time. But there is nothing simple about it. Only to the ear of a spouse does all sports conversation sound alike. In fact, the subject comes in millions of pieces, from local school football to Olympic boycotts, and every fan has his own hierarchy of interests, so that it's hard to arrange a coherent agenda even in a single saloon. A sportswriter is like a man trying to address a hundred saloons at once, not to mention dining rooms and bedrooms. And now, to add to his woes, he must wonder if "they" have seen this or that event on TV and know as much about it as he does.

TV has certainly scrambled what was already a confused picture. In the arts, critics are those who write for the people who already know the work in question, while reviewers are perennial introducers, booming out the names and credentials of new arrivals. Each task is agreeable enough in its thin-lipped way; but the sportswriter has to do both, because his clientele is mixed for him daily in unknown proportions.

For this reason, the locker room has become the favored arena of many a columnist, with the game serving as so much fodder for interviews. The recent hullabaloo about women in the locker room was based largely on this development. The public mind, being what it is, fell back on its *other* subject, and fantasized much hasty snatching of towels, attempts to interview in the shower, and all the other jolly things we like to think about. But if the story is in there, women writers obviously have to go in and get it, let the towels fall where they may.

But what a flat story it generally is. Like many another club women have fought to get into, there isn't much *to* a locker room when you arrive. A score of articulate people can be found jabbering questions at a gaggle of tired and frustrated, or tired and elated, men who are not paid for eloquence. An artist like Red Smith can tease their mumbles into funny stories, and a safe-cracker like Dick Young can extract better mumbles. But the rest are left scrambling for the small coins, the "I hit the real good curve" and "we've been picking each other up all year"—thus contributing to another of the functions of sports-writing, as defined by another friend, namely "to keep those clichés circulating."

The phrase "in depth" usually has even less to do with these hairy confrontations than it does with a Washington press conference. The masters, the Smiths and the Youngs, have a certain small edge: the jocks remember them and occasionally treat them like friends and not answering services. But I suspect that even the best expect little from the postgame hog call. Only after the sweat has dried comes the quote; and by then frequently only the Smiths and Youngs, the trusted retainers, are around to hear it.

The quote they finally do pry loose seems these days to have less and less to do with the game that's just been played. Often the athletes appear to have seen the game slightly less well than the TV cameras, and have been known to mutter "I'll have to

see the films on that." What they do know about is their own
grievances and those of their playmates and these the surliest
of them seem willing to enlarge upon endlessly. "They treat us
all like meat," says Dave Kingman, breaking a silence of several
years. And if the great Steve Carlton ever breaks his monastic
vows, one can bet it will be with some similar keening growl.

So the focus has shifted not just from the arena but from the
whole world of liniment and leather and into the souls of men.
These in turn divide into two departments: fiscal and medico-
spiritual. A sportswriter so inclined can now write about money
every day of the year without giving a thought to bats and balls.
And if he can't, George Steinbrenner will help him. When the
Yankee dictator, with his iron fist and his wooden tongue, observed that some of his batters were being thrown at, he hollered,
in effect, "That may have been okay in the old days, but I pay
these guys a lot of money." This startling evaluation of human
life was all the more gripping for having gone, so far as I know,
completely unquestioned. In the steamy bazaar of the sports
pages, mowing down the peasants while sparing the millionaires
seems almost as reasonable as boxing.

Just in case the fan in the street ever starts to choke on all
the bankrolls he has to read about, along come drugs to change
the subject. Slightly. In fact, it is just a short stroll from one
subject to the other. If athletes are going to be paid like movie
stars, they are inevitably going to start acting like them, which
includes, nowadays, snorting, mainlining, and—felicitous
phrase—freebasing. After which, chances are they will find Jesus.

Back in the fifties, the crusty Jimmy Cannon accused his young
colleagues of being "chipmunks" because they asked so many
personal questions. But the chipmunks must have sniffed something in the wind and foreseen a day when there would be no
impersonal questions left. They were the first TV generation of
Tracys, and they knew that the best seat in the house wasn't
worth a single indiscreet remark from a famous ballplayer's ex-
wife.

So the human-interest story went into place as a basic column—and mighty insipid stuff it could be, as Muscles McGurk conquered fear with the help of his priest and his seeing-eye dog. It needed a shot of something and it got a massive one: the great national shoot-up went coursing through these drab pieces, lighting them up like pinball machines. Even the news items began to read like *General Hospital*: shortstop agrees to rehabilitation, relief pitcher comes out of rehabilitation (but still looks kind of funny), basketball player disappears. All you needed to cover this circus was a degree in pharmacology and the soul of Rona Barrett.

Finding Jesus has, up to now, proved harder for our boys to handle than dope; in fact it could be called a downright handicap. The born-again game hero won't even tell you whether he hit the good curve or the bad slider before he launches into the Man Upstairs, and how *He* did it. Although I would dearly like to know in that case exactly how *He* did it and indeed would welcome a hot theological discussion in the clubhouse, followed by a pillow fight, these pious fellows seem to have given up thinking about anything at all, even the last thing they said. So a story about a born-again has to stress the lamentable drug years and the unfortunate bar brawls before homing in lightly on the homogenized happy ending. Sportswriters are versatile, but only a few of them—and those, specialists—can do much with uplift.

However, there is still work to be done in the other direction, the sin beat. When I covered Muhammad Ali back in 1975, I found myself, like everyone else, covering *for* him. Although he was clearly stepping out with a lady other than his wife, the writers agreed to a man simply not to see it. It goes against the grain of this (let's get it over with) remarkably decent profession to cover bedrooms—even when they begin to show in a subject's work. At the moment, with so many sinners turning themselves in voluntarily, one doesn't have to go looking for them. But even with privacy everywhere in tatters sportswriters sit on spicy stories with a frequency that would get them fired from other parts of the paper. Gallantly, I believe, many of them consider that stuff is simply unworthy of the sports pages.

Even if all the closets flew open at once, we would be left with the condition we came in with: namely, that sports, however described, are local and particular. Drive through Massachusetts or North Carolina on a fall Saturday and you will imagine that the state has been completely overrun by football teams: colleges with funny names like dummy corporations, high schools beyond measure—each demanding its mead of talk.

For this reason, there is hardly such a thing as a national sportswriter.* Jim Murray of the *Los Angeles Times*, who is perhaps the closest, has no regular New York outlet. And when you do see a syndicated column in out-of-town papers it looks oddly abstract and out of place, like a paid ad, among the regional chatter. The syndicated writer must stick to national personalities like Orel Hershiser the Good or John McEnroe the Bad—but these are themselves commercial images, clumps of connected dots, brand names from another world. Or he can try to interest you in, say, some Dallas middle linebacker: but people have their own linebackers to worry about. Above all, he needs national subjects, which translates into endless coverage of championship fights, tennis players' manners, and the grotesque hype of the Super Bowl. All these matters fit quite comfortably into sports magazines, written by zealots for zealots, but seem like more fuss than they're worth in a daily paper. *Sports Illustrated* houses genuinely national sportswriters, but only for Sports-nation: if one wants a larger bowl to swim in one must still turn, like Lardner and Broun and Westbrook Pegler and so many others, reluctantly to other matters.

Meanwhile the best sportswriters remain what they always were, local guys talking to people they know about common, not manufactured, enthusiasms. Red Smith, to end this on a proper note of reverence, used to sweat out a column and then talk away several more of them at the nearest pub. Smith spanned several eras, so he is a useful gauge of possible change

---

*This was written before the *National* came into existence and I'd have to say I'm impressed by how ingeniously that paper has coped with the local v. national conundrum. However, the conundrum remains.

in the genus sportswriter. When he died two years ago at the age of seventy-six I doubt if there was a single apprentice in the game who didn't think of him as in some sense a model. And as long as the kids want to be like Smith, breasting the bar with a porkpie hat and a *Baseball Encyclopedia*, all the electronic flimflam in the world won't seriously modify this early American type. Upon rereading the old masters, I was startled to find that some of them barely seemed to know how each particular sport was played. What they knew were stories. And so do their successors. The stories may be different now, and fewer people may be listening, and conditions may be straitened, but Spencer Tracy lives—even if he is sometimes to be found in a broadcasting booth where the best announcers, like Vin Scully and Joe Garagiola, tell funny stories between pitches and frequently talk more like old sportswriters than young sportswriters do.

Even on film, it may still be the best way to do it.

Terrific

This is the too-judicious book review mentioned in the preface. As you'll see, I also reviewed Roger Angell too judiciously, deciding not to mention that he had once been an extremely helpful editor on my first short story. The particular books under the knife will introduce themselves as we go along.

"Hollywood," wrote Johnny Mercer, is the place "where you're terrific when you're even good." But you don't have to go to Hollywood to attain this pleasant but vaguely humiliating condition; sportswriting will do.

Selected sportswriters get canonized by the faithful in every major city, and a precious few become national cults, but no matter how glibly or fervently they are honored, their impact on the outside world of letters remains slightly less than that of a movie starlet—and the best of them know it. When the late, wonderfully fluent John Lardner tried a regular humor column in the *London Times*, he became as awkward as a circus bear, as if he were performing for his betters; and in *The Red Smith Reader*, the few political pieces just read like sports pieces without the sports. Smith's jauntiness seems for once out of tune and self-conscious, because politics is a different *kind* of joke.

Both Smith (also, alas, late) and Roger Angell, two of the very best, seem well aware of this deforming bind, and it affects their work. Smith was often praised for reminding his readers that baseball was a game that small boys could play; but so are mathematics and the violin. It hardly seems worth repeating. But Smith was a super self-deprecator, midwestern Catholic division (see under Eugene McCarthy) and this was one of the ways he did it. "I never had any soaring ambition to be a sportswriter per se," he writes in a stuttering sort of preface, "I wanted to be a newspaperman... I respect a good reporter and I'd like to be called one... I haven't been ashamed of what I've done. I seem to be making apologies for it. I don't mean to..." In short, a soul, or at least a *persona*, on the rack.

In real life, Red (it seems pertinent to say that I knew him) was capable of forgetting for weeks at a time that baseball could be played by small boys. In the late, bad hours, when lesser men may be found wrestling with the meaning of meaning, Smith would most likely be grubbing gleefully through *The Baseball Encyclopedia* to prove that Travis Jackson did so belong in the Hall of Fame. His world was sport, small boys or no, and he strayed from it at his peril.

But he did get some outside fame anyway—a mention in Hemingway, an appointment to a board of language purists for the Random House Dictionary—and the guess here (a phrase he used to bypass the first person, which he avoided like *Yaweh* in the Old Testament) is that recognition flustered him a little. Hence the ungainly attempts to apologize and not apologize for his subject in the same breath; hence also an increase as he went along in think-pieces: analyses of the players' union and other sub-athletic matters. He came to write less about the game as played and more about the game as paid for and manipulated. This edged him closer to straight reporting and the coveted other side of the newspaper where the big boys wrote.

Yet his method remained blessedly the same. All those chortling evenings had not produced the razor mind that some of
his fans wanted and celebrated (in fact Red's logic could wobble
like an old-fashioned bicycle, puffed along by his sentiments)
but they had produced a wonderful cartoonist in words, who
could skewer the guilty parties in a dispute even if he couldn't
quite skewer the System. After he had done with the wimpy
commissioner Bowie Kuhn* and the fat, bland, scheming owner
Walter O'Malley, he had no need of dialectics.

His collector for the *Reader*, sportswriter Dave Anderson, is
at least half right when he says that there is no best of Red
Smith: his vintage lines (and you read him for the lines) are
scattered all over the map. But Anderson may still have done
him a slight disservice by favoring columns about "big names,
big events, big issues." Anyone can do the big issues; Red was
a master of the small ones. As with A. J. Liebling his eye wan-
dered constantly from the stage to the cutpurses in the audience.
His piece about the famous Bobby Thomson playoff game in
1951 starts with three paragraphs about a drunk crashing again
and again into the ushers and special police until he makes the
diamond: a symbol of the Giants that year. And the day Floyd
Bevens lost his no-hitter to Cookie Lavagetto in the 1947 Series,
Red notes a hapless chap at the end of the press box whose
letter "v" has jammed on him.

Smith's long career spanned from a time when relatively few
readers had seen the games and the rest depended on the thoroughness of his accounts to the polysaturated TV era when some
clowning around is almost mandatory. Thus do changes in convention unleash genius. Red's play-by-play reports had only
been so-so—you can only make so many jokes while imparting
information, and his knowledge of technique seemed to be
mugged-up rather than experienced. But for clowning around,
his gifts were formidable: a computer-bank mind crammed with

---

*I believe in retrospect that he was unfair to Kuhn. Baseball commissioners are bound
to seem a little wimpy so long as they are answerable only to the club owners. But
Kuhn like Jimmy Carter has grown since leaving office, and whatever else one may say
of him he is now the very model of a *former* baseball commissioner.

anecdotes, a deadly retrieval system and a tongue that liked to play, viz. the following on the occasion of Ted Williams being fined five thousand dollars for spitting: "It was a $4,998 mistake when Ted Williams chose puritanical and antiseptic New England for his celebrated exhibition of spitting for height and distance. In easygoing New York's unsanitary subway the price is only two dollars . . . The price the Boston general manager set upon a minute quantity of genuine Williams saliva, making it the most expensive spittle in Massachusetts, suggests that the stuff is rarer than rubies," and on. No pair of desperate TV announcers on a rainy afternoon could go further with less.

A third gift Red had was a small boy's fascination with athletes as such. This becomes clear in *Absent Friends*, a goulash of eulogies in which it seems that if any funny saying or doing could be wrung from these deceased jocks, Red would wring it and massage it into a story. The net result is like a string of Lite beer commercials full of jocular ghosts round a celestial bar. The reader is coaxed not to cry but to smile and shake his head: "There was a boy-o."

Taken one at a time, these eulogies are real artifacts to be pondered by anyone who has to write a condolence letter. But in bulk, the limits of the form become oppressive: the need to find "class," that Humpty-Dumpty word, in everyone, the automatic conversion of grouchiness into integrity, etc. Each of his subjects seems to have left the world with a little less warmth or laughter, which could become a problem.

Absent Friends also gives the impression that Red was all heart—a curious condition which he would have considered unprofessional. To balance his admittedly outsize generosity, Red would hastily revert to his tireless baiting of Kuhn and Happy Chandler and Avery Brundage and to his sometimes unholy gloating over losing teams' incompetence (he gave this up later). As a once shy and always undersized boy, he delighted in running with the virile roustabouts, the Toots Shors and Bill Veeks and Stout Steve Owenses, and sometimes he took on a tone of mocking banter suitable to such.

Sportswriters have inner lives just as surely as the next artist, but because their output is taken less seriously, it seems only fair that they should be spared the heartless scrutiny we accord the Bellows and Mailers. Still, it is not probing much further than he would to say that the quirk that gave Smith's stuff definition and force was the craving of a myopic, highly literary homunculus to be one of the guys whatever it cost him in other ambitions.

And the guys were his subject, not the games, even when he was covering fishing and horse-racing. He had a good ear for clubhouse quotes, but he couldn't have gotten his best material without those marathon drinking sessions. Ah, what a man will sacrifice for his art. Weight for age, Red was a world champion drinker and proud of it.

But what made him famous was his phrasing. In Smith's world, coaches didn't just tear their clothes, they rent their haberdashery; his teams not only overwhelmed their opponents, but occasionally underwhelmed them or just plain whelmed them. To quote these felicities is to suggest that they were rare. On the contrary: they were the sparkplugs in every single column, the quality of which could often be judged by how much work the phrases had to do to get the column up the hill.

When Red talked about opening a vein and bleeding into his typewriter, this must be what he was talking about. He had a sure sense of the essay form and he didn't need to send the waiter out for an anecdote, so there was nothing to bleed about there. But those phrases, which had carried him from the Midwest to Philadelphia to New York to Olympus, really drained him. His favorite sport was fishing and there is no better metaphor for the passivity and guile, the planning and touch it takes to catch bons mots. Without them Red was (to use another of his favorites) just another working stiff.

The case of Roger Angell illustrates other pressures, other tactics. Angell is doted on by the dabblers, the people who pick baseball up and put it down as the mood strikes, but is not, I believe, fully approved of in Red Smith's kingdom, the press box, because he doesn't have to meet deadlines. In fact, most journalists wouldn't know what to do with the extra time if granted, as their occasional books show. But the Deadline is a stern discipline which makes for a brotherhood, and Angell isn't quite in it.

In fact, as a *New Yorker* writer, he has no natural allies in the business. He talks of dedicating *Late Innings* to the Fans— by which he seems to mean something very close to E. M. Forster's "the sensitive, the decent and the plucky," a band of fellow spirits whose existence one just has to take on faith. And speaking of Forster, imagine the following clip being passed around a locker room to appreciative chuckles. "As E. M. Forster said (I can still see him, with one spiked foot on the top step of the dugout and his keen, Ozark blue eyes, under the peak of the pulled-down cap, fixed on some young batter just now stepping up to the plate), 'Only connect.'"

Neither a jock nor Forster specialist would make much of this, but Angell soldiers on gamely. In his earlier baseball musings he seemed to accept his distance, and watch baseball under glass, like *The New Yorker's* Eustace Tilley peering through his monocle. But in his later books, especially this one, he has decided to go out and find those allies or quit. Among the players themselves, he notes that a surprisingly large number don't really like baseball or think about it more than they have to. But every now and then, he spots one of his phantom fans disguised in a baseball uniform, and his faith is restored temporarily. These conversions lend a pinch of drama to what would otherwise be a random collection of pieces.

Late Innings records a cycle of little deaths and rebirths as each spring he determines to give up the game, not because he thinks it unworthy of him but out of a sheer Sisyphean *angst* rare in his dodge. "Is there no cure," he wails, "for this second-hand passion, which makes me a partner, however unwilling, in the blather of publicity, the demeaning emptiness of hero worship, and the inconceivably wasteful outpourings of money and energy that we give professional sports now?

"I would happily avoid ever again having to watch the beery rage of a losing crowd in some dirty big-city stadium on a sweltering night in August, or—just as bad—suddenly noticing across the room the patronizing stare of some certified baseball hater, a certified adult, when he hears me mention Reggie or Yaz or Willie and watches me wave my hands and take up a stance at a make-believe plate . . ."

Thus our hero, stranded between two wastelands, too sensitive for one and too hearty for the other—but look, isn't that Bob Gibson or Pete Rose or Catfish Hunter, all of them fellow humans who love the game? Or it might be a fellow teaching the fundamentals to kids or a Ph.D. poet persuading her husband to take up professional pitching—always our hero is rescued (John Updike would probably call the book *Angell Is Risen*) in time to enjoy another surprisingly good season and an epiphany of a World Series.

There is nothing stagey about any of this. It is exactly what many of us go through every year and Angell is our spokesman. How good does it make him? Previously he had been a crack utility-infielder at *The New Yorker*—short story writer, film critic, fine editor—but hardly a household word. Then suddenly he found a whole new field to himself. Baseball had no Weltys or Updikes or Kaels to go up against; Angell's natural rivals were all chained to deadlines and space limitations and the hardened expectations of sports-page readers.

Angell could write any way he liked for a bright audience with no expectations—a heaven-sent opportunity to be terrific if you're even good. But there's usually a reason for such vacuums. Just try making spring training interesting sometime, with its unknown casts, its changeless routines, and it's fly-me-to Florida (or Arizona) settings, and you will see why other writers have left it to Roger. Angell's apparent freedom is like having the run of the Gobi Desert. Yet by a kind of hunt-and-peck method, a promising rookie here and a ruminating veteran there, he floods these encampments with color. In his glowing vision, there is hardly such a thing as a dull ballplayer or a meaningless game: he will spot something in a pitcher's motion or a hitter's eyes that rivets you on the inessential until it fills the canvas.

The heresy "it's only a game" which bedevilled Red Smith becomes meaningless. Anything as sweetly concentrated on as this becomes as important as anything else—while the spell lasts.

So this is not, after all, some journeyman writer stumbling on a lucky subject. Angell was born to write baseball; it consumes him, as artists are consumed, and there's no point asking how he'd do at something else. His feel for the game is sensual, and this seems to come through even to the heathen. He can describe a batter's swing with the thoroughness and exaltation of a man carving a statue, and the effect is almost as graphic.

Other sportswriters know all that they need to know about a dozen or so sports, but Angell is a man of one sport, one god, so reading him is quite different in intensity from reading anybody else. He is indeed the Apostle to the Gentiles, and not in the same racket as the others. Like M. F. K. Fisher or Isaac Walton, he can be enjoyed by the unwashed and may even have wiped a sneer or two off the faces of those cocktail party ghouls.

But note how he has reversed Red Smith's tactic for dealing with a basically trivial subject, by removing it from the world of value altogether: baseball for baseball's sake could be his motto. Small boys can daub at it if they wish; insofar as they come into it, they are all to the good. "[Watching Tom Seaver] we had become children too, and this could not be permitted to last."

As for old men, Angell tells a nice story about watching a college game with Smoky Joe Wood, a hero from the trolley-car days. Angell wants breathlessly to talk about the past, but Wood is too wrapped up in the game right here in front of him to pay much attention. Gradually, watching it through the old man's eyes, the author sees that this Yale–St. Johns game is one of the greatest ever played, if not the very greatest,* and he might have missed it if he'd had his way. Angell has just been taught a lesson of a kind one usually turns to *him* for.

---

*This was the classic ten inning 1–0 duel of no-hitters between Frank Viola and Ron Darling and it would indeed have been a pity to miss it—even for the sake of Smoky Joe Wood.

My one caveat about *Late Innings*, an elegant chronicle of four seasons (1977–81), is that the extramural stuff—the baseball strike, women in the clubhouse and whatnot—could as well have been handled by any concerned citizen and I'm only sorry that this fine pictorial writer had to be bothered with it.

Another and yet more hag-ridden form of transmitting fun and games is TV announcing, and by chance, the titan in this modest field has also committed a book, *1947: The Year All Hell Broke Loose in Baseball* by Red Barber. That was the year, you will recall, that Jackie Robinson broke the color bar and Leo Durocher was suspended for consorting with gamblers, and Laraine Day: a diverting year, and Barber, as Dodger announcer, was well perched in his famous catbird seat to watch it; but the best writing in his book mainly consists of quotes from other people (including Red Smith). Since I have only seen bound galleys, and wonders are supposed to occur between these and publication, I assume that the many mistakes of fact will have been fixed by now; but if the repetitions are also removed ("Yogi could swing that stick") it will be a very slim volume indeed.

However, the author has a couple of interesting things to say about his calling. He was famous in his day for a soft, somewhat homogenous southern voice proper to the early forties when streamlined sound-mixing was a new toy, giving us singing groups like the Andrew Sisters, bands like Glenn Miller's, soundtracks like Walt Disney's, and the worst years of Bing Crosby; but also for Barber's urbane, non-partisan, and altogether independent commentary.

Something else happened in 1947 which would render this kind of commentary obsolete in no time flat, although this was not clear at the time. Up to then Barber, and all the little Barbers, had been employed by radio stations or networks. But in the hairy wars between Larry McPhail and Branch Rickey, Barber found himself being fought over by the clubs themselves, and he wound up in Branch Rickey's pocket. The Old Redhead, as we were obliged to call him, went on in his own blithe way, although his career may have been shortened by a tendency to review the new plays in town or whatever else came to mind. But the floodgates had been opened to a host of dismal company shills, whose collective sophistication sometimes suggests that baseball can also be *announced* by small boys.

Even before that, Barber had been asked by Commissioner Judge Landis (baseball's version of de Gaulle, an autocrat famous entirely for being autocratic, and who is for some mysterious reason universally admired) just to report the games and keep his opinions to himself. Baseball has never been too keen on free speech—what big business is?—and the owners have even been known to demand loyalty from newspapermen, with indifferent success. So baseball, in its odd way, needs its books— if baseball matters at all. And this, I believe, is where I get off.

Red, One More Time

loser, but still not quite right. Something I'd completely forgotten was how married and husbandly he seemed when I first met him at sixteen (my years not his). This has led me to rethink the message of his last house the night we visited and to settle finally on the version of Red in the introduction—positively my last word on the subject.

People expect an awful lot from their newspapers, and the news isn't the half of it: they also expect the Last Word on practically everything. Thus the poor drudges who blunt their taste at bad plays night after night, and the drones who have to master two books a week—books of a kind that most people put aside a whole summer to read—are assumed to be the most important critics in town, while the hurry-up sages of the editorial pages may be the only voices some people will ever hear on the Middle East or the decline of the yen. (All the above, by the way, is supposed to be done entertainingly.)

It's a lot to ask for thirty cents, but certain hardy souls devote their lives to bucking the odds and making newspapers just that good; and of these, none delivered the goods more consistently than Red Smith, the subject of Ira Berkow's skillful biography. Uninitiates might object right off that sportswriting is too slight and easy to count in the Sisyphus League, but it is easy only in whatever sense six-day bicycle racing is easy. The sports guy merely has to pump his way round and round the same old sports calendar "making it new," in Ezra Pound's words, every time around. To do this, he is advised to maintain, or simulate, the fresh heart and clear eye of a rookie—not to mention the zest for motel rooms of a political candidate—until he drops.

Smith kept on pumping for fifty great years, and according to him (and Mr. Berkow, who watched him from down the press box) not one of them came easy. Column writing can be deceptively and, for Smith, excruciatingly difficult—harder in some sense than a sonnet a day, because it has no fixed form: each column hacks out its own forms, and is one of a kind; it will not help you to write the next day's one.

Red (and you had to know him very well indeed *not* to call him that) was a self-proclaimed bleeder. Since a good lead paragraph will sometimes deliver the whole column for you on a platter, Red really agonized over these. But he never took the second paragraph for granted either. Altogether his stuff was the most thoroughly "written" in the business, to the point where one occasionally wished that he would take his hands off the controls and let 'er rip. But his search for the perfect sentence precluded that.

These technicalities are worth going into, because Mr. Berkow's "Red" is essentially the biography of a career, with a little fishing thrown in (Smith was mad about the sport). To a degree Red's columns *were* his life—the in-between bits sound agreeably humdrum—and Mr. Berkow, being a *New York Times* columnist himself, concentrates on what he knows best. In a field where two good outings out of three may be considered a hot streak, it may take a peer to appreciate and convey the worth of a man who, in his prime, routinely turned in five, six, seven, if they'd let him, gems a week.

Red Smith was born in Green Bay, Wisonsin—a good omen for both of them, although the only Packers in town back in 1905 were honest-to-God meatpackers. His family sounds wonderfully nice and uneventful, and in fact his whole private life seems to have been magically free of abrasion, until he ran into a nest of stepchildren in the 1960s, and even that sounds not much worse than a sitcom.

But it's hard to tell with a man like Smith. He was much too decent and old-fashioned to air his domestic woes, if he had any; in his day *all* Americans had wonderful parents, wonderful spouses, wonderful kids. And it's none of your damn business anyway. The only minor revelation here concerns his brother, Art. After the usual infantile pummeling (with Art usually on top) it seems that they settled into a sort of joshing friendship, of a kind that can get pretty edgy at times. When Art died, Red the Reticent mysteriously thought it worth mentioning in print that his brother drank too much. Since Red himself was a prodigious drinker who got away with it, I can only take this parting dig to mean, "I did it better than he did."

This at least would be in line with Red's low-key but unrelenting competitiveness, which for years was stoked by his conditions of employment. Although his talent was quickly recognized, his early (and middle) career was almost a guide to the number two papers in town. The *Milwaukee Sentinel*, the *St. Louis Star*, the *Philadelphia Record*—these are not the journals you associate with those cities. And when he finally did reach his dream, New York, after twenty years or so of bleeding out great columns, it was, naturally, with the *Herald Tribune*— good enough you might say, but the *Trib* was not so far from going out of business itself. After that happened, and as if to round out the cycle of near misses, he did a stint with *Women's Wear Daily*. Before reading Mr. Berkow (who has been there himself), this reader had no notion of how much luck is involved in hitting those magic slots on the great papers.

Small wonder, then, that Red was fiercely jealous of his stature. Without a major employer in back of him, he felt he was only as hot as his last column, and he watched the competition like a buzzard. Mr. Berkow suggests that he was actually jealous of Jimmy Cannon (who was jealous right back), and over the years he found himself in mini-feuds with the likes of Dick Young (which is not hard to do) and Howard Cosell.

A sportswriting feud is by necessity a muffled affair, since the feuders are constantly thrown into each other's laps, and feuds only stand out in Red's case because he was otherwise so courtly and unflappable. His killer instinct only responded to one thing, his pet, his column. Perhaps the closest he ever came to outright cruelty was in his column-related contempt for Arthur Daley of the *Times*. Long before the graceless but likable Daley won the first Pulitzer ever given for sportswriting in 1956 (the contempt was *not* caused by the prize, as Mr. Berkow seems to suggest), Red was making merciless fun of him everywhere but to his face. It seemed that Smith needed just such a whipping boy to contrast with his own elegance.

He was rightly proud of his prose. It gave him in later life a reputation not unlike E. B. White's, as the English teacher you never had, and the guy you would have liked to write like yourself. Mr. Berkow is particularly illuminating on this because he was a protégé of sorts himself, and it is clear that Red more than made up for whatever small sins of envy and rancor he committed against the competition with his incredibly generous advice to just about anyone who wanted it. (Ironically, he once lent his name and blushing photo to an innocuous scam—not mentioned here—called the Famous Writers School: the gag being, of course, that the Famous Writers did not actually teach anything. It's nice to think of Red being paid a little, never mind how, for what he so often did for nothing.)

Red's home life comes through as dutiful but a bit shadowy, and this sounds about right. As traveling men go, he seems to have been a loving and conscientious husband and father, whose idea of a perfect vacation was to take everyone on a fishing trip. When I visited his house one time, I got a strange feeling of transience, as if Red had just arrived there himself too. His natural habitat had for so long been a hotel room that there seemed no permanence to any of his goods and trappings. This was definitely not a retirement home, nor would it ever be.

His family did, however, make one significant impact on his career. The aforementioned stepchildren apparently "politicized" him a touch, to use the jargon of the sixties, and it showed in his work. He had always been bothered by accusations of being lightweight (which he thought was exactly the right weight for sports, but not for himself), but now he found that there was no limit to how hard or heavily he could hit out at the *management* of sports. Red had always used owners, commissioners and such as figures of fun, buffoons capering around the edges of his canvas. But now, as he devoted whole columns to the reserve clause in baseball and the mean hypocrisies of the Olympics, management was plumb in the center and blazing merrily.

The change in Red was never one of personality: he still walked in the door laughing and left the same way. Ideologically he had always been a players' man—never met one he didn't like, nor an owner he did—so he didn't have to change that. Thus, the unpoliticized Red of 1947 was strangely slow to welcome blacks to the big leagues, because too many of his player-friends objected. But then the *politicized* Red of the seventies turned out to be just as slow to accept women reporters in the locker room: again on account of the players. He even believed in the teeth of the evidence that that idol of the sixties, Muhammad Ali, was overrated, because his friend Jack Dempsey thought so too.

The difference was that Red no longer thought of sports as *just* entertainment but accepted that social issues were a legitimate part of the sports beat. And this was enough to bring him abreast of the times and buy him a whole new generation of fans and friends and a rollicking new life in his sixties and early seventies, when he sat at last, unchallenged, on top of his own world, at the *New York Times*.

Mr. Berkow does justice, insofar as there's enough in the world, to Red's mighty capacity for friendship. Sportswriters on the road tend to peel off in twos and threes according to taste: some for wenching, others for toping, and the precious few who can still recognize the stuff, for good food. Red's trio, formed with Frank Graham and Grantland Rice, was legendary, and one pictures them chortling from event to event in assorted jalopies: on his worst day, Red never forgot that this was a pretty nice way to make a living.

However, even in these sunlit sequences, I find a small part of Red missing. Put it this way. The first time I met the great man, he happened to be singing, loudly but not well, a ditty that went something like this: "Oh hurray for the Jones Junior High / It's the best junior high in Toledo." The Red in this book doesn't sing, or come even close to it. And one imagines the author leaving his subject long before the hour for that sort of thing arises, and picking him up again the next morning.

Back in the sixties, Red wrote a piece for the *Trib* lamenting the vanishing tribe of sportswriters who could sit up all night over a bottle and still work the next day. He probably wouldn't find *any* today. Red had triumphantly outlived his own breed, and became, by grace of those magic sentences, a hero and model to a new one. I believe he died a very happy man.

Nobody Asked Me but...
The Art of Jimmy Cannon

*J*f Jimmy Cagney was a sportswriter, he would have been Jimmy Cannon (we couldn't afford a subjunctive on our block). A tough guy who cries a lot, a staccato marshmallow, also the fellow you have to clear it with to get into the gang, and the guy who defends you best on the way out. His speech was rough but fastidious, because he had found the words himself and he valued them, like a gangster's jewelry.

So much for style. Jimmy Cannon knew you had to have a voice of your own to be heard in the din of an evening paper, and he developed a riveting one. There were a lot of rich voices around in his day: Dan Parker, Joe Williams, Frank Graham. You didn't read them for information, of which you got choking amounts elsewhere, but for mood and attitude, as you would choose a guy to talk to in a bar after the game. Laconic, witty, indignant, the closest thing you could find to talking to the mirror.

Cannon fans were the most addicted of them all, ripping their way blindly past Mary Worth and Murray Kempton in the *New York Post* to hear the voice. His detractors were passionate too, finding him just too lush and mannered, which he was. But his one-man turns were not to be compared with regular writing, but with, let's say, swing trombone solos, in which the sentimentality is controlled and entirely suitable to the form. Jimmy Cannon was a Broadway writer, as professional as George M. Cohan singing "Mary," and his rendition of a tough-tender Irishman is as good and resourceful as anything in his master, Damon Runyon. You may not like it, but it couldn't be done better.

Without the orchestration of an evening paper, his pieces can seem thinner, but if you should run into a collection of them you might conceivably try clipping them out and stuffing one a day into your regular paper, which would be improved magically. In bulk, they provide a fascinating study of a gifted writer confining himself to a lifetime of sports in a seven-hundred-word straitjacket.

Obviously such a one must use sports to speak his piece about everything else. Cannon's real subject was courage, and its visible manifestation, class. More than once he questions his own courage, and his right to judge other people's from a press box; and later he says, in virtually the same breath, that Hemingway was very brave and probably our best writer, as if these were the same thing.

Conversely he sticks it mercilessly to the phonies: a phantom fight manager, who "wouldn't fight to defend his own mother," a horseplayer who can't read a racing form but is ashamed to ask how, and all the name-droppers and blowhards of Broadway. Yet these are his people too, and he dissects them fondly, like a relative. One feels that if Jimmy Cannon wrote about a sportswriter like himself, it would be his harshest portrait yet. Like Scott Fitzgerald, he is both inside the party and the kid outside watching.

This turns out to be a good vantage point for gazing up at his heroes: DiMaggio, Louis, Hemingway. Although the phrase "no cheering in the press box" is his, Jimmy Cannon's loyalty to these totems is almost obsessive, and he invokes them like saints' names to remind us of class before we get on with the day's work.

This may well consist of a study of some athlete ("You are Yogi Berra") in which we are asked to shoulder the problems of this worthy for a minute or two: the sore arm, the passing years, the darkening future. He sometimes turns the poignance up too quickly with precious phrasing—"You are Willie Mays, trapped in the prison of your skills..." floats back to me over the years—and he used these columns to hotdog his talent more than usual. Yet his acute observation of physical mannerism and its links to character often gave him the essence of these athletes and froze them in time like old sporting prints.

Everybody feels that sportswriters should be rescued and placed on some higher ground, and everyone is surprised when the trapped maidens refuse to budge. Jimmy Cannon found room in a sports column to do everything he wanted: war, his old neighborhood, show-biz friends, all in the style of a sports column—with friction, vitality and loss all playing their licks and winding up together on the downbeat.

His outsider's gift of social observation found its happiest outlet in his famous "Nobody asked me, but" one-liners. Sometimes these are a bit mystifying, as in "men with high freckled foreheads favor small knots in their ties," but at least they show he's out on the job; and others are just plain right. "Neat cab drivers are the hostile ones." "People in bus terminals look tired even before they start the trip." "The stingiest guys I know favor heavy starch in their collars." An Emily Post for tinhorns. A novelist of manners, short about three hundred pages.

And always he is oneself, the perfect mirror behind the bar. "I can't remember ever staying for the end of a movie in which the actors wore togas." I believe that says it all. You had to be in the mood for Jimmy Cannon—and so did he—but when everything went right, he was simply incomparable.

Ring (An Introduction to
You Know Me, Al)

ing Lardner is perhaps our most accidental writer, and *You Know Me, Al* is certainly his most accidental book. Young Ringgold Wilmer Lardner apparently had never thought of being any kind of writer, and only backed into it because, like so many in this business, he proved unemployable at anything else.

His love for baseball being considerably deeper and more intense than his interest in letters, Lardner compromised by covering the White Sox and Cubs for sundry newspapers in Boston and Chicago, at which chore he might have been blissful forever if marriage hadn't conflicted with the traveling schedules. So he began backing into things again: first (after some misfires) into a daily sports column and finally into fiction.

In those days "daily column" meant what it said, and Ring scratched desperately to fill his space seven remorseless days a week. He took to writing whimsical bits on his kids' birthdays, light verse on this and that, and anything else that came into his head—including some accounts of real games written in the baseball vernacular, as if by one of the players. He was getting closer.

Lardner liked playing with slang, even in his private letters, and a daily column is nothing if not a playpen. At long last, when every other evasion seemed to have been exhausted, he invented the Busher, whose letters to the sainted but invisible Al would constitute his first book. Once invented, the Busher took off and ran. In no time flat, the six stories in the book had poured out of Lardner's suddenly steaming typewriter and into the *Saturday Evening Post,* and the author had gone from being a local sports stiff to a national treasure.

When I first read *You Know Me, Al,* I didn't know this background and I assumed that it was a polished later work. The pacing of the narrative, the expert changes of lens and focus— this could not be the work of a beginner. But it seems that as a storyteller, Lardner was born fully armed. He never knew where the stuff came from and was always uncomfortable with his gift—in fact, in later years he kept slipping away from fiction every chance he got. But in this, his first outing, one still finds the serenity of a man at play, making all the right moves because he doesn't know the game is supposed to be difficult.

Although Ring always insisted that a novel as such was beyond him, *You Know Me, Al* is surely the next best thing. The development of the characters, major and minor, including Al, the long-suffering recipient, is not circular as in most serial stories, but incremental: one cannot profitably read the stories out of order. Likewise, the turning points actually lead somewhere and not just to themselves, as in the Sherlock Holmes books or other collections. In fact, one sometimes wonders what Lardner thought a novel was, if he didn't think it was this.

But it's no use wondering too much about Lardner. This midwestern aristocrat, or walking contradiction, who was too proud and shy even to call himself a humorist ("It's like calling yourself 'a great third baseman'") was certainly not going to have truck with two-dollar words like "novelist." In fact, he refused ever to say anything serious about his stuff, and as Ring

Lardner, Jr.'s book *The Lardners* (to which I'm indebted) testifies, he was at some pains to conceal that he worked at it at
all. This most fastidious of writers was happy to have you think
that he typed with his elbows while swapping wisecracks with
his children.

Never mind how he did it. The Busher is an eternal American
type, and you know him too, whatever your name is: the ever-
ready explainer, the guy who always does the right thing but is
always let down by others—why, such a one might even grow
up to be president. But Jack Keefe the Busher is not just a
caricature: he is a loving study of a real type. Keefe's goofy self-
confidence is actually a necessary part of certain athletes' equipment. Out there on their own, they will buy any delusion that
keeps them flying, whether the name is Muhammad Ali or Bill
Johnson, the puffed-up downhill skier. The Busher has indeed
had many strange children, from Dizzy Dean ("If you can do
it, you ain't braggin' ") to John McEnroe, who feels booby-
trapped and misunderstood everywhere he turns.

It would have been a cinch—and the natural path for a "humorist"—to make Keefe a self-deluded bum. But Keefe is actually pretty good; almost as good as he says he is, a self-deluded
champ. And as such, he is just a few steps behind those lords
of the Golden Age, Americans like Bill Tilden and Walter Hagen
who strode the world like colossi because they never doubted
their right to.

To a polite foreign competitor, *all* Americans must have
seemed like Jack Keefes in those days. The early twentieth century was an age of bursting self-confidence over here: the worms
of self-doubt and self-consciousness hadn't entered the American garden, and there was no "inner" game of tennis to calm
your nerves, nor yet any support systems (unless you count
teammates carrying you home after spiking your drink). You
got by, if you did, with the crude psychic equipment of the
Busher, or a suaver version of the same.

What distinguishes Keefe and his descendants from the ruck
of jocks is the impregnability of his solecism. He often suspects
he is being kidded, but can never be sure. Although he's a

gregarious fellow, he learns nothing from the company he keeps
because his self-absorption is too pure. Yet through the ears
and out the mouth of this somewhat dense figure passes a whole
vivid world, of baseball and boardinghouses and *lumpen* America circa 1912. Virginia Woolf went so far as to call what comes
out of Keefe "the voice of a continent."

The other thing about the Busher is that he is a genuine letter
writer. I understand that he *has* to be in order to provide us
with the letters and the story in the first place. But there's more
to it than that. This guy would write letters whether we were
there or not. By chance I happened to know a Keefe once myself,
a natural letter writer; and although she was in fact a teenage
girl living in a very different era, her "sound" was exactly the
same, even her misspellings were the same (she got the hard
ones and blew the easy ones), as well as the uncertainty about
kidding and being kidded. She, too, was active and athletic, but
no day was complete without a volley of letters to a raft of
friends.

The difference is, of course, that she has since grown up and
become more literate and her letters have lost those haunting
cadences. Keefe would never have allowed that to happen. *Au
contrary,* as he might write (he is always looking to improve
himself), the Busher still stands out there on the mound like the
statue of Peter Pan in Kensington Gardens, for new generations
to wonder at, while his support collapses eternally behind him
and various lucky stiffs attempt to connect with his smoke. Two
things you know for sure about him: he will never grow up and
he will never die. And you can count on that.

A P.S. for pedants. According to Lardner, the original for
Keefe was actually not a semiliterate but a totally illiterate White
Soxer who once asked Ring to type up a letter for him to send
to his girl. The fellow's suggestions as to how the letter should
go were all that Lardner needed to know about Keefe's endlessly
ramified and poignantly side-splitting love life. The letter-writ-
ing passion that Lardner endowed his character with was, of
course, his own.

Howard Cosell: A Riddle Wrapped Up in a So-Called, Self-Appointed Enigma

*I*f you ever went to Ebbets Field, you know Howard Cosell through and through, and ear to ear. He was the guy who always sat directly in back of you, yakking to beat the band. At first you were impressed and made a note: "New York fans are very knowledgeable." Then you observed that he seemed to be talking about every game ever played under the sun or stars, except this one here. His friend had to break in to tell him that the lead run was on base, at which point he would become unduly—but all-too-briefly—excited.

At various times, he would pronounce this the best game he had ever seen and indubitably the crumbiest. But in either case, it left him plenty of time to discuss Don Newcombe's tragic drinking problem, Hack Wilson's home run in *that very spot* in May 1929 and Ethel's (or Angelina's or Brigid's) irrational dislike of baseball, fine woman though she was in other regards.

You breathed a sigh when he went out for a hot dog during the winning rally. But later you thought, well, he added to the color of the day, you won't find this at home; and you went back for more, to be maddened all over again. The ball game was his palette, on which he painted his personality—and there were thousands of him, clones kidding and being kidded about thinning hair and thickening waistlines, showing off about the infield fly rule and hollering "balk" every time the pitcher moved a muscle. "I think I locked the keys in the car" were his last words on earth.

Now, of course, you *can* find him at home and the whole Cosell issue (which, as he would say, has been blown out of all proportion and should not be dignified by a rebuttal) boils down to that. To begin with, do you want a guy, any guy, talking right through a game? Most fans I've asked about this say no, they'd prefer total silence.* But that's not the way the networks are betting. The word from the truck is, keep talking—either because time is money or because the nets think fans like noise more than they admit. For better or worse, Cosell simulates game conditions.

Anyway, sports announcing has to be an unpromising vehicle for a superstar. It's like being a spectacular butler or a boastful tour guide. Don Meredith and Joe Garagiola have their own irritation capabilities, according to taste. But they don't have nearly Cosell's range or his intangibles, his ability to bore you a lot of ways.

Okay, suppose that our fan at Ebbets had been given his own TV program. He would certainly have become mighty pleased with himself, which was the last thing he needed. But he would also have become proportionately touchy. Two thousand hate letters a week (or whatever he gets) is a lot of booing. And repeated uppers and downers of praise and blame can render a man edgy and self-conscious, alternately aggrieved and braggadocious.

The story of Howard Cosell is basically the history of a ner-

---

*NBC did indeed try a football game without announcers a few years back, except for the public one in the stadium, and I found the effect quite powerful in a sci-fi sort of way. But apparently viewers considered the experiment unnatural, and it has never been tried again.

vous system. At first he seemed just a brash young fellow whose
trademark was blitzing weary athletes with outrageous questions. Since the victims were frequently too stunned to answer,
the question itself had to be the story. Howard was telling it
like it is, though all the world was silent.

I wrote a little something about him back then, and when we
met he joshed me good-naturedly—said I'd been picking dan-
druff off his collar, but have a drink anyway. A nice guy, no
complications. At that point, he hadn't overdosed on mixed
notices. The next time we met, he obviously had because he
quoted that same aging column to me, only this time word for
word; and he followed it up by casting aspersions on my pugilistic expertise (he really talks like that) or accusing me of doing
that to him, I forget which.

Something had gone wrong around here. The self-importance
that had once seemed like a gag, a Falstaffian flourish, had grown
like a tumor. The actor had become his act. The very last time
I heard from him,* it went like this: "This is Howard Cosell
calling. I am deeply saddened by your book [a piece of froth
about Muhammad Ali that couldn't have saddened Sorrowful
Jones]. You obviously don't like me and that's your privilege.
[I like him fine.] For three-and-a-half years one man and one
man alone defended the U.S. Constitution...so-and-so [who
had also stood by Ali] is only a print journalist, I am a network
...that [a playful question about boasting] is *ad hominem* and
beside the point...I would not be Howard Cosell if I hadn't
made this call."

So, there he is: disdaining criticism even while he memorizes
it. (Writing about Cosell is a particularly intimate experience,
because you can actually picture his face working as he reads.)
Humor is a problem for him, because the guy at Ebbets Field
never thought of himself as primarily a comic: it would have
spoiled everything. So although Cosell may snigger along with

---

*Since writing this, I've run into Howard several times and find that in retirement
he is quite his old charming self. Like Richard Nixon, Ed Koch and how many others,
the limelight had, as he would say, "blown him out of all proportion." But he seems
to be okay now so long as he *stays* out of it, and bless him.

the laughter he causes, he could live without it. I had at least assumed that his use of fractured legalese was meant to be funny, but apparently not so. According to a recent interview, he actually thinks he is educating the public with those gorgeous garblings of his.

In fact he takes his whole work seriously, and must be frustrated that it so seldom gets talked about as such. (Like Farrah Whatzit's I.Q., there is simply too much else to think about.) On my own scorecard, Cosell has improved quite a piece as a boxing announcer. It seems like the one sport he could have played himself—unlike ball games, which don't seem to come naturally at all—and he is exceptionally resourceful with unknown fighters in unknown towns in Mexico. He can make a show out of nothing better than anyone around. [Shortly after I wrote this, Howard turned on boxing with a snarl—showboating no doubt, but a real sacrifice.]

At football, his homework is prodigious, if sometimes irrelevant: all that background can swamp the foreground. But he is not supposed to do play-by-play, and he has to do *something*. Here, as so often, the problem is not Cosell but his role. Do we need *anyone* to give those pious readings (so-and-so played at Palo Alto Normal) from the official program during games?

Baseball is his one disastrous area. Unless he's had a change of heart since we last spluttered together, he doesn't even like the game, and he'll do anything to avoid talking about it on the air. The human interest runs completely amuck when Cosell does baseball, barreling through important moments, because there are no important moments to a non-baseball man. Baseball fans, a crabby lot by and large, are the last people in the world to try this on. We want to know where the invisible fielders are placed today and how the curves are hanging, and to hell with what Tommy Lasorda said to him at the top of the telecast anent this fine young individual.

Baseball may be responsible for the latest wave of Cosell haters, and this one he has brought on himself. It seems condescending of him to have taken on a sport for which he has no feeling, and the howlers he inevitably makes simply accentuate the bear-baiting aspect of Cosell's persona. There has always been an uneasy feeling that Cosell is hired *because* of the hate now, like the bad guy in a wrestling match, and that yahoo anti-Semitism grows fat on this *lumpen* New Yorker. So his masters should take special care not to go fishing for extra ridicule. It's just too painful to keep a man in the stocks these days.

A cooled-off, melted-down Cosell might make a better announcer, but just being good might be a fatal come-down for one who has aimed so high. The things that make Howard a laughingstock are the very things that make him famous, so he's stuck with the cap and bells, even while he swears they're really laurel leaves.

No wonder he can be tense and irritable. I would be jumping out of my skin in Cosell's position. Like many celebrities, he has worked his way onto a spot on the roof, where it seems hard to stay up but impossible to come down, and only the fire department can help. But I do believe that, if he piped down a pinch and pruned back the mannerisms, which may be starting to lose even their hate value, there would be enough Cosell left over to make a very noticeable announcer. And a grateful public would honor him for his sacrifice, and remember that he lent some color to the day, and go back for more.

What Do Men Talk About When They Talk About Sports?

*R*ecently I had the simple-minded pleasure of watching a cliché come true. A small dinner party had peeled off into its constituent sexes, as groups still do despite all the browbeating we've had, and somebody asked both sides what they were talking about. "Needlepoint," chirped the women. "Baseball," growled the men.

Needlepoint will have to fend for itself here, although my uncle does it between innings (all relatives mentioned in this space are myths, but instructive ones). But why baseball? My wife, who watches sports avidly and endlessly, glazes over in seconds when the stuff is talked about.

The physical charm of games is either self-evident or completely impenetrable: in either case blessedly undiscussable ("You mean that putting a tiny ball in a silly hole is *fun*?" "Yes, dear.") But sports chat is a real oddity, a keep out sign between the sexes that goes up regularly across the nation's living rooms determining wide-scale patterns of marriage, courtship and child neglect. Worth a look, perhaps: if one can't have one-sex clubs anymore, a one-sex topic may be the next best thing. Anyway, it's worth a fast brood.

"I'm not sure," wrote Dashiell Hammett, "[that] talk oughtn't to be limited to women and sports." This may strike one as a pretty dull remark to come from such a bright fellow. Didn't the old detective know that what he proposed had already come to pass, and that his precious limitation was in full effect in all forty-eight states? Of course, Hammett was also suggesting that all talk should be done by men, but this might have had something to do with living with Lillian Hellman, and is beside our point.

That these two subjects, women and sports, should make the all-male small-talk finals year after year, easily trouncing religion and less easily politics, is actually no fluke. As many a small Catholic boy can tell you, sport is the only image in his pubescent arsenal bright enough to compete with the female body. And a man whose business it is to consult with Catholic priests once told me that an obsession with sports was a telltale sign of clerical crack-up. Let the chosen few sublimate sex with art or the lives of the saints; the man in the crowd will reach first for the long pass and the double play, to the point where these images can become quasi-erotic and torments in themselves.

But short of these fevers lie the hours of harmless gabble that have to be gotten through somehow everyday; and here again men who are too genteel to talk about sex are likely to subside into sport. The only other universal subject, politics, usually either angers people or bores them, or both. Art, even for the initiate, does not provide fresh stories every day as sports does.

In fact art is surprisingly hard to talk about. Even professional critics become pretzel-tongued in its presence, mumbling about tonal values, while the rest of us can only stamp and roll our eyes. Without fresh stories, one is left with the experience itself, color, sound, texture, the ineffable, and try having a bull session about that. Most art talk is simply chitchat: openings, those ungodly prices, gossip. A sports fan would find it all rather

insubstantial, however noble the subject. Sublimity doesn't guar-
antee good conversation, and I've known more than one person
in the arts who'd rather talk baseball.

Politics is better on stories, but significantly the best of these
are not about the deadly, numbing business of government but
about winning elections, which is the closest politics comes to
sport. Even a game like Running for Office which seems to
consist entirely of dealing and bluffing is not without interest—
except, as I say, that people tend to claw each other's eyes out
over it, unless they already agree about absolutely everything
in advance.

Sports talk is, at its purest, like politics without the rancor.
Although stadiums have been known at times to sound like the
French Assembly just before lunch, this is not the work of the
talkers, those wise, serious men who sit in quiet bars and living
room corners. Here the equivalent of Republicans and Demo-
crats, vegetarians and anarchists meet in friendly muted con-
clave. The Red Sox fan is delighted to swap pleasantries with
the horse's ass who favors the Yankees. The best of us even try
to understand hockey lovers. It is the Socratic ideal: the dispute
is constant but civilized; ranters and shouters are patiently out-
waited. It is timeless and circular and, to the outsider, it is
possibly the dullest sound on earth.

Sports talk is by no means the same thing as sports-play or
even sports-watch. Some athletes have little time for it, and seem
mildly to resent these pale-faced amateurs who think that games
are about numbers (statistics are exclusively for talkers and their
home is taverns). And some talkers haven't been to a ballpark
in years. Our game is sociability, but not the crude bear-hug
sociability of the grandstand, which we view with Jamesian
distaste.

Our kind of thing, if I may use myself as a specimen, is a café
in Rome where, over espresso and strega, my father and I drone
dreamily about English cricket. My mother, maddened beyond
endurance, resorts to female guile. "I don't know which of you
is humoring the other, but I know *one* of you is."

Fiendish. Hot protests from the males, of course, but a nasty seed of doubt is planted. Each of us knows *he* isn't guilty—but what about the other one?

My mother was trying blindly to pry apart the clubability of sports talk, no doubt for good evolutionary reasons. To my knowledge, sports talkers are seldom great ladies' men, and vice versa. And although they may make up for it at times by being ploddingly faithful husbands and fathers, this may be more a tribute to their sheer capacity for sitting around than to any strength of feeling.

There are, there's no denying, some heavy fellows and lack-wits in the Hot Stove League. It is the price we pay for democracy. You can't shut somebody up in a sports conversation—it isn't done. Every remark is created equal, as at a P.T.A. meeting, and there are dull rogues who take advantage of this. With such one may even be driven to the extreme of changing the subject.

These oafs give sports talk a bad name, and I think they're what wives have in mind ("how can you spend five minutes with that guy?") when they denounce the whole business. This is too bad, because behind these gloomy sentinels and their barbed wire of trivia lurks a subject that can be anything you want it to be. Take merely the feast of low life served up every day. If drug scandals are your thing, sports boasts the very finest. Or for pathos, how about the superstars who wind up robbing gas stations? or being shot dead by groupies? The first I ever heard of wife-swapping was in the sports pages. And for political hugger-mugger you can hardly do better than the funding of new stadiums.

In short one can talk about sports all day without actually mentioning sports. George Plimpton, for instance, can converse all day in "parasports" anecdotes that would tickle a Martian; and I doubt if a quarter of them even take place on the field. The rest are likely to be set in press boxes, locker rooms, or Pullman cars, where a vast unruly cast of characters, constantly involved in volatile activity, give George all the material he needs for a life-work. In England, the great stylist Bernard Darwin found golf sufficient. Indeed, the slower the game, the more time there is to talk.

People who miss all this richness should be pitied but not coddled. They can still lead perfectly useful lives among their gray bric-a-brac (concerning which most of them can be pretty boring too): it is no worse than being tone-deaf. But some among them, glorying in their infirmity, actually sneer at sports talk and call it childish. These are outright Philistines, and of course they come in all sexes. Even if they were to hear Beckett and Pinter talking cricket (which is all those great men *do* talk, I'm told) they would learn nothing. Private sections for them in restaurants is one solution that comes to mind, except that the whole race might then be endangered; private sections in living rooms is what we've got, and where we came in, and it isn't much fun. Imagine being trapped by some statistics bore while on all sides fascinating women refuse to rescue you.

Surely talks should begin about this immediately.

4

Lesser Sports

◇

Meditations on a Statue

he Statue of Liberty was about to have a birthday (I forget her age, as I was raised to with ladies) and I was asked to contribute to a symposium on the subject. And if you think this work is easy, just try writing about the Statue of Liberty and sports sometime.

She may not look like an athlete to you, but to this particular immigrant she has never looked like anything else. To my British eye, the Statue of Liberty has always just run her torch straight down from Olympus. But perhaps my experience is unusual.

For my first two years over here, age circa ten, baseball was the only language I spoke (except for the King's English, which *nobody* understood); and when I finally learned to talk football, I encountered the Lady for the first serious time. To my surprise, she turned out to be a *football* play—remember it? The one where the passer raises his arm as if to welcome the huddled masses, and hands the ball off behind his back instead?

Anyway, every time I look out there at the symmetry, balance and calm power of the Lady and at her patiently alert face as she scans her beat like a centerfielder, I know that if she ever stepped down from her perch it would be to swing that torch like a toothpick and hit the ball over buildings.

I don't know—maybe she just looks like whatever you most want to do in a free country, within reason. At any rate, I cannot have been the only youthful arrival in America to find sports more glamorous and pertinent than the Four Freedoms of the Bill of Rights, which didn't apply in your own house anyway, as you found if you tried to push free speech or the right of assembly too far. To many immigrants, finding any games at all here, never mind which ones, must have been a revelation. To see so much arable land turned over to people at play must have seemed almost unnatural, if not un-European. The freedom to frolic is seldom listed among our basics, yet what gift has done more to shape the happy-go-lucky, take-on-anything Yankee character that foreigners so goggle at?

But this freedom did have its limits, depending on where you found yourself. The booming northern cities in which most immigrants got stuck did not have *that* much space, and what they did have tended after a while to drift into the hands either of professional associations or schools. The rest of the public was simply there to watch, bet a little perhaps, and then, if it so wished (and the traffic allowed) to reproduce these games as parody in the cramped streets and alleys of home.

Thus came about the two most striking features of American sports as such: they are pre-eminently spectator events, and they are intertwined inseparably, sometimes morbidly, with education.

To take the first first: the city kids I knew might well have watched a hundred major league games without ever touching a hardball themselves, because a hardball is murder on concrete (and vice versa). A country boy, contrariwise, might find his hand contoured from infancy around a baseball, but his mind innocent of the big-league game. So baseball became not precisely the country game, but the game played by country boys for the entertainment of city boys, who then wrote funny things about them (Ring Lardner's baseball stories being among our quintessential documents).

For its part, football was not precisely country *or* city, but academic. In pre-TV times, even city kids saw very little first-class football, because all the seats were taken by huge men with hip flasks, and they themselves were consigned for life to improvised games of touch football, that most ersatz of imitations, the margarine and powdered eggs of sport. In the country, on the other hand, where space was no problem, it was hard to muster the complex organization that football requires. So the sport battened on the one organization the kids had to go to anyway, the school, and made that its exclusive home. To play, and rise, in the game you had to pass through successive garrisons of education, which still dot the landscape like military bases, and stay there till you were mustered out. To this day, the number of successful professionals who skipped school can be counted on one hand. No skilled profession could be more exacting educationally.

One result of these two imperatives—spectatorism and academicism—was to make football for years easily our least played sport. If you were too small to make the team, you didn't play it, and if you were too dumb to make the school you never found out if you could play it. In fact, until the Kennedys ushered in their famous wave of national fitness, many able-bodied kids went right through school without playing anything at all, because if you didn't try out for some team or other there was no other way to do it. And teams were there to *watch*. The freedom to play was grossly neglected and the Lady with the torch must have wept an ocean.

Times have, as usual, changed out of sight, and today you are more likely to see that same kid jogging to his tennis lesson bouncing a basketball. But the years of inertia left an interesting legacy in how our major sports are played. The "nation of spectators," as we were once called, made its silent demands with the consequence that our sports are uniquely designed among world sports to please the viewer first and the player second.

If I linger on football once more, it is because I consider it to be our most distinctive sport, the one least like anyone else's and hence also our best example. Strangers are especially baffled by its policy of unlimited substitution. Surely no red-blooded player ever wished to be rushed off the field every few minutes just to sit on his hat and watch from the sidelines? If he has just been tackled, he must wish to tackle someone, anyone, right back, *n'est-ce pas?* But, you explain to your guest, fate has ordained that he will *never* tackle anybody (unless the ball is intercepted) because he is an *offensive* player. The defensive player for his part will never take part in a scoring play, except by accident.

Everybody gets to play only a fragment of a football game, the smallest portion going to that *reductio ad absurdum* of specialists, the kicker—himself now divided into two, the punter and the place kicker, the last of the bivalves. Even those legendary quarterback duels are illusory, a species of montage, because the duelists are never on the field at the same time: in a pinch their parts could be filmed on separate days.

In short, and with the same daunting efficiency that produced our great industries, football has evolved a division of labor beyond the dreams of Adam Smith, and all in the interests of more polished entertainment. When games were played for the fun of the players, anyone who felt like watching just had to take what he got. If the players happened to be dropping with fatigue, that was their business; you couldn't keep sending out for fresh ones. Kicks were made by legs that were never meant to kick, because you needed that man for his stamina, this one for his brains or his bulk. And so on. The guys got to finish what they started, life's keenest pleasure, and to hell with what it looked like. (It is interesting, apropos of this, that many Americans have taken a step backward to two more elemental, all-involving sports, rugby and soccer.)

Now, of course, you get devastating ensemble work from ever fresh spare parts, and it can be breathtaking to watch. Coaches, who existed once chiefly to make sure everyone got on the bus, have become master choreographers, and they along with quarterbacks and a few middle-linebackers (all of whom are semi-coaches) have become the only significant personalities in the game: the rest are basically employees, fieldhands, if you will, of the above.

It might be argued that as long as all our sports are played for fun by the rest of us, there may be something to be said for sacrificing some purity on the professional level for the sake of appearances. The opportunity to watch may not be one of the Statue's promises, but she has a kind heart for the old, the infirm and the clumsy, who can *only* watch. The question for now is how much can a game give up of itself and keep its soul?

The designated hitter rule is an interesting case because it suggests the influence of creeping footballism on the easygoing world of baseball. Picture if you will the Recording Angel hovering over the delivery room intoning, "You, my son, will grow up to be a very great pitcher, but you will never, never get to hit so long as you live." Or worse, "You will hit all right, but you will never enter the field of play outside the base paths." This is simply no way to talk to a ballplayer.

The dh rule is a prime example of how to give superficial pleasure to superficial fans. It means you never have to watch a lemon at the bat, with all his mad hopes and sorrows, and life becomes one unbroken parade of experts. It also means that half the game strategy which you didn't understand anyway disappears forever for your greater viewing pleasure.

One game which seems to remain pretty much itself, if only because it can't help it, is basketball—our ingenious answer to the city guy's space problems and the country guy's solitude. Just one hoop and two players can kill an afternoon very comfortably. To be sure, you have to be excessively tall to play with the best; but who has to play with the best? Basketball, unlike its older brothers, does not need to be diluted at the lower levels into the likes of softball or touch football. You are playing the same basic game as Larry Bird, whoever you are, minus only the twenty-four-second clock, basketball's one concession to streamlining; and you don't need special pads, helmets or other forms of harness to play. It is hardly a coincidence that this most accessible of sports is also our only large export among the Big Three.

Baseball, football and basketball remain our most popular spectator sports, precisely because they have taken such care of their looks. Football is actually so pretty that it has developed a large audience abroad which has not only never played it but never even seen it played, except on the tube. This puts it in a class with figure skating, gymnastics and other approximations of ballet.

For those who resent the tyranny of the ball, the spheroid, over our capers, there have always been some venerable alternatives. For one thing, Americans will race anything against anything, from thoroughbred horses to diamondback terrapins to every conceivable species of motor. If you can drive it, fly it or float it, if it trots, crawls or gallops, there has to be a contest in it someplace. All in all, we have probably raced more objects against each other than there are kinds of pie in New England.

But what do Americans actually *play?* Everything under the sun by this time. Tennis courts seem to be sprouting like fungi and municipal golf courses no longer require you to rise at dawn and defend your starting time with your life. But beyond that, the Olympic brouhaha has made us interested as never before in minor sports. Volleyball, the ultimate beach game, has been promoted all the way to the high table. Nothing is really too humble anymore if a gold medal can be attached to it. And every Olympics sees more Americans competing in arcane activities like cross-country skiing and the hop, skip and jump— rejoining the rest of the world, but of course, we being Americans, trying to beat its ears off at the same time.

To end on a pompous note: Great Britain is not only the mother of parliaments but of most modern sports, and in this respect, America is its true child. And I don't think it is cant to say that if sports, with its absolute *need* for fair play and the rule of law, does not entirely prepare one for democracy, democracy does at least prepare one very nicely for sports.

The Origin of Football and Other American Species

*T*hirty years ago this month (I lie about the dates—what do you care?) I published my first piece. The subject of my juvenilium was the tedium of explaining football to Englishmen and cricket to Americans—in particular of fending off the moss-covered jokes that each national thinks he is making for the first time about the other guy's sport.

It all set me to thinking, with the speed of mulch, that our games *are* a little peculiar; quite unlike anyone else's, in fact. So over the years I've hatched out the following little set speech, to be delivered with a frozen smile, and preferably with a blackboard covered in zodiacal signs to help explain. The advantage of this method is that no foreigner can politely interrupt, or indeed will ever be likely to bring up the subject again.

Once upon a time, if you were a good little English boy, as God intended us all to be, you believed that the Almighty created every sport on the same day, and in its perfect form—especially cricket. Now, alas, we know better: the rise of *Homo ludens* from the muck has been infinitely grimmer and slower and tackier than that. It's just that he doesn't seem to have gotten very far yet.

When man's first sport came grunting out of the woods, one fancies it consisted mostly of shoving, gouging and mauling— very much like American football today. Early man, to judge from the pretty pictures, was superbly designed for football. His head virtually *was* a helmet, and a pointy one at that; and his thick neck, long arms and grasping fingers suggest that evolution had precisely football in mind for him, and nothing but football.

Just to fill in the other puzzling gaps in Darwin: at some point, perhaps a rock was inserted into the primal scrimmage, or a piece of meat or simple banana (ideal for passing), and eventually a ball, and the genus *Sport* split into species. In England, which is as rich as Mesopotamia in specimens, dozens of local maul games came crunching together at Oxford and Cambridge and bred down their differences into two families— *homos soccer* and *rugby* respectively. Soccer, suitable for any climate, terrain or physique, went on to conquer the world and to claim exclusive title to the name *football* in every corner of the globe except one.

This one corner, which airily calls its natives Indians and itself America (as if it were the whole continent), had no trouble commandeering the word *football* for its own game—which is actually a loose derivative of rugby and has as little to do with the feet as a sport called football can decently have.

Football, baseball and basketball, the great American trilogy, are all interesting examples of how regional climate and circumstance can deflect evolution. American football immediately demanded a breed of very large men, which promptly appeared and proceeded to mate with cheerleaders, thus producing even larger men. These behemoths in turn made football ever rougher and meaner, even as the lanky basketballers on the next reservation were making their game more floating and swanlike. (If all this genetic hanky-panky sounds far-fetched, consider the miraculous emergence of tall Orientals, just in time to play basketball.) The cost of this heavy breeding was a trifling loss in jockeys and bantamweight boxers, and a surplus of shot putters and other large, lonesome men: a routine change from light industry to heavy.

But size wasn't the half of it. Although America's self-portrait is big on individualism, most people's actual experience is of formidable organization, starting out with those great gangs of men racing the clock to build bridges and railroads before the other gang got there, and writhing under the gaze of some steely-eyed sumbitch or other. The foreman/sweathog relationship is perfectly expressed in American football—and remains a puzzle to Europeans, if not to Asians (some of whom helped build those railroads).

Old Father Rugby by contrast is totally spontaneous. Since rugby's action is continuous, a coach could not get a word in edgewise even if there were a coach. The players make the game plan up as they go along, which is fun for them but muddling for spectators, who don't matter anyway. The idea of redecorating a sport for the sake of the spectators never occurred to our English progenitors, who have hatched racetracks where the horses disappear for minutes on end behind the bushes. Their crowning achievement, cricket, cannot be witnessed from less than fifty yards away in any direction.

Wooing the public is built into the DNA of every modern American sport. Our racetracks are fast, flat and short, yielding quick, close results as opposed to England's cross-country straggles. Pro basketball has been souped up by the twenty-four-second clock—lots of scoring for those brief attention spans of ours. Baseball began putting "rabbit" (a magic new yarn that Baseball still swears was a happy accident) in the ball in the 1920s to make it fly farther, and now there's some kind of rabbit in the turf as well for more bang-bang action.

Even in the games we play for ourselves, similar streamlining has occurred. Pool-table pockets are wide and inviting compared with snooker pockets, which are harder to enter than the Kingdom of Heaven; ditto our croquet hoops. As for bowling, small children who would be blown off the boccie court by sheer adult breath, can sometimes make a go of it. Whether watching or playing, Americans want things to happen.

The agent of change in football has been the forward pass, a fairly obvious addition to rugby that the British have sternly resisted, presumably because it would make the game too easy. Without the forward pass, American football would be virtually unwatchable. "Three yards and a cloud of dust," followed by interminable huddling, and then more of same: about as stimulating as trench warfare.

The first forward passes were rickety, humpbacked affairs, like early aircraft. The new toy had to be nurtured, by the blind cunning of nature, to make that much difference. The shape of the ball mysteriously began to change in the 1930s, till you could no longer drop-kick it because it bounced so funny. With its tapered ends and huggable waistline, it was becoming a throwing ball instead of a kicking ball. (At the same time, Billy Mitchell and others were preaching the virtues of aerial warfare in real life.)

Next, trick formations had to be introduced, which through excruciating flimflam bought the receivers more time to get downfield. The T-formation used the linemen as screens, as opposed to just battering rams, and the backs as decoys, enabling large bands of wide receivers to roam farther into the savanna, or open field, thus spreading the tight little game out for observation and making way for the ultimate weapon, the Bomb, the most satisfying sight in football.

None of this could have happened without the fanatical discipline that was already there in the very bones of the game. Football strategy advanced enormously during World War II, again in strange harmony with the aeromania of the times, and it needed the enlisted men to implement it. Players began to memorize playbooks fatter than college reading lists just to crack the code in their own huddles. And an unparalleled apparatus grew up *around* the game—coaches with clipboards and guys making films, and high above them all agents crouched on the roof like U–2s, spotting defensive patterns, forming probability theories and war-gaming the hell out of things. Enemy codes got cracked, disinformation got fed, traded players got de-briefed. Spies were even unmasked at rival practice sessions. Surely no game has ever acted out a nation's fantasies so faith-fully.

It was inevitable during the Vietnam War that football would become a symbol of hawkishness, and we football-loving doves had to watch meekly as the air force flew over during half-time or old generals were dug up and honored. On the plus side, soccer snuck into the country, and it became for many the antiestablishment sport, the anti-body-count, anti-quick-results alternative. Which meant either that America was joining the rest of the human race or that soccer was in for some fiendish streamlining: widening the net, greasing the ball, or just plain throwing it.

The popularity of both soccer and rugby may well indicate terminal impatience with the rigid formalities of football, with its fixed schedule and its daft rituals and its officious role in academic life. Football's Ivy League roots, and its colorful flow-ering on slicker campuses, seemed equally dead in the "burn, baby, burn" sixties and the "did it my way" seventies. But the game itself has acquired a sort of intellectual elegance that makes its own quite separate appeal to a generation that has also gone ape over electronic puzzles and such. Football is now so com-plicated that at first sight it gives away nothing at all, except the caveman gouging and shoving mentioned above. But every year the fan sees a little bit more, Delphic mysteries become clear to him, and he advances in the priesthood. With such a base, the game could shed all its historical trappings, its very reasons for being, and still be a beauty.

Football's one real strength and weakness is that it is always in flux. Unlike baseball, whose fearful symmetry needs and gets very little tinkering, football is constantly up for negotiation, as the superpowers of Offense and Defense maneuver for an edge. So the game is only as good as its last rule change. New York, as Confucius once said, will be a beautiful city if they ever get it finished. Not so football. If they ever get it finished, which God forbid, football is dead.

Unnecessary Roughness

*T*he literature of nausea has come to professional
football: the "I Was a Vampire for the Chicago
Bears" school for one crowd, and "I Was a Rich
Owner's Plaything" for the other. On the constitutional principle that anything we enjoy that much must be evil, we have
begun gobbling up exposés like health food—book upon re-
lentless book proving the essential rottenness of coaches, players, hot-dog purveyors, and even us fans. It is a brand new
chapter in the history of meaningless outrage.

Because if we took the exposés seriously, we would simply
have to stop watching the game altogether and cease tax-sup-
porting new stadiums. And nobody seriously expects that, not
from one reader in a million. So we are just reading the books
for fun. In fact, if I may expose the essential dinginess of the
football reader, I suspect we buy the books for the football
parts—as the authors will discover when they write that next
book about the Esalen Institute or the power of prayer. We
listen to the sermon for the dirty bits, as we always have.

As literary entertainments, these books depend heavily on the unfathomable innocence of the old yellow-press client, who never ceases to be shocked that businessmen like money or that athletes have sex lives. When it comes to more specialized information, the exposers fall to babbling in tongues. For instance, where does the sickening violence come from in football? Hear Bernie Parrish in *They Call It a Game:*

"I think a lot of the more evil problems of pro football might be cured if the owners were forced to cover one kickoff—and to repeat until they made one tackle, however long that took." In other words, the violence comes from effete owners sending young men to their deaths, like Lord Cardigan. (Unfortunately, the one owner who *has* played, George Halas of Chicago, is known as one of the meanest men in the game.)

Yet a few pages later, Parrish is denouncing coaches as pussycats because they're not violent enough. "When an opposing runner goes down they don't have that urge to stomp him into the turf so he won't get up again." Coaches have no feelings. Parrish himself has the urge to stomp in spades. "I relished hitting people, I could hardly wait for the next collision. I even enjoyed being hit," says he; and this was in high school, before he'd met his first rascally owner.

Turning to Dave Meggyesy, the pioneer malcontent, we learn that the violence and sadism were "not so much on the part of the players or in the game itself, but very much in the minds of the beholders—the millions of Americans who watch football every weekend in something approaching a sexual frenzy." So that is where the trouble lies—not in the owners or the players, but the fans. How he knows how we watch I don't know—at my place, aphasic torpor would be closer to it. Yet Meggyesy admits that he, too, liked to hit. In fact, he played the game more ferociously than anyone asked him to; and it seems possible that he quit the game because he actually frightened himself.

One is reminded, on a miniature scale, of Lieutenant Calley's confessional style: the system may be evil, but you don't have to embrace it quite that ardently. If we are all guilty for Meggyesy and his pals, it would mainly be for tolerating a game that feeds and clothes the beast in them. What would happen to this beast if we took away its ball none of our philosophers quite gets around to analyzing. Chip Oliver in *High for the Game* says that football players behave like animals because they are expected to. But Oliver, like Meggyesy, so exceeded beastly requirements that his own teammates called him Rudeness. Both authors stress how football indoctrinates you. But no one seems quite as indoctrinated as they were.

Does pro football tear down character faster than it builds it? It depends on what you're trying to prove. On one page, Parrish calls the players "overgrown, self-conscious children," on another he says they are "even more sophisticated" than the players of the fifties and sixties. Parrish's children "foolishly fight over their toys; and they live beyond their means, as the recent rash of player bankruptcies illustrates." But in Joe Durso's *The All-American Dollar,* another pro complains that football is no fun anymore because "players sit around checking their investment portfolios," just like boring old grown-ups. And Oliver chips in with praise for the black players who "knew there was no sense in holding onto their money or sinking it into a bank." What the devil is an adult anyway, and is it a good thing?

Ideally, the exposers' first fight would be with each other. Like all of us, they were raised on at least two completely contradictory moral codes, and can preach from either one interchangeably, and with their ears ringing from clothesline tackles, they can be as confused as anyone. There's another reason for their baggy-pants logic. Happy the man with a book-length grievance—and rare. Each of these books contains one possible magazine article surrounded by more padding than an offensive lineman: every little indignity that ever happened to them, and every two-bit feud, magnified to a Horrible Example to justify a larger printing. Bernie Parrish's article would simply be a demand for a bigger piece of the commercial loot for the players, and he has some nice, dull facts to back him up. But nobody's going to buy a whole book about athletes' pay scales. With bad times here again, it's uphill work feeling sorry for fully employed football players clamoring for their share of the TV cream.

So Parrish tarts up his message with this fuzzy stuff about violence and dehumanization and throws in a chapter about how games *might* be fixed (e.g., the referee could make some bad calls in spite of being monitored by millions of sexually aroused bettors on instant replay). As often happens, the useful part of the books is the dullest, and the sensational part is just a come-on.

In Meggyesy's case, he has some convincingly damning things to say about two particular institutions—Syracuse University and the St. Louis Cardinals. Once again, not enough for a coast-to-coast book. He would like to say more, but so far it's all he knows. Athletes are hampered by narrowness of experience, though, as Benchley might say, not always hampered enough. It seems the Cardinals were a racist outfit, overripe for exposure. But Meggyesy has to do a book exposing all of football as well, and he generalizes feebly. According to a black player, Johnny Sample, in his book *Confessions of a Dirty Ballplayer,* Joe Namath has routed racism from the New York Jets: and no doubt, other cities, other tales, dimly known to Meggyesy.

His real story is about himself, and it's not a bad one. His father's beatings were his first contact with violence, and after that it drew him like Swinburne. He says he hit people to please his father-figure coaches. But Ben Schwartzwalder, his coach at Syracuse, says that "you couldn't go up from behind and tap him on the shoulder. He'd turn around and hit you." So even father figures weren't safe.

Meggyesy had none of the juice or joy that George Plimpton found among the Detroit Lions, or the boozy good fellowship which might make this life tolerable. He just doesn't like the football player type. So he tried solemnly to turn himself into a hippie, for which he didn't have the juice or joy either. The book jacket shows him with a beard and headband and an uncertain frown; and the text is no adventure of an expanded spirit, but a heavy laborious tract written with the help of his new coach—Jack Scott of the Institute for the Study of Sport and Society.

Meggyesy's gloomy grapplings with the counterculture make one wish for a third choice—the clergy, maybe. Chip Oliver, on the other hand, fits cheerfully into both cultures, and anything else that's going. He is an old-line extrovert, who once frightened some tourists by appearing naked in a college corridor, and a new-line love child throwing himself into the latest jargon with a rookie's enthusiasm. Of his new friends, he warbles, "Their philosophy that the problems on this planet are only the effects of acquisitive behavior really turned me on." Wild. Or how about "The Chinese have been eating a rice and vegetable diet for years, and despite the propaganda that they are starving, they don't have the health problems that come from obesity that we do." A rip-off of a book, but a diverting character.

On his high-for-the-game days, old Chip couldn't tell a football from a sunflower anyway. Both he and Meggyesy have dropped acid and it sometimes clouds their message in the clichés of *that* sport. LSD may expand consciousness, but it sure as death shrinks vocabulary, and these two very different characters sometimes sound as if they're talking from the same sack. Also they keep expanding way, way beyond football to call on the whole of straight society to repent—in which case football becomes a silly detail. Oliver would like to turn it into an Elysian love dance, but mescaline can do that for you already, without the game being changed at all.

The matter of pro football is serious enough to be referred to the philosophers or professional arguers, except that nobody buys their books. (Any clown sporting a jock outsells the most talented noncombatant.) When Ara Parseghian played for a tie against Michigan State, he defended himself by saying, "I think I know more about football than they do." Quite true. The only thing a philosopher could have told him was why people play the game in the first place. Coaches would be the last to know this, and college presidents would be the last to tell them.

The autonomy of the coach with his large jaw and his tiny outlook is the one clear evil that each of our authors agrees on. A coach can mislay or bury a player he doesn't like more effectively than in other sports and can use this threat to manipulate private conduct and thought, play injured men, and work out his own scoutmaster kinks. How much is this un-American tyranny necessary for the best functioning of the all-American game? Unfortunately, our authors are too bogged down in petty grievance to put the question sharply, and so far the pompous football establishment has been able to duck it with, of all things, pious talk about American values. Here's Oliver mulling his damnedest: "The Chiefs played more creatively, and creative people, the ones who do the unexpected, are the biggest winners in football." But here's Oliver versus Oliver: "Vince Lombardi was a great coach, not because he was a football genius *who was constantly coming up with new things to surprise the opposition,* but because he worked the hell out of his players." (My italics.)

How much of football is played in the head is a moot question, and this probably is not the place to moot it. Our four playing authors (I include Sample) were all veteran defensive players who needed less coaching than most (they were also shifted in youth from offense without consultation, and may harbor resentments; offensive players write dreamy accounts of their coaches). The psychological hold of coach over player belongs to social history. Vince Lombardi probably won't arise again in quite that form. Vince had the world view of a parochial school nun, determined that the Irish and the Italians would not be the slobs that people expected; but those schools are closing. The Chip Olivers wouldn't obey him now anyway. And the Meggyesys must look for a new kind of father.

For a decent perspective on all this, I would recommend two books by authors outside the pit: Neil Amdur's *The Fifth Down* and Larry Merchant's *Every Day You Take Another Bite.* Amdur can be rambling and earnestly sentimental, but he sees the size of the question: football is one more excuse for today's kid and yesterday's adult to have at it—or if the coach tries something new, yesterday's kid and today's adult. Merchant goes him one better. He laughs at the whole thing. Could this be the answer?

Well, the greed can be sent to Congress (Parrish's book is being used in an antitrust investigation, where it belongs), and the violence can be sent to Esalen. But the self-importance, the idolatrous "mystique" that coaches and owners grow fat on must be stamped out in the home, and Merchant's is the brightest and funniest contribution to that task in some time.

The Unknown Football Player:
No. 65 Replacing No. 63

*O*nce upon a time, before the age of specialization, there were two kinds of football players: forwards and backs; or, as I remember them from the old programs, players who needed big necks and players who didn't—but had them anyway.

Of the two, the forwards were slightly heavier and the backs slightly faster. But since everyone had to do so many things— block, tackle, and look lively for sixty minutes—there were few glaring disparities in type. If you saw a team waiting for a bus, you would know they were all in the same line of business.

"We had two guys who weighed 230 pounds," reminisces Irwin Shaw of his Brooklyn College days in the thirties, "but they were just substitutes. Too clumsy." Yesterday, contrariwise, I heard a man of six feet three inches and 246 pounds described on television as "possibly a bit too small for the game."

Too small for *his* game, that is. Specialization has riven the overall game into several quite separate activities, so that walk-

235

ing around the field is like visiting different kingdoms. There is no longer a single football type but a linebacker type or a wide receiver type. Our tiny 246-pound friend was simply caught in no man's land: too small to enter one kingdom, too large, like Alice in Wonderland, to enter another.

Modern players do have one thing in common with their ancestors, which is an uncanny willingness, bordering on exhilaration, to hit and be hit. My own recollection from school days is of one's face constantly crashing toward the ground, so that one developed a special relationship with topsoil, whether hard or mushy. You might not like it, but it was your brother.

I don't know if Astroturf has changed this relationship, but I still imagine your basic football player as a man who will hit anything, from a brick wall to a near relative, at the bark of a signal. How much of this sheer "hittingness" is inbred is obviously anybody's guess, but I do know that it can be acquired, as dread of contact gives way to relief and finally to a curious pleasure. And it does not imply violence in one's other pursuits. Although football players are, like most athletes, abysmal practical jokers, their horseplay is not notoriously aggressive—perhaps for the good biological reason that they would all be dead by now if it were. For whatever reason, the last superstar to get hurt in a locker room scuffle was not a football player but a baseball guy.

So much for what f.p.s have in common: hitting and more hitting. Beyond that, differences in size and assignment dictate differences in temperament. A study reported in *Sports Illustrated* some years ago indicated that our gang are overall the most intelligent of athletes (or, as an announcer might say, "very smart for a big man"), but this again must vary from position to position. Anyone who can memorize any part of a modern playbook has to have some smarts, but some obviously have to memorize more parts than others. Which brings us not to the steely-eyed quarterback—the one player that *everyone* knows about—but to the interior offensive lineman, about whom little is known or possibly cared.

These men in fact constitute a fascinating breed, if only because, quite against the American grain, they seem content to remain obscure and relatively poorly paid. Try naming an all-time all-star team, and you will likely come up with twenty-five quarterbacks, fifty running backs, and a great hole up front. If it hadn't been for Jerry Kramer's *Instant Replay*, one might never have heard of any offensive guards or tackles at all.

How content these beasts of burden actually are we'll probably never know, because we hear so little from them; but we do know that your wise superstar like O. J. Simpson never misses an opportunity to praise them. A guard or center may never become a free agent or a household word, but he holds the key for those who can. One doesn't think first of loyalty in terms of the other positions, but here it is everything. When, for instance, the talented quarterback Vince Ferragamo went to Canada and had the most miserable year in history it seemed fair to deduce that he'd forgotten one of his lineman's birthdays, or more seriously, that they didn't cotton to rich Yanks up there.

It would seem too much to ask of these anonymous, brutally overworked citizens that they also be intelligent, but nobody ever said that football was fair. In fact, every play in the book requires of them a different nuance of blocking—whether to make a hole or only appear to, whether to brush block or steamroller or even occasionally to let a man through while appearing not to (the primeval "mousetrap" play)—and these plays are often changed at the line of scrimmage, while our man is staring at an enraged, hyperactive gorilla a few feet away and trying to decipher the quarterback's signals over the howl of the crowd.

Although in aggregate, offensive linemen may look like fugitives from a chain gang, they are highly disciplined and intelligent souls—many of them, I would guess by the names, from coal mining country and grateful to be playing anywhere at all where the sun shines.

They also tend to be slightly smaller (let's say 260 versus 280), and perhaps slightly less good natural athletes, than their opposite numbers on the defense because coaches like to fill up the defensive line first. These two groups of mastodons are condemned to spend their lives within about five yards of each other, yet they tend to be quite different in type. Where the offense is quasi-military in its planning, the defense must improvise, seize the moment, think on its feet. Defensive signals are only suggestions based on guesswork (unless they come from Tom Landry, who *knows*).

Defensive linemen tend accordingly to be buccaneers and free spirits. There is some glory to be had by them, even if they have to share it with the other People Eaters or the rest of the Fearsome Foursome, and unlike the stolid Palace Guard across the way they have the mouthwatering pleasure of sacking the rich instead of defending them.

The intensity of this pleasure used to be testified to on Monday Night Football by Alex Karras' cackles of glee every time a passer was hit. Apparently a lineman is never too old to light up over a writhing quarterback. Karras himself was particularly menacing on the field: reveling in the limitations of his position, he actually used to play without his glasses, which was somewhat equivalent to a fast-ball pitcher working blindfolded.

Behind these marauders lurk perhaps the most vicious creatures in the bestiary, linebackers. Up to now we have been dealing with men who don't look as if they could play any other sport, except maybe the shot put. Karras' bad eyesight is unusual but symbolic—what other athletic work can be found for the blind or near-blind? It is nice of football to provide a home for these large but sometimes limited men; but this ceases abruptly as one leaves the pit, or line of scrimmage.

Linebackers are built closer to the size of heavyweight fighters, which is clearly the optimum size for speed combined with strength (linemen are too big for boxing, as one "Too Tall" Jones of Dallas recently discovered in a brief ring career), and their nervous systems seem to be at some equivalent juncture of aggression. In a world of giants or linemen, they are the little guys, feisty and ferocious; among more normal specimens they are the enforcers, the cops. Either way, they are among the hardest hitters in football. Ray Nitschke, Dick Butkus, Jack Lambert, and Chuck Bednarik were all bywords in terror: yet

each is now quite genial in repose. Action seems to alter personality more radically in their case than most.

The middle linebacker in particular must do his best to cope
with the Mack truck elements, the Jim Browns and Earl Camp-
bells, as they thunder over the tundra, breaking jaws and snapping necks; but he must also cut with the scatbacks as they go
out for short passes. His rage is inflamed by concentration. Every
play ideally begins for him in thought and ends in violence.
Having read the mind and history of the quarterback, the linebacker must decide like a tennis player, or a yo-yo, whether to
move in or out, become a forward or a back, for both of which
he is half-equipped. His natural rival physically is the offensive
tight end, usually a slightly taller version of himself, who must
for his part block with the big boys and play catch with the fast
ones. A Butkus stalking a Mike Ditka is one of the finest match-
ups in nature or anywhere else.

Which brings us at last to the pure athletes who make the
game so pretty to watch. The cornerbacks and safeties on defense and the wide receivers and halfbacks on offense look as
if they could play any other sport they choose, and they often
have. Some have been recruited from track, others from baseball
and basketball (has *any* middle lineman ever been offered a
baseball contract?), and as they approach other athletes in type,
they seem to recede from the football essence: I'll bet there are
even some wide receivers who don't like to be hit.

These belong to that special elite which gets to play with the
ball and not just with each other. Out in the outback where
the receivers roam, far from the noise and urban congestion of
the scrimmage, the game becomes pastoral, a bunch of kids
fooling around, ducking this way and that, sidestepping, stealing
the ball.

For the offense, this randomness is mostly illusion. As with
the running backs and linemen, whatever can be planned is
planned and the receiver had better be where he's supposed to
be by the count of three or four, however he elects to get there.
The defenders are as usual the gamblers. Play deep and get
burned, play close and get incinerated. No one's mistakes are

plainer to see, no one gets more egg on his face per season. Yet guess right, and he may find himself strutting down an empty lane with a picture-book interception.

These rangers are often converted running backs, and they thirst to get the ball back one more time, and with it the glory, that was rudely taken away by some coach. They also live on their reflexes and their wits and are the most likely to write sassy books (see Johnny Sample, Jack Tatum, et al.) upon retirement. The fact that they also tend to be black may have something to do with the legendary Negro foot structure and its awesome capacity for leaping. But here, as with other positions, notably quarterback, a lot also depends on how much early coaching is needed and how much is available. And you can't coach a reflex.

We are now approaching the high priest himself, the quarterback, and his henchmen the running backs who, as far as statistics are concerned, are the only people besides receivers who play the game at all. Middle linemen who put in ten years or so depart the scene without a trace: they leave no records behind, except minutes played, to prove their existence. The only other statistically existent players are not really players at all, but those strange little footnotes who bob up and kick field goals during the intermissions in real life. When I recently saw one of these gnomes give the high sign and scamper round in a tiny circle after a success, I thought, by God, he's *trying* to be a football player. But that's as close as it gets.

Statistics have little to do with football, as one might guess from the sloppiness of the math: a statistical yard is just an estimate (how far has Franco Harris actually run? every yard is raised, as in banking, to the nearest round number); a dropped pass is not recorded, any more than a miraculous catch, in a passer's percentage; and a five-yard pass followed by an eighty-yard run is listed, incredibly, as an eighty-five-yard pass. As for the gnomes, on any given (or withheld) Sunday, incongruous headwinds, bad snaps from center, and missed blocking assignments can play the very devil with their precious numbers.

Statistics are designed to hide what every player knows,

namely that football really is a team sport, from the spotter on the roof down to the man shooting the films for next week's game, laboring under a publicity-enforced class system. So let's for once skip the sky pilots throwing their bombs and the solipsists running for eternal daylight, and give the game ball to the man whose name is only heard when he steps offside, the enlisted man who risks his knees and his neck in the trenches every Sunday—the Unknown Lineman.

P.S. A surprising number of linemen have made great coaches, including the likes of Vince Lombardi and the three great pioneers George Halas, Steve Owen, and Curly Lambeau; by contrast, I find it hard to think of a single running back in the top rank. Which supports a belief that running backs know less about the total game than anyone else on the field except the kickers.

Soccer: England's
Number-One Killer

f you're a city kid, crowds are the element you swim in. When they seem to thicken slightly, that means you're at a ball game or riding the subway. When they thin, you're having a quiet night at home. But at any size they don't bother you much: they are the city equivalent of the farmer's dog that slams you against the wall and pants in your face. Tiger is just being friendly.

Move to the country and of course it's another story. On your trips to the city now the crowds who belt eternally along the sidewalks begin to look and sound like roller derby to you. And when you're in a real crowd, at a sports event or political rally, you pick up all sorts of hostile, menacing growls that weren't there before. You are now in the city guy's equivalent of the woods at night, without a compass or a flashlight.

There is nothing paranoid—I repeat *nothing paranoid!*—about either reaction. There is danger galore in dogs, woods and crowds. What you lose without practice is alertness to the benevolent counterforces, the training in the dog and the civilized antibodies in the crowd. Take those protections away and we are all cowards together. Faced with a forest full of wildcats or a stadium full of Yankee fans—but I go too far, revealing my own brutish biases. Let's just say that something seems to have gone wrong when city dwellers increasingly fear crowds even in those palaces of play, their sports arenas. So herewith some notes on the subject, found in a Long Island potato field.

Once upon a time, a fight at the ballpark was one of life's minor pleasures. All heads would turn to gaze and applaud as some pair of tipsy citizens squared off and attempted to paw each other without tottering down the ramp. There was no danger of the thing spreading beyond the next row, because everyone was laughing too hard; and if it lasted more than the usual three seconds, we got bored and turned back to the game.

Nowadays, these happy warriors have largely disappeared, to be replaced by a sleeker breed of cat, and one tends to watch a fight, or kindred ruckus, with mild apprehension, looking for the flash of steel. Nothing to panic about just yet—but then last summer, some English soccer fans staged a near-massacre in Belgium, and some of our own qualms burst into vivid color. Up to now our aggressives have mostly worked freelance, or in small foul-tempered knots that don't even like each other, but if they ever balled themselves together, as the Brits did, into a single fist, could our walls come tumbling down too?

"Can it happen here?" is, of course, all that most of us want to know about anything, so let's get on with that. But before miring down comfortably in the bogs of sociology, let's consider a few Brit particulars, in order to compare them with our own particulars.

"The English disease [a.k.a. vice]" has undergone quite a change in the last few years. Old-timers may remember it wistfully as "the love that dares not speak its name." Now it is closer to a hate that is practiced outdoors in front of thousands, and it isn't too shy to say anything.

By chance, I happen to be the world's leading expert on the subject. Lord knows, it doesn't take much. Back in 1969 I wrote an interminable essay on this disease of men making war not love with each other and I talked to every manner of shrink and cop and loudmouth-at-large, and you've never heard so many explanations—at least since Mr. Nixon last discussed the Watergate tapes. Specialists had sprung up everywhere, in their infectious way, to report that violence came from poverty, new-found affluence, status envy, loss of empire and the Bomb. It's nice to know that those specialists are all still there, spouting off as ineffectively as ever: it gives one a sense of tradition and continuity.

The only glimmer of obvious truth I got issued from a wizened lad in Leicester City (age somewhere between twelve and sixty), who suggested that rioting might be kind of fun. "We have some grand poonch-oops with t'lads from Notts Forest" he averred. It seems that this had nothing to do with the course of the particular match: the stadia were simply open-air trysting places for these claques of merry half-wits, and win or lose, the fight must go on.

Just to show they had no hard feelings about soccer as such, the visiting fans would then proceed to break windows randomly and rip out telephones (you couldn't make a call within a mile of a soccer ground), until their stately progress would lead them at last into special trains where the light bulbs had already been removed along with the cushions and toilet seats, making these trains the closest thing to padded cells on wheels that British Railways could devise. What is particularly touching is that the sixties are now looked back on as a kind of Golden Age, or boys-will-be-boys period, of English soccer violence. So you can imagine it now. Multiply that by the sensitivity of invading armies in general, and perhaps you have Belgium— but not quite, so far, the U.S.

Next culprit, please. Soccer is the most amiable and civilized of activities, a least likely suspect among sports. Yet it seems time after time to be found lurking at the scene of the crime, and its overall death toll, from Buenos Aires to Brussels, probably exceeds that of all other sports put together, including boxing—impressive when you realize that this is just among the spectators. There is something about soccer that makes the mildest of nationals want to kill, and go on killing, until the paddy wagon hauls him away.

To the untrained eye, soccer consists of twenty-two men in shorts pattering endlessly up and down a vast field, minding their own business. But something about its rhythms seems to set the pulses pounding. Compared with our own leading sports, the action is continuous (no time-outs or substitutes), but comparatively slow. At a basketball game you simply have no time to fight: twenty points will have been scored while you are squirming out of your coat. In hockey, on the other hand, you can fight as much as you like, but only when the players are fighting, too. The moment they stop you stop, at whatever point your affairs have reached. Since the players fight most of the time you could possibly contrive a sort of herky-jerky battle right through the three periods. But very few people would get killed that way.

Soccer, on the other hand, provides countless blank patches, little phony wars where the ball seems becalmed in mid-field. The enemy seems to be mounting an offensive—whoops, out of bounds. Now its our guys—sorry, back to the drawing board. Again. These troughs are never quite dull enough to put you to sleep (as in some sports I might name), but they do give you plenty of time to attend to your neighbor's thoughtful comments on your home team and on the bewitching town you and it hail from.

In short, there is a vacuum, in fact a whole mess of vacuums, in soccer clamoring somehow for *you* to do something, to complement the game in some way. With scores of 0–0 not infrequent, a man might almost feel that nothing much had happened that particular day unless he started it himself. Pity to travel all the way to Pudsey and have nothing happen.

What such a man is likely to start is, naturally, the one thing the players are not allowed to do themselves—punch people, plus the trimmings. No game, even basketball, seems so constantly to approach the edge of violence without quite crossing it. The athletes stalk each other *mano a mano*, malignantly but decorously, with their arms at their sides like Irish dancers (and perhaps for the same reason). Everything about their bearing suggests what they would do with their hands if they were allowed to, and their feet too (the poor blighters are not even allowed to kick each other).

But there's nothing stopping the bloke in the stands. Everything that can't be done on the field is done in spades on the sidelines, down to biting and carrying concealed weapons. The loyal supporter is only doing the team's work in another fashion. At day's end, he has shared body and soul in their triumph or defeat, and deserves his spoils: his light bulb and his toilet seat.

Perhaps such more openly violent games as boxing, rugby and our own football exhaust this need to throw one's own weight onto the scales (I say "openly" because a surprising number of soccer players fall to the ground, writhing mysteriously). After watching Marvelous Marvin Hagler, do you really think you can do better? And what precisely can you add to the mayhem in an Eagles-Cowboys game?

Well, maybe a little something. Actually, the end of a match is a tricky time in all sports. Fight fans have been known to riot after bad decisions and pelt the ring with stuff—it's a great target, brightly lit and central; great for converging on, too, screaming and waving your arms. Football fans are great trophy hunters, as befits a sport of acquisition and possession, who are especially captivated by goal posts. Baseball fans at World Series time do some of their best work outside the stadiums afterward, mainly because most of them never got into the game in the first place. Club ticket policies can, as we'll see in a moment, do wonders to get violence out of the stands and into the streets where it belongs.

What else, after the Ball? Horse players hang themselves, chess buffs go home and study. Every game leaves you with a little something extra to burn off. Soccer is not unique in its aftermath, only in its play-by-play. And even this could be cut back to nothing by America's last line of defense, the season ticket, which renders all crowds equal. When Giant fans mashed up the Polo Grounds in 1958, the General Admissions window was closed the next day and forever. And this very year, some of the famous but sometimes scary bleacher bums of Wrigley Field will find themselves rousted from their aerie to make way, no doubt, for mild-mannered businessmen and their hangers-on. (Scare talk: if those are mild-mannered businessmen, spare us from feral ones.)

Season ticket holders start few fights and make no mess; they leave their seats as they would like to find them, and they exit quietly by way of the Stadium Club, not pausing to riot on the way home to Scarsdale or Grosse Pointe. Ideally they do not even show up at all for games on end, thus averting whatever little trouble they might have caused. Safety can ask no more than this: empty seats that have been handsomely paid for.

According to this expert here we haven't yet come anywhere's near meeting the conditions for a really world-class riot, but trust management to take no chances. The phrase "general admission" may soon pass out of the language altogether and that volatile age group from ten to twenty-two, which Shakespeare thought should all be locked up anyway as being good for only "venery and burglary" (and which is heavily represented at English soccer games), may just have to wait until it has graduated from business school before attending its first ball game.

Season ticket holders are, in a most literal sense, the wave of the future in sports, since weeks of practice can also enable them to execute this simple-minded maneuver about as well as its rather limited nature permits.

Yet for all their housebroken perfection I wouldn't trust them not to go berserk and set fire to the stadium if they had to watch a nice quiet game of soccer every week. It seems to be that kind of game.

The Old Man and the Tee

*T*here are certain things you never get to see in life because there aren't enough cameras to go around. For instance, the look on a painter's face when he stares at his latest baby and decides that it's finally finished—one more stroke and he could have blown it; or the novelist coming down the homestretch; or the scientist contemplating his slide and realizing that that unappetizing blob of muck on it spells either glory or twenty years down the tube.

We did, however, get to see Jack Nicklaus play the last four holes at the Masters Tournament this spring (spring for us, that is, autumn for him—non-golf fanciers should be apprised that this was the second oldest man ever to win a major tournament, coming from four strokes down with only four holes to play and passing a menacing herd of young tigers on his way).

To go with his sizzling performance, Nicklaus happened to be wearing the most expressive face I've ever seen on an athlete—because in his own special world he *was* an artist working on a masterpiece that one extra stroke would literally ruin, a scientist with a pack of rivals baying at his heels as he pondered each putt. But above all, he was playing a sport that allows one to show, indeed almost forbids one not to show, one's thoughts.

Consider the alternatives. Football players, bless them, never have to show their faces at all. Baseball hitters' mouths, as photographed, open foolishly at the moment of contact, while pitchers do their best to look like poker players or shell-game operators, which in a sense they are. In track, sprinters' faces tend to burst at the seams, while long-distance guys run as if they were down to their last tank: one animate expression might dislodge something vital in there.

Tennis players have the time to look interesting, but they waste great gobs of it glaring at the linesmen or the umpire or at anything that moves—still, they have their moments. Basketball players seesaw interminably between goofy elation and grim determination all the live night long. With hockey players, who can tell? A man without teeth looks like the Mona Lisa at the best of times, bomb damage at the worst. Jockeys probably look fascinating, but who has time to notice? Golfers for their part do not exactly whiz by: for days they move like snails under glass, until we know every last twitch, with time left over to memorize their wardrobe and decipher its meanings.

However, there was more to Nicklaus' face that day than simple visibility. He is a disciplined man, and there had to be a lot in there for so much to come out. The first item in the Making of the Face was simply that of his age; at forty-six, Nicklaus is at least old enough to *have* a face, as they say in Ireland. But he is also much too old to win a major golf tournament, and this thought must have followed him around the course like a playground pest jumping on his back and trying to pinion his arms, all the while jabbering, "You can't do it because it can't be done, *you can't do*..." Scat, said Nicklaus' face. Get that bum out of here. But not until the Face lit up, like Broadway, on the eighteenth green, could we be sure the bum had left.

Then there was the Occasion. The Masters is far and away our classiest tournament—the one the Duchess of Kent would attend if we had a Duchess of Kent. And since Nicklaus' appearances anywhere at this point are on the order of royal visits in themselves, the combination is enough to make even a spectator's knees tremble. The gale-force waves of adulation that crash over the guest of honor on such occasions must make it all the victim can do just to smile and wave weakly like the queen. So imagine her royal self being handed a set of clubs and commanded to play right through the crowd, all the way to the coronation, pitching her ball up the steps and into a little tin cup, before she can claim her crown.

That is more or less what King Jack had to do to get his green jacket, and he admitted that he had to fight tears several times as he strode down those last ringing fairways. Wouldn't it be pleasanter just to relax and enjoy this? It's such a lovely course. . . . No, said the Face.

A third, more mundane factor in the Making of Nicklaus' Face was the simple fact that Nicklaus can't see as well as he used to and no longer has the pleasure of watching those intergalactic drives of his return to Earth. For the Masters, therefore, his son had to double as caddy and long-range seeing-eye dog, which added for this reporter a curiously Biblical touch to the proceedings. But besides all that, myopia in itself can produce a slightly strained appearance that, as I learned back in school, can pass for thinking if you play it right.

Of course, the fourth factor, or facet, in the Face was that Nicklaus wasn't "playing it" at all. By the fifteenth hole, he probably wasn't even aware that he *had* a face, and he certainly didn't give a damn what it looked like. In fact, if the Devil had popped the question, I daresay old Jack would have willingly put on a fright wig and a bright-red nose in exchange for just one more twenty-five-footer.

Or at least *I* would have. I guess it hardly needs pointing out that all the above was going on in my mind, not his, and that watching a game can be even more nerve-racking than playing one, as I learned from a priest friend who bit clear through his umbrella handle while watching a cricket match. What Nicklaus actually said when this seeming agony in Bobby Jones' garden was over was that he had felt "comfortable" (comfortable!) over the twenty-five-footers and that he hadn't had so much fun in six years.

Well, a champion's idea of fun may not be everybody's. Amounts of tension that would send a normal man screaming into the woods act on him like a tonic, or a wake-up call. Athletes have been known to complain of not feeling enough of it ("Man, I was flat out there"). Basketball's super-cool Bill Russell—and doubtless many others less cool—used routinely to throw up before outings, so that it became almost part of his regimen. John McEnroe favors a level of constant embarrassment to light his phlegm, while Muhammad Ali's weigh-in tantrums used to send his blood pressure into the stratosphere.

But a golfer has no need of such paltry devices. All he has to do is think about putting. The great Sam Snead for one could never resign himself to the idea that this dwarfish stroke, the putt, should count every bit as much as a booming three-hundred-yard drive, and he actually wanted putting declared a separate sport.

It certainly *looks* different. Every other stroke, I am assured, can be played with the same basic swing, variously adjusted— that is, until one approaches the pressure pit, or green, at which point the whole exercise changes its nature from a robust, swinging affair to a pinched little game of skill suitable for saloons. The lords of the fairway are suddenly called upon to hunch over like bank clerks and not move a muscle. The result is almost an anti-swing, a total negation of everything they've been doing. The shoulders remain still, the hips don't swivel, the wrists break not. From behind, the golfer appears to be doing nothing at all, but that's not quite so; what he's doing is growing an ulcer.

That low growl that hangs over the nation's golf courses at all times is mostly about putting. At least in the rough you can hack your way out and mutilate some of the course in revenge, while with water hazards you get to roll up your pants and have a nice paddle. But putting is like drinking tea with your pinkie raised, or more precisely, like threading a needle with a thread that bends at the last moment. (Tournament greens, by the way, are not to be compared with miniature golf; they are more, if you can stand another metaphor, like ice that tilts.)

Testimonials to the human toll exacted by this disgusting practice can be picked up anywhere the strange game is played. The incomparable Ben Hogan had to quit the game because of it. Although Hogan's nerves had won him the name of "Iceman," and although the rest of his game still glittered, he suddenly succumbed to something known as the yips, a degenerative ailment that freezes the hands in terror and renders them incapable of so much as lifting the club head back.

Out of sheer and unprecedented compassion, the unbending masters of golf bent just enough to let Snead use a club shaped like a T square during his later years, with which he could practically putt from between his legs like an aging croquet player (it didn't help). Gene Sarazen, the Grandma Moses of the game, once suggested, but was *not* granted, a six-inch hole. And if the word of an outsider is of any help, Dick Groat, who played shortstop for the Pirates in the hair-raising seven-game World Series of 1960, said that he didn't know what pressure was until he stepped onto the eighteenth green in a pro-am tournament.

This is the stuff that Nicklaus feels "comfortable" with? Well, saints be praised. One falls back in awe as a champion so simply and casually defines what the word means. He didn't *look* comfortable, but that had nothing to do with it. He looked, among other things, eager, speculative, and about ready to cry. But inside he apparently felt the kind of joy that inhuman pressure brings only to heroes, and you didn't need to be a golf buff to have felt happy to share a species with such a man as the green jacket was finally slipped over his shoulders.

The Vanishing Tennis Brat

O ne of the small but quietly satisfying happenings of 1986 may turn out to be the decline and fall of the tennis brat. Call it wishful thinking, but last summer's U.S. Open looked to me suspiciously like the Brats' Last Stand. First, we saw a subdued, verging on polite, John McEnroe going down without a whimper to a perfectly behaved young American gentleman, Paul Annacone, which was rather like seeing a fighting cock drenched in water.

Then, in another corner of the Open, we witnessed that elder statesman of brats, Jimmy Connors, taking *his* lumps like the good husband and father he is, and instead of storming off the court in a rage, bouncing chirpily into the announcer's booth to make bland, cooing noises about his lifelong enemies, the competition.

So what does all this bode for American tennis? Can it stand up to this sinister wave of politeness, or is surliness now part of our arsenal? And, come to think of it, where have all the young brats gone anyway? (Hollywood doesn't count.) Perhaps even as I speak, some evil-minded toddler is working on his foul court manners in some unknown sandbox; but there is no one in sight right now, either brat *or* champion, and the question obtrudes itself: after McEnroe, what?

Well, after McEnroe, *more* McEnroe for a while, if we're lucky. Although American tennis cannot lean forever on this agitated reed, one always wants to squeeze the last drop out of such beautiful talent: "for sure," as the European players never tire of saying, we shall never see anything like him again.

My only complaint about McEnroe, before we go on to deeper things, is that he didn't spend his recent sabbatical, his forty days in the desert, taking voice lessons. There he was, out on the West Coast, and practically married to an actress of sorts, and what does he do? He searches his soul: a fool's errand in most cases, but doubly so if your soul seems to consist entirely of what other people say about you. "Why does everyone hate me?" is the gist of it, and I have a suggestion about that.

It is generally accepted by tennis fans that, owing to some strange muck-up in his wiring, McEnroe can play his red-hot best only when he is behaving like a pig: well, that's okay, it's the price we pay for art, the mess in the maestro's studio and all that—but does he have to *sound* like that?

Bad King John has always reminded me of one of those glamorous silent actors who were utterly undone by the coming of sound. There must be ways of misbehaving on the tennis court that have artistic merit. Ilie Nastase's Transylvanian glowering, for instance, showed some promise, although it needed a hell of a lot of work, while Jimmy Connors' Cagneyesque growls have their own teeth-grating charm (nobody hates Jimmy much anymore, if only because he so manifestly *never* searches his soul).

But what do you do with that ghastly adenoidal whine of McEnroe's? It is simply *wrong*, a desecration, for a great player to sound like that. I understand that, as a denizen of Douglaston, Long Island, John probably spent his formative years in a traffic jam, but that's no excuse for those infantile, virtually prenatal squawks at his age and income.

As it stands, that voice of his reminds me of nothing so much as some guttersnipe blocking one's view of a great painting, and *that's* what we hate about him: the lousy way he treats his own genius. But imagine for a moment how different it would be if McEnroe stepped smartly up to the umpire one day and said mellifluously, "I say, sir, this is simply an outrage"—well, I leave the dialogue up to him; but it's something for him to think about on his next vacation. If he would just curl up with some old Ronald Colman movies, with maybe a dash of Walter Pidgeon, all his spiritual problems would vanish overnight. We would love him forever, and beg him for just one more tantrum, please ("My kid has never heard one").

However, outside of giving us the world's classiest brat, I don't know that this switch would do anything very solid for American tennis, which is in a strange kind of doldrums right now, owing, I believe, to a peculiarly flaccid public, which is celebrity-curious about tennis but not really wrapped up in it, as they would be in a *real* sport. (In other words, if we cared as much about football, we'd probably lose that to the Swedes, too.)

It's my experience that the average American, outside of a few fever pockets, probably feels about tennis pretty much the way he feels about the America's Cup: he would vaguely like us to do well at it, the few times he gets around to thinking about it, because he vaguely wants the United States to be number one in everything. But the moment we lose, his interest snaps off like a light switch. Instead of snarling, "We'll get those Czechs next time or I'll know the reason why!" he says, "McEnroe's out, honey," and switches to baseball.

Paradoxically enough, it is in this thin, unresponsive soil that the curious American hybrid, the prickly tennis brat, has flourished like a cactus. Brathood is, of course, always a scream for the grown-ups' flickering attention, however hostile this may prove to be, and it is downright perverse (but perfectly routine) for brats to expect to be loved as well as noticed. But at least in the cases of McEnroe and Connors, maybe they *do* deserve to be thanked, if not hugged, for keeping the game on the air at all. American tennis has, of course, boomed enormously, but its tenure as a major, or TV, sport is constantly negotiable, and waiting for Ivan Lendl to smile may not prove quite enough.

Since Muhammad Ali also "saved" boxing by calculated outrageousness, we may take it that brathood serves as a respiratory function for marginal sports. But public apathy has shaped our Bad Boys in other, less predictable ways. Since we don't have anything like what the Czechs refer to constantly as their "national program," the brunt of grooming our heroes has been seized by a handful of fanatical parents, who tend to treat their charges like little Amadeuses rather than athletes—and can't you just imagine McEnroe stomping off the stage with two violins under his arm instead of tennis racquets, because his accompanist has played a clinker?

When Jimmy Connors first came grunting into view, John Newcombe commented mildly that he would have thought Connors' mates would have straightened him out by now. But Jimmy's best mate to that point had been his mother, who had played with him through the endless afternoons of childhood. As for John McEnroe, his father still defends the young rascal's antics occasionally, in the manner of a parent bursting into the principal's office to protest his kid's (perpetual) innocence.

I call parental influence unpredictable because Ivan Lendl also grew up under his mother's care, tethered to the net at times, like a goat, watching his mama at play; and although Lendl's parents sound more like a branch of government than a recognizable family, the example does show that excessive attention can repress as well as spoil.

In either case, there is nothing to cry about. All three men *were* still kids when they came along, although we persisted in analyzing them like old men, and all three, including the fretful McEnroe, show excellent signs of growing up.

But when one sees the serene stream of young masters issuing out of Sweden and elsewhere, one thinks of how much pain might be avoided over here if we had, if not a "national program," at least another Harry Hopman or Perry Jones, i.e., a super-coach, organizer and baby-sitter. Our current alibi, that the Czechs and Swedes beat us only because they can't play anything else, doesn't really hold up: if you can coax a young Czech off the soccer field, he'll probably head straight for the nearest hockey rink, while just getting a Swede out of his skis is probably more trouble than it's worth.

But what they have, they use, and the results are fine by me. The players from both countries are articulate, manifestly unbrainwashed and speak better English than we speak anything. It might even be that their unearthly poise has begun to rattle our brats—although why do we keep insisting that they smile? Why should they bend the knee or flash the gum to this strange American custom?

What's mildly sad about all this is that American players used to be just like that, too. In the days of Don Budge and later of Jack Kramer, Budge Patty, Gardnar Mulloy et al., you could take a tennis player anywhere.

It could happen again—maybe *is* already happening. If suspenders can come back, why not gentlemen? And if they do, John McEnroe actually has some interesting qualifications for First Gentleman: he has never ducked an interview, even in pain; he always speaks respectfully of opponents; and, a sure sign of sanctity, he plays Davis Cup matches for his country in places like Pago Pago even when the billion-dollar King Midas Classic is scheduled that same week in some place like Monte Carlo. If he could just learn what every Englishman knows, that impeccable manners are much more intimidating than yipping at umpires' knees, he could have his country playing the palace again in no time, and find himself "number one" in a sense he has never, tragically, quite been taught to understand.

Author's Note: When I wrote this Andre Agassi was just around the corner—the first completely pointless brat and surely the end of the line (he looks like the end of the line anyway), because behind the corner after that lurked the saintly Michael Chang and the new boy, Pete Sampras. And never were a pair of squares more welcome.

Another development since I wrote this is that women's tennis seems to have become more interesting than men's, having reached that equilibrium between power and touch that comes and goes with the men's game but right now seems mostly to have gone. In other words we need John McEnroe—either the original or *another* original—more than we ever did.

Cricket: What Do You Mean, *Lesser*?

*I*t is an iron, unwritten law of American journalism that any article about cricket or, for some reason, croquet *has* to be facetious. I don't know. Maybe it's the white pants. Tennis wasn't taken too seriously either until it took off its long pants, which obviously stand for buck teeth, monocles and silly money. Or maybe it's the silence: no cricketer, or croqueter, ever ran around the field screaming "let's get 'em, guys!" or administering high fives (although watch the West Indians for developments on that) or even whimpering at the ref.

Whatever. *Something* ridiculous is going on out there, as the men in white bend solemnly to their business. And as a consequence, Americans can't even talk about cricket without giggling and saying "pip pip," or words to that effect. All of which gives a born Englishman like myself a lot to put up with (especially the jokes; I can hear cricket jokes coming in my sleep by now, and wake up sweating).

It also means that we have no one to talk to when the seizure is upon us, and that *Americans* have no one to talk about in such seductive corners of the globe as Australia or Sri Lanka or Pudsey-on-the-Mold. The sun never sets on cricket and neither does the fog, however devoutly an American might wish for both. The fall of Empire actually seemed to increase its value as a souvenir—it may have been the only bond with England that some of the dominions ever really liked whole-heartedly, while even space exploration to a cricketer would simply mean super new places to play with wickets hotter and stickier than Ranjipur itself.

So it is with the grim certainty that the thing is here to stay that I herewith tender the first totally serious piece about cricket ever to appear in an American publication, starting with the Great Slowness Fallacy and pretty much grinding on down from there.

Cricket is indeed a hard religion for Americans to swallow— much harder, for instance, than Zen or Hinduism, although these too are slow and uneventful. Speed is not an issue for us when we go fishing or bird-watching; in fact, we only remember what a restless, energetic people we are to be sure when it comes to this one activity, cricket.

Clearly, Americans have a built-in resistance to the game, but its name is not slowness, it's baseball; if baseball just blew away (which God forfend) we could watch this other thing on its own weird merits. But the two games are just enough alike to force nagging comparison.

Cricket *looks* all wrong: the fielders stand around in bored-looking clumps like kids just hanging out, the bat is too wide, the fielding too lackadaisical, and it all goes on for days, etc. The fact that golf also takes several days and is slower than ketchup doesn't bother us, because there is no jazzed up version, no golf/baseball to compare it with. So perhaps it might help if one thinks of cricket primarily as a tournament, in which fortunes can turn overnight, depending on who didn't sleep and on who had a tactical brainstorm at 3:00 A.M. The suspense between days is a genuine part of the game although, yes, that too is *slow*.

The next complaint (which is really more of a whine) is easily dealt with: "I can't understand the rules." In fact, the game is completely self-explanatory. When the batter scores, it is recorded on a great big board; when he makes an out, you will immediately deduce why, except in a case of l.b.w., or letting the ball hit you instead of the wicket—ask the guy next to you. To make matters even simpler, the out batsman leaves the field completely, and the fielders all sit down. Any questions so far?

It's true that I've put many a tableful of people to sleep trying to describe the rules of cricket. But just try explaining the rules of *anything* over dinner. Football, laid out in its full panoply of by-laws and nitpicks, sounds like a nightmare Bertrand Russell might have had while working on his *Principia Mathematica*. But cricket's essence is, literally, child's play and my guess is that an American reasonably versed in the baseball rule book would be surprised to find how little there *was* to cricket.

The next gripe can only be baseball-related, to wit, that they score too many runs in cricket. The answer to this is that a run has a totally different value in cricket. In itself, a run is merely an incident, a hiccough, a notch on a stick. Only in accumulation do these notches begin to matter. Individually, a run is slightly less important than a single ball game in a 162-game season or the first point in basketball.

What the game is really about is domination, not numbers: who shall call the tunes, the batsmen or the bowlers? If a run is nothing in the early going, an out is everything, and the bowlers will probe with every trick known to baseball, including not only a screwball but a make-believe screwball, or googlie, at each batsman's concentration until it either snaps or overwhelms everything.

These transactions between bat and ball are genuine mind-probing duels compared with the brief encounters of baseball where the batter changes every few seconds. But alas, it is hard to see them properly. There is (and this is a *real* complaint) no such thing as a good seat at cricket, for the simple reason that the batsman can hit the ball in back of him as well as in front and needs an equal amount of space in every direction (hence the number of ovals in cricket).

So unless you can contrive to wheedle your way onto a playing field your best bet might be to watch your first match on television, which does pick up some of the ball's flight as it leaves the bowler's hand, and the ensuing spin off the turf—and shows in that same split second the batsman deciding whether to go forward or back and which stroke to use when he gets there.

A great batsman in full flight has a vast repertory of choices compared with the baseball hitter's basic one (or at most, four). With the whole field at his disposal and command, he can wield that flat bat like a bullfighter's cape, flicking the surface this way and that to foil the panting fieldsmen, or driving fiercely straight ahead of him like a golfer faced with a moving ball. And just like that the game is transformed from a gawky, hesitant affair into one of the most graceful sights in sport.

This is cricket at its self-explanatory best, and you don't need a good seat to enjoy it. If you have been lucky enough to witness the game catch fire like this, and you still don't like it, so be it. But it's my guess, as a bi-gamist, or lover of both games, that in that case you probably don't really like baseball either, except as a stick to beat the mother sport with. There are moments when these two estranged relatives, slick, brash, utterly perfect young baseball and shambling, dreamy, absent-minded old cricket, become simply quintessential bat and ball games, at which point, to love one is at least to appreciate the other.

But. It does take time.

Now for some details: 1) the bowler may bend his wrist all he likes but not his elbow. He compensates for this stately inhibition with a run-up, which can at times produce velocities exactly equivalent (90 mph+) to those in baseball, and curves which whip in either direction, and 2) he doesn't *have* to bounce the ball in front of the batsman, but he'd be a fool not to. It causes the batsman to delay his decision whether to attack or defend or just plain duck to the last conceivable split-second, and it takes any possible advantage of oddities in the turf.

In recent years, fast bowlers, especially West Indian ones, have taken increasingly to banging the ball down a little shorter than usual to a distance from which it may either spring up in the batsman's face or skid on through to his wicket, the three sticks he is sworn to defend. The victim then has just a split of his usual split second to decide exactly how much value he places on his face as such *vis-a-vis* three pieces of wood. No beanball ever delivered was more intimidating than a barrage of these lovelies (known as bouncers), which can only be closely compared to slap-shots in hockey.

Luckily for him the batsman doesn't have to run every time he hits the ball, and this of course is another offense to the baseball-minded; but he does, contrary to appearances, have to run *sometime*, or lose any hope of dominating, or even of making the team next week.

A run, as noted, is a simple affair: a trot to the pitcher's mound, in terms of distance. However, there can be much quiet skill in this as two experts slipper back and forth like cat burglars, stealing runs that were never meant to be; and occasionally a master batsman can use the system to protect a stumble-bum partner from having to face the bowling altogether by scoring his own runs in twos and fours and switching to odd numbers only toward the end of an over, when the whole game changes ends.

This turnaround is, I grant you, somewhat bizarre looking. It is as if, after every six or eight balls, home plate sprang up in some other place, and all the players had to face in the opposite direction. The result is almost a whole new game, as the batsman gropes with fresh sightlines, subtly different turf (each end experiences a different day, in terms of wear and tear) and a brand new bowler who is working on his own private game of Domination.

Having been burned with speed at one end, the batsman may suddenly find himself having to cope with a wily little gent who floats the ball up like a fizzing balloon at the other. Giddy with relief, he is likely to lash away like a kid out of school, which is of course exactly what the little man wants. He didn't get that look for nothing.

Meanwhile, the fielders are far from aimless in their arrangements: they are more like pieces in the bowler's brain who form a quite precise map of his plans. To take two simple examples out of an infinity: if he plans to spin the ball away from the batsman he will likely pack that side of the field with bodies, daring the batsman to "hit against the spin" into the empty spaces and probably up in the air where it can be caught. Fast bowlers for their part prefer to place their henchman behind the wicket in hopes of foul tips, which come at such speed that one of the damn things once actually shot between my legs and crossed the boundary before I realized I'd been supposed to do something about it (and there endeth my personal stock of cricket anecdotes).

Once again, baseball rears its lovely head: a fielder without a glove looks insane to a baseball fan; a fielder *with* one looks like a Martian to a cricketer. But, also once again, the difference is less than it seems. Protection is the least interesting, and most dispensable, of a glove's virtues. A good fielder's hands can always learn to "give" to cushion speed. What the glove does for you is enlarge one hand and liberate the other, making possible the instant release upon which one sport depends, the other doesn't—or at least, not so often.

What cricket fielding occasionally lacks in elegance (slovenly types have been known to stop the ball with their boots—what the hell, it's only a run) it amply makes up for in variety and guile. Where most ballplayers are sentenced for life to fixed positions, which they patrol as if on leashes, the cricketer may find himself placed literally anywhere in the arena, which is divided obligingly into zones with sixteenth-century names like mid-off and gully and cover-point.

Some of these names are on the quaint side and are no doubt good for a giggle (although try not to overdo it—you may be depressing some Englishman), such as short leg, long leg and silly mid-wicket. ("Silly" incidentally applies to any fielder standing suicidally close to the batsman: thus one might also talk of a "silly third baseman" on bunt plays.)

The blessed thing about all this clackety nomenclature is that you don't need to learn a word of it. Just as you read a map without even noticing the lines of latitude, so you can enjoy cricket without knowing the names of anything at all. My otherwise encyclopedic father, for instance, relished the game for over fifty years without ever knowing a late cut from a square cut or an off-drive from a cover-drive. He just didn't want to cloud his mind.

Nevertheless, desperate cricket-resistors do like to go on about the game's arcane vocabulary, as if it somehow made the game itself *as played* more impenetrably confusing. So here are absolutely the only translations you need. The on-side is anything to the left of a right-hander's legs and the off is just about everything else: all the rest is pedantry and pettifoggery, except perhaps for the word wicket itself which refers both to the sticks, or "stumps," at either end and to the ground in between, which is the part that becomes "sticky" (sunshine on wet turf makes it gluey and unpredictable). The wicket in this special sense is sometimes also called the pitch, which—oh, never mind. Believe me, it doesn't matter.

In fact, you don't even need the words to be *bored* by cricket. For the many incurables out there, I have a word of good news about this: millions of Englishmen are bored by cricket too—so much so that the lords of cricket allowed the unthinkable a few years ago and decided to speed up the game, introducing a sort of carnival facsimile called one-day cricket. To a purist, no jazz Mass was ever more painful. Before you know it, think we, the fielders will be racing out to their positions, batsmen will be running on everything they hit and bowlers will be hatching out their plans at the speed of Charlie Chaplin—and we will have baseball all over again, only not so pretty.

Meanwhile, though, for all you *im*purists, I am advised that one-day matches can also be sinfully exciting, so if the invitation says cricket, maybe you'd better make sure it's one of those, at least for your debut. Who knows, the pleasures of slowness may grow on you gradually—they have all the time in the world—

but if they don't, they don't. One-day cricket is like a basketball game consisting entirely of final seconds, which, if you're not much interested in the game itself, is certainly the way to watch it; and just think of the jokes your host will be spared about too many days, too many runs, and too many damn tea breaks. For my part, if I have helped stamp out just one of those little beggars, I will consider my time and yours thoroughly well worth wasted.

And now, about croquet...

The Anti-Boxer Rebellion

*T*he last decade was a very bad one for boxing: death came in murderous combinations and Muhammad Ali took to mumbling. Celebrity being what it is, Ali's mumble (which I pray to be temporary), was perhaps the more damaging of the two—partly because the joyous sounds of Ali-babble were still so fresh in the ear, and partly because it showed the irresistible forces of self-destruction in this business.

Muhammad Ali enjoyed two of the most civilized and solicitous of cornermen—trainer Angelo Dundee, who loves fighters like an Italian mother, and Ferdie Pacheco, the renaissance doctor. Yet when Pacheco suggested that it was time for the boss to quit, he found himself in a jiffy working for CBS (now NBC). And if Dundee had seconded the motion, he would have been as swiftly replaced by some less fastidious (and less skillful) trainer. Ali loved the glitter of a big fight, and the creatures who live in a champion's pocket wanted another payday, and another, and the combination would have rolled over any boxing commission or board of health yet devised.

So the cry has gone up once again for Abolition to save the Alis (and they are legion) from themselves and their friends. And the defenders of boxing have adopted for now the rope-a-dope (Ali's tactic of covering his head and letting the other guy punch himself out), occasionally throwing back a feeble peck of an answer. Boxing has, say its pals, rescued many a kid from the ghetto—but so have war and munitions work. Overall, football is even more destructive—but you can't compare knees with brains, limps with slurred speech. And so on.

To the lover of boxing, the question has to be posed slightly differently, somewhere between athletics and aesthetics. To take a parallel from furthest left field: supposing ballet suddenly turned out to be dangerous; the balletomane would have to ask, how dangerous? Prohibitively or just regrettably? He would not give up his passion without a struggle. And neither can the fight connoisseur who sees his own beauties in the feintings and parryings of bodies perfectly sculpted for their task and of minds at least as bright as ballet dancers.

Danger and beauty are not incompatible, and a life in the arts is not necessarily a safe one. Poetry has certainly caused its share of brain damage, not to say premature death. And on a lower level of being—should rock music be banned to protect future Janis Joplins? Dubious analogies aside (and all analogies are dubious) there is a real issue here between those who accept the possibility of a short life and a merry (or intense) one and those who would call that a fancy phrase for suicide. Boxing, like mountain climbing, auto racing and such, cannot win with the safety-firsters, the long-life-if-a-dull-one crowd. But perhaps it can make a little ground with the moderates, not precisely as an art, but as an addition to life and a possible source of art in others, worth a risk or two. (And I promise not to mention Bernard Shaw more than once.)

Ban-the-box tracts generally seem to be written by people who, while well enough up on their pugilistic medicine, know virtually nothing else about the sport and don't want to know. This is understandable. Simply watching men punch each other sounds pretty second-rate to me too (though you should see how many of them miss). But in place of reality these critics seem to have conjured up something much worse, though easier to argue with: something based, I suspect, on a primal vision of John Garfield's body being scraped onto a stretcher or nailed to the wall by gangland bullets. Nearly all boxing movies are anti-boxing for the time-honored Hollywood reason that they can be gorier that way, under the mask of disapproval. In the gruesome world of movie boxing every punch lands and draws rivers of blood; eyes glaze over at a touch, and knees turn to jelly, so that by the second bell both fighters look like bullfight horses, more than ready for the knackers.

But even this is not enough, nothing is enough for the sadistic fan we keep panning to in the balcony. This portly citizen, who seems to cover three seats at a time while holding a hot dog in each hand and a third in his mouth, still manages to scream through the crumbs and spit, "Moider the bum!" And as for his wife . . .

The portrayal of apoplectic harridans is a special pleasure of these films. Presumably if boxing just went away, these ladies would return to their senses with a start and take up bridge, while hubby would lower his hot dogs shamefacedly and join the Book-of-the-Month Club. Since *all* the other spectators shown are gangsters, one can only hope that these would now proceed to peddle their slimy wares elsewhere (maybe even in Hollywood—there's more than one way to fleece the public) and leave poor Mr. Garfield alone for a while.

All in all, the Japanese in World War II were treated more evenhandedly in films than the fight game. Yet the Hollywood version is the only one many anti-boxers have ever been exposed to. And though it may seem surprising that these gentle humanistic souls should swallow so easily such a hilariously debased view of humanity, that's boxing for you: the fatal touch of leather that turns men into beasts and their wives into banshees. The medical news props up the caricature at this point and together they make the case.

The actual world of boxing has to be quite a come-down from

this Goyaesque jamboree. The fans at the old St. Nicholas Arena in Manhattan tended to be thoughtful, slightly dyspeptic fellows who watched the preliminaries as if they were chess matches in Washington Square. When the inevitable traditionalist (himself a mild enough chap) piped up "spare me da next waltz," as the killers hugged their way through round after round, the cry died on the air. Instead the guy next to you would mutter "I like the kid in the white"—there never was such a sport for muttering—"but he don't look so good with lefties." The fat fan and his wife would long since have gone mad with boredom, and headed screaming for the nearest roller derby. But it was a nice little culture, with an Old New York taste all its own, and I miss it more than Penn Station.

There were no gangsters in sight at St. Nick's—at least not to the eye of a teenager (and I wasn't the only one present) and there wasn't enough money in the house to fix a fight. Nor did the kids look like desperate animals shanghaied from the slums to be set up for a killing by Mr. Big. Some of them looked a bit scrawny, because they'd been trying like actresses to make improbable weights, but that was the cruellest thing about it, and not likely to make the medical journals.

Otherwise, they were in much better shape than most athletes. Whatever the evils of boxing, its training is saintly—and even, ironically, good for the mind in some ways, because a boxer must reach peaks of concentration unknown to most sports: one opening missed and another given, and the training unravels in split seconds.

Meanwhile, under a hail of leather, our hero must try to remember and constantly revise his game plan and apply it under battle conditions. Anyone who has tried it knows that boxing is mentally stimulating—unless and until the lights go out. Before the much advertised brain damage, if it must come, are moments of fierce clarity and, I would guess, exhilaration.

Those lights going out are the sticking point, though. Isn't it the whole aim of boxing to render a fellow human unconscious? Well, not quite. Knocking the other guy out is indeed a happy

conclusion to one's night's work, a (frequently unexpected) div-
idend. But a good boxer is much too busy to brood about it.
Looking to his own defenses is enough to keep a man tolerably
occupied. The "manly art of self-defense" is not a euphemism,
like the U.S. Defense Department, but the very heart of the
matter. At the old St. Nick's one's most reliable pleasure was
that of watching men *fail* to hit each other. If those preliminary
boys were really bent on slaughter most of them kept it a dark
secret.

As with many sports, the better boxing is played, the harder
it is to follow and the duller for the uninitiate to sit through. (I
know the feeling: once, having grandly pronounced a soccer
game boring, a nearby expert said, "That's funny. I thought it
was one of the best I'd ever seen.") Anyway, some of the most
beautiful fights are as superficially uneventful as pitching duels.
When one such occurs, a knockout can be a positive irritation,
a rude ending, like Fred Astaire breaking a leg in mid-dance.

So why have knockouts at all? Why not wrap the men in
thick towels and riveters' helmets and let them practice their art
in safety? Alas, even if one could devise armor plating that did
not impede motion, the knockout would still be necessary, if
only as a brooding possibility. Grace without pressure is a different kind of grace. A matador working a safe bull may make
some nice moves, but they won't be a bullfighter's moves, they'll
be pretty imitations. And even the most elegant fighter must
perform under the gun. It keeps him, as they say, honest.

So much must be conceded, but not a whole lot more. I know
I'm not the only fight fan who actually dislikes violence in its
more feral forms. I don't go for barroom brawls, gory movies
or thoughtful sitcoms about rape. But the controlled violence
of boxing is quite a different experience. These are highly disciplined men guaranteed not to go berserk or pull knives on
each other. The few fighters I've known have been highly affable
souls, with no hint of trouble about them. Why would they
want to get into that stuff when they're not getting paid for it?
When the new breed guys glare and snort at each other at weigh-

ins, you never saw a more peaceful sight. No one rushes up to grab them. They are thinking pure and beautiful thoughts of money.

Which brings us at last to the seamy side of the sport: the way it's promoted. I doubt many fights are thrown these days, because it just doesn't make sense. Winners' purses are not worth sacrificing for rematches that may never happen or other *nebulae*. But grotesque match-ups are still made and logical ones avoided for reasons of greed. Contenders can be kept waiting for years until their skills dull, because right now they are too good for the champ's taste. And old-timers with name recognition are encouraged, like Ali, to hang around for just one more. These things are not the norm, as they are in the movies, but they happen.

They happen because the sport rejects organization as strenuously as it rejects padding. Attempts to clean up boxing must go back at least to Cain and Abel, yet it remains its raffish, riverboat self, subject only to the customers' whims. If referees now stop fights sooner than they used to, it must be because, contrary to myth, the fans really prefer it that way; otherwise the slaughter could go on forever, for all the promoters care. It's just that death seems to be bad for business.

When Eddie Futch surrendered on Joe Frazier's behalf during the famous "Thriller in Manila," he demonstrated the other great safeguard in boxing: the wise trainer. Predictably, rumor has it that Frazier now doesn't talk to the man who may have saved his life (the rumor was wrong I'm told); but when he made the decision, Futch was in danger of losing Joe's conversation either way. And at least the voice Frazier doesn't talk to him in now is clear and free from mumbles.

One day sometime back I saw a kid walk into Angelo Dundee's Fifth Street Gym looking for an audition. He was a well-dressed, handsome Cuban fellow, not at all the dregs of the ghetto but the cream, and brimming with eagerness to learn this strange craft. And I thought, I'll admit that I'm glad he's not my son, but that if he were, and if he insisted on this, he couldn't have picked a better place. Besides the million laughs that form the atmosphere around Dundee, the kid would be as safe from harm as you can possibly be in this dodge—unless he himself someday, worn down and self-deluded, positively demanded it.

Incidentally, Angelo Dundee is also Sugar Ray Leonard's trainer, and if you can imagine persuading that cantankerous creature either to fight or not to fight against his will, you will have grasped the scope of the problem.

The Greatest:
Ali with the Sound Off

*W*hen Muhammad Ali, né Cassius Clay, first hove into view at the Rome Olympics in 1960, he was still nine parts boxing to one part mouth—and the boxing was something to behold. His technique at sixteen and seventeen in the Golden Gloves was of a sophistication unknown in that hairy shambles of an event. He could already hook off the jab, which is beyond some professionals, and he had mastered his great gift of depth perception—judging the length of his opponent's arms and bobbing an inch or so out of range. In one match with a burly Army champion, he fell to his nemesis, a left hook, but he was up in no time, poised as ever (most kids go completely to pieces and wander off in the wrong direction) and ready to kill. His opponent's legs were still twitching minutes later.

It is sometimes forgotten that, like many great entertainers, Ali had put in a full career before we'd heard of him. He'd had over one hundred amateur fights (which might account for his head-hunting; body punches counting for less in a short bout) and his defects were by then as ingrained as his virtues. Eddie Futch, the trainer, who has had a hand in both of Ali's professional defeats (by Norton and Frazier), says Ali had so much natural ability that he never learned some of the fundamentals: he could always outrun his mistakes.

His technical shortcomings actually served to make him more exciting and saleable, by adding a cliff-hanging or Perils of Pauline quality to his work. At Rome, the experts immediately spotted not one but two fatal flaws. Ali sometimes keeps his hands too low to protect his face properly, and he pulls his head back from punches, which could get him killed by a follow-up. Futch noticed a third: he always moved clockwise.

To be fair to the experts, these really are fatal flaws. Many young fighters have come to grief imitating Ali—in fact he may be the worst influence since Ernest Hemingway. But his speed and judgment always allowed him to escape by a whisker. "Defense ain't the hands, it's the legs," he says, and by dancing so precisely out of range, he can actually fight like the Venus de Milo, without any arms at all. Then, like a parent playing with a child, he can offer his face to be hit, only to snap it back, until the child collapses with frustration. Thus, Ali versus Foreman.

Anyway, at the Rome Olympics, he was felt to be promising, but not as promising as Floyd Patterson had been in 1956. As soon as he cleans up those flaws, we'll see. Then when he turned pro and began moving up in class with triumph after triumph, the warnings continued, more ominous than ever. A minor fighter called Ernie Banks dropped him on his drawers with a left. Then Futch came in with a boy called Charlie Powell who made appointments with Ali's clockwise rotation and rocked him for two rounds before missing an appointment himself. Vulnerability was part of the package, and it was given a lifetime lease by one Doug Jones, who not only hit him over the low hands and with the head back but lived to tell the tale.

A couple of other things showed in the Jones affair. One was that Jones, a journeyman whose sole mission in life seems to have been to fight this fight and demonstrate this one point, stumbled into the best way to fight Ali, which is simply to dull him down. Jones positively refused to dance with him, but stood stolidly in the middle of the ring waiting for something to happen, and fighting in flurries. Ali responded well enough to win— I only said that Jones' way was the best way, not that it would succeed—but he couldn't fight his classic fight, and sometimes he gets angry and bored when this happens, and he fights like a stuffed panda.

The other thing the Jones fight demonstrated was that the propaganda machine had already gotten in its deadly work and no one was quite rational about Ali. His famous practice of predicting which round his opponent would fall in had taken on a certain sacred impressiveness with the assistance of the two-thousand-year-old Archie Moore in his last fight. Moore had waddled around the ring at Ali's pleasure, collapsing on cue. So the prophetic mumbo-jumbo became briefly believable, perhaps even to Ali himself. In Jones' case, he said he would win in four and when he didn't, it was like the death of God. People rapidly assumed that he was a total fraud, and they booed when he won a unanimous verdict.

Reviewing the fight films now, it is clear that Ali fought a most satisfactory fight that night, adapting himself to his loss of divinity and falling back on layers of professionalism. The fourth round itself was terrible—Ali was so eager to make his prophecy come true that he swung with his arms instead of his body, like a beginner—and the fifth round was rueful and melancholy, as he came to terms with mortality. But the rest was crisp as lettuce.

Anyhow, the scribes and pharisees now sought ways to put him down. They brought up the fatal flaws again and again. They said he lacked a single knockout punch, that freak of nature, as if a hundred knockout suggesters weren't good enough. "He jabs you so sweet and cool," said Willie Pastrano— sort of like death from drowning. But he's obviously never

jabbed the critics. And they said he couldn't take a punch himself—a myth as far-fetched as Jack Johnson's yellow streak.
There *had* to be something wrong with such an obnoxious fellow.

Once a prejudice gets rolling, there's no stopping it. Sonny
Liston, his next port of call, was the most awesome thing in
boxing at the time. He had twice demolished the ever-promising
Floyd Patterson in something under six minutes all told, and he
was good and ready for Clay. Even if the famous pre-fight
needling was 90 percent promo, pretend emotions can become
real ones with a dark spirit like Liston's, and he trained like a
Stakhanovite for this fight. Yet no sooner had Clay beaten him
than he became a washed-out bum. His physical condition wors-
ened retroactively—he hadn't really trained at all. He was over
fifty, with grown-up grandchildren serving time. Besides which,
he had thrown the fight.

A pattern had set in of downgrading Clay by belittling his
opponents after the fact. Again, upon viewing the Liston films,
this becomes incredible. The first two, three rounds are among
the most beautiful ever fought by the big men, with Liston
prowling and charging at jungle speed, and Clay dancing clockwise away from the deadly left hook, but reversing himself just
often enough for the hook to whistle past the other ear. He
pulled his head back and he didn't get killed. He fought the fifth
round half-blind from some caustic in his eye, but Sonny was
exhausted by then from the fastest pace ever set in a heavyweight
fight and Clay held him off like a matador, sticking and jabbing
blindly and defending himself by Braille.

Liston characteristically managed to leave a dark stain on ring
history and on Clay's reputation. He didn't come out for the
eighth round because of torn muscles in his arm—quite genuine
as it turned out, but such is Sonny's aura that no one in the
world believed him. Then in the return match he managed a
fainting spell in the first round, which again may have been
genuine (microscopes later turned up an actual punch), but when
referee Joe Walcott blew the count and gave him all evening to
get up, Liston's rendition of a coma wouldn't have fooled a

possum. He later said he was afraid Ali would hit him again on his way up.

So Clay, by now Ali, was again short-changed by the critics, and might reasonably have become bitter about it. Yet, oddly enough, Ali the publicity machine that was growing alongside Ali the boxing artist seemed to relish it. In his role of public enemy, it suited him to be underrated. It meant that he could draw crowds even with the dogs of his division—which was going to be more and more necessary (the heavyweight division is chronically overpopulated with dogs). Clay would even challenge himself, come in overweight, change his style, anything to fill the house. Against George Chuvalo, he even tried standing still. His famous shuffle, which he had used as early as the Olympics (a crazy little war-dance, more suitable to entering an end zone) became more prominent. I used to suppose he only did it when his opponent was too weak to interrupt—again like a matador, when he kneels in front of his bull—but I find that he did it against Cleveland Williams in the second round when Williams was still zinging them in at top speed. (Williams was, it goes without saying, over the hill, a bullet-riddled ex-con, but he looked awfully good that night.)

I have intentionally separated Ali the boxer from Ali the media freak, because (a) the freak has only the most glancing relation with boxing—it is his occasion, his launching pad, but I'm convinced Ali would have found some other way to be famous, and (b) because the freak has too often obscured the fighter and even held him up to ridicule. In this sense he has debased himself like a black entertainer after all—or like Jack Johnson. Ali is quite possibly the greatest fighter who ever lived, but many whites won't admit it under torture because of his Mouth. Instead, and to prove they are not bigoted, they have promoted Joe Louis, the good nigger, to this spot. Thus does Ali help his brothers.

After his disposal of such worthies as Ernie Terrell and Williams and Zora Foley (who fought him the Jones way, and made a nice dignified showing before going down in seven), Ali's critics had to concede some merit in the chap. A fighter can only fight what's there, but this was not at all a bad crop by division standards. Jack Johnson's opponents were a scrawny bunch (Tommy Burns weighed 175 pounds), and Joe Louis was reduced to forming a Bum-of-the-Month Club.

In fact, the critics were down to their last trick. They said that Ali was all speed; that once that went, he would have nothing left. One thing you have to say for critics: they have endurance. Ali left the ring to sit out three long years of the Vietnam War and he lost some of his speed, and a new crop of heavyweights came along led by one Joe Frazier, an authentic star of the kind that dominates eras, and Ali came back on rubber legs and became champion again. And still there were critics—you can recognize them on sight—mumbling like spaced-out old boxers. No knockout punch. Foreman was out of shape. Marciano would have licked him. Yah.

Let us leave them to it. Ali's comeback was not only an astounding exhibition of character, it also proved as conclusively as anything can be proved in the impressionistic world of boxing that he is indeed the greatest, even if he does say so himself. Older people were raised to believe that braggarts are always bluffing, but the new breed has no trouble believing. As the late Leonard Shecter remarked, "he had the kind of body that was revolutionizing football"—and he might have added track and swimming and tennis. That is, he was a big man with the speed and reflexes of a small one. Films indicate that his jabs are one-third faster than those of Sugar Ray Robinson, the great middleweight—so he is not just fast for a big man, he is fast for a midget. What seemed like over-confidence was simply a judicious assessment by a very knowing professional. And don't be fooled about that. He is, for all his flighty image, a meticulous student of old fight films and of the game in general. He learned to jab better from Willie Pastrano and to move side to side from Louis Rodriguez and to lie back on the ropes from Sugar Ray against Jake LaMotta in 1952.

Beyond his studies though, Ali simply thought and moved so much faster than his opponent that he always had time in hand, like Ted Williams in baseball. He spent the extra time promoting his business: shuffling, talking, relating to the crowd. He also used it to psych his opponents—since once you have a fighter thinking consciously, the battle is half over. But the real marvel was that he had the time and the spare strength to do this stuff at all, against highly trained sharpshooters who can hit you between blinks. Again Ali the clown eclipses Ali the super-athlete.

When he came back, all the talk was about his legs. Gone for sure, said Joe Louis, the voice of God. And they certainly had slowed down some. He fought flat-footed now like a normal human. Against Jerry Quarry and Oscar Bonavena, the kind of pugs who are always around and who could be extras in a John Garfield movie, he was good enough, but the bounce was gone. Perhaps the legend of his speed had grown in his absence, even beyond the reality—he never danced more than a few rounds, or needed to—but the legs lacked enthusiasm now: they just carried him around, like an old station wagon.

Time now for the rendezvous with the new boy in town. Joe Frazier had taken over Dodge City and Tombstone and he wasn't the kind of man you want to meet on rubber legs. His fists went off like cannons, exploding through the TV set like Sonny Liston's—especially the left, Ali's weakness. His legs were like tree trunks, and if you allowed him to plant them, they were a source of biblical strength. He was something of a trolley-track fighter, who might have had trouble with Ali's old lateral speed, but to make up for this he had an irresistible forward charge that no number of punches would discourage. If old-timers wanted to know how Ali would have done against Marciano, here was their answer: Frazier had the same bull-like qualities, the same courage, stamina and armor plating, plus, in my opinion, a better punch and a smarter brain.

It is an odd law of physics that there can never be two great heavyweights at the same time: one rises as the other declines. The smallest edge in sharpness is multiplied infinitely in Big Man fighting: the slightly better man becomes the totally better man when such artillery is used. Hence the first Ali-Frazier fight was something of a suspension of natural law, as befits one beloved of Allah. There were two great heavyweights that night, and it was that mythical event—the Fight of the Century—as improbable a happening as the Great American Novel.

What made this particular masterpiece even more unlikely was that it also carried the burden of the biggest, bitterest build-up since Jack Johnson fought the Great While Hope Jim Jeffries fifty-some years before, with half the nation seemingly squared off against the other—and you're lucky to get even a good fight when that happens. Yet we got the greatest. Ali's pride demanded it, and Frazier's skill was equal to it. No one has ever fought better than Smokin' Joe that night. Most fights, like most books, contain one or two good ideas at the beginning and a lot of puffing and blowing in the later stages. But Frazier was still able to fell trees in the fifteenth round, and Ali was still able to dissuade him from it. In fact, that round alone was worth the price of most fights.

The immediate question was, what was Ali going to use in place of legs? He was still fast, but not superhumanly so, and Frazier bounds in at an agile, tireless trot that even the old Ali would have had to stop and confront at some point. The new Ali was down to hand-speed and intelligence, of which he has enough.

His early plan seemed to be to hit Joe with lightning combinations and then tie him up. The clinch was a comparatively new weapon for him, not to mention the head-in-the-armpit hold, but he took to these old man's devices with a resigned ease. Of course, no one plan can last fifteen rounds against the likes of Frazier and before the fight was over, Ali had improvised a whole grammar of styles.

"I'm going to fight ten more years and people still won't know if I can take a punch," Ali said once. "I'm not in there to prove whether I can take a punch." But that night, he reluctantly proved it, again and again. At times he made Frazier a gift of his mid-section to protect his head. But he made some mistakes with his head too, and Frazier came in with some shuddering shots over missed right leads. Each time, Ali found some way to show wobbly derision. He couldn't just take a punch—he could take one better than anyone who'd ever lived. Incredulously we watched as he reluctantly unwrapped perhaps his greatest gift. Courage.

By the middle rounds, Frazier was dominating the fight in that mystical sense which makes scorekeeping an interpretive art. You can dominate from the ropes or you can dominate from the center of the ring; you can do it running or you can do it standing still. You don't even have to land the most punches (by count, Frazier didn't even come close). All you have to do is call the tune and assert your will.

When a man like Frazier does this, it is usually a question of guessing the round. Yet, after each one, Ali managed to summon a sneer and a mocking flip of the hand. He would not be dominated *psychologically* so long as one brain cell remained lit. He would at least be on top between rounds.

During the mid-game, Ali took to jiggling his fist in Frazier's face and smirking, another Ali first. Later on, it enabled him to say he shouldn't have played games like that, but it looked at the time like a council of desperation, a calculated use of his superior reach to keep Frazier off him for a few healing moments. It did not spare him a terrible beating. Frazier would slap once, twice at the offending fist and then would leap past it with a murderous hook. It became like a schoolyard game: how many slaps before the real one.

Ali could no longer dance out of range so he took to resting against the ropes and nesting his head in his gloves like peek-a-boo Floyd Patterson, while Frazier pounded him with rib-crushing body blows. Some rest. "Kill the body and the head will die": boxing's most revered maxim also took a beating that night.

By round ten or so, we were learning to live with not one but two miracles. Ali was still on his feet and Frazier was still smoking. Joe had landed his best shot and Ali had done his jelly-leg stagger—being a clown has its uses. He was damn near out but Frazier didn't know it.

After that they would both have been excused for waltzing out the clock in time-honored style. Most fighters would have had no choice. Yet incredibly the best of the fight was still to come. A third miracle occurred: out of God knows what resources, Ali found the strength to come back, and Frazier's face began to wash away under Ali's snapping jabs. In the fifteenth, Joe came back with a killer left hook, Ali's old enemy, and it appeared over. The dedicated Ali watcher, Eddie Futch, had come up with a new trick. When Ali commences an upper-cut, he leaves his whole right side exposed: so Futch had advised Frazier to move in, let the upper-cut graze off his stomach, and unload. And unload he did. It says much for Joe that he could wait fifteen rounds for this situation to arise and still have the kitchen sink in readiness. My back teeth still sing at the memory of that punch. But Ali got up somehow and fought in a coma for a few seconds and then, my God, launched a counterattack of sorts as the fight ended. They have given Congressional Medals of Honor for less. "I hope they appreciated my artistry," said Ali.

The scoring of fights is, as indicated, a mystic pursuit, depending on how one interprets dominance, but the consensus is that Ali's greatest fight was ironically a defeat. Referee Arthur Mercante gave Frazier eight pounds, Ali six, and one for the pot, and the ref usually knows best, especially if he's Mercante.

Both fighters left the ring as slightly different people. Forty-five minutes' work can do that in this business. Frazier left his greatness behind—that witch's brew of talent and passion, of physical and mental vitality—and became merely sporadically excellent. As a public figure, he deflated instantly, until such time as Ali chose to pump him up again for their next fight. People love or hate Frazier entirely in relation to Ali; otherwise they have no feelings about him whatsoever. The non-fight fans who yearned for him till the sweat ran that night have probably not given him a thought since.

As for Ali, another change of persona is no news for him. The public hatred which he'd so carefully nursed came to a head that night and burst and may never be the same. To some people, he went back to being an irritation, to others he was suddenly a familiar institution, like other young rogues whose badness

has been blessed by time, but very few people hated him anymore. The old-timers would never like him, but they loved boxing and they'd seen the best. Can a ballet fan really hate
Nureyev? They may also have felt the mixed respect they'd feel
for a homosexual who beats up a bar bully or wins the Legion
of Honor—a respect tinged with pleasure. Above all, they'd
seen him beaten, that great healer of hate, and they'd seen the
Mick Jagger smirk smashed off his face.

Ali's lack of conventional masculinity may have bothered his
critics' psyches more than his race and his youth. Who can read
the heart of a critic? If so, the cat was out of the bag now. Ali
was no specimen of the unisex counterculture but an old-fashioned lion-hearted hero. Ho hum. The publicity freak has met
his greatest challenge: acceptance.

Epilogue

◇

Wrapping It Up

TV Guide had asked me to write a piece naming in effect one good reason why Muhammad Ali, who was trailing clouds of glory by that time, should be bothered to fight one Leon Spinks, a hacker who could add nothing to Ali's reputation except conceivably embarrassment. So after a paragraph about the Great One's finances insofar as it was then given to mortals to understand them, I launched into the following meditation on the horrors of retirement in general—a fitting epilogue to a book that began with Willie Mays stumbling around in center field and must now reluctantly end itself.

Sports are habit-forming, even the ones that hurt. (We'll get to the others in a moment.) Floyd Patterson, the old champion, actually liked to train, and if you've trained you might as well fight somebody, just so you can start training again.

Ali, to judge from his hideous groans, does *not* like to train, but he does like to break training. His carbon eyes gleam as he talks about his first postfight peach cobbler—wouldn't be the same if you could do it every day. Training also keeps him young and beautiful, so he does just enough of it for that, but not nearly enough to go fifteen rounds with a fellow killer. (Luckily for him, Spinks has been known to train even less.)

For all his hysterical activity, outside the ring Ali can be the most bored-looking man I've ever encountered. He's been around the world, but he hasn't really seen it (how much can you take in while you're waiting to meet George Foreman?). So you can imagine the world view of a boxer who's barely been outside the gym. Even pain is better than sitting around the house; and pain is the only sensation boxers are permitted for months on end.

Of course, fame has its own pleasures, and being a celebrity is a great way to kill time. So I first began to worry about Ali when he stopped enjoying the weigh-ins. I figured that this would be the last thing to go, that he would train and fight forever for this one moment, when the lights are on full blast and the mikes surround him like herbaceous borders. But lately he's been sleepwalking through this too. Fame without performance can be embarrassing. Mickey Mantle quit baseball after he struck out in an All-Star game on three pitches he couldn't see. A standing ovation takes on a funny sound when you haven't earned it.

Yet there are those who stagger on in the limelight, collecting residuals, like Arnold Palmer, or refusing to admit that anything's happened, like Johnny Unitas in his last years. And it isn't always just for fame and money, but to appease some personal devil. Take Unitas. From the outside, he seemed a graceless figure, hanging around much too long, willfully hurting the team and blocking the light for younger quarterbacks. But Unitas from the inside was another story. He had made it to the pros off the sandlots on absolute self-confidence; he had faced down the cattle stampedes known as pass-rushes more bravely than anyone in the business and taken more beatings than Elisha Cook Jr.; and he had radiated such a fiery sense of self that teammates who fouled up were scared to come back to the huddle.

Self-belief elevated him above mere talent, and made him the *only** quarterback on most all-time all-star teams. And it was this warrior pride that would not break down, surviving grotesquely without arms or legs through weekly humiliations.

Usually football players give up more easily than that. Of all professionals, they are likely to be the best educated, and to have the best business connections in their cities. Even in retirement Joe Namath probably sells more products around New York than the whole current Yankee and Met line-ups put together. Also they are the most likely to collect broken bones, housemaid's knee and mysterious twinges, all urging them symphonically to quit.

In football, the bigger the star, the more incentive there is to do something else; viz. James (formerly Jim) Brown, the movie star and Merlin Olsen, the priestly flower salesman. Lumbering linemen, who just run a few feet and fall down, tend to hang around the game longer than backfield guys. As with boxing, but not with tennis or golf, the joys of their sport cannot be duplicated in the afterlife. There's no turning back from four hundred pounds (ex-linemen can inflate like blow fish), and no recapturing the team feeling: that special brew of personalities, pressure-cooked each year by success and failure.

Baseball players may hang around just because they don't know what else to do with their summers. From childhood on, their life has had the hypnotic dedication of concert virtuosi. When they quit, they talk of "getting to know their children," but the prospect doesn't seem to excite them enough to prevent them from trying out one more time for Spokane or Tuscaloosa with a brand-new knuckle ball and a seeing-eye dog. And base-

---

*Now, of course, he would have to share the job with Joe Montana. Although Unitas had the better arm, it's hard to argue with Montana's superbowls. As for temperament, I don't rule out one of them killing the other to have the job to himself.

ball has an additional macabre attraction: every time you breathe, it goes into the record book. So a Stan Musial keeps pumping away at some mythical number, three thousand hits, four thousand hits, that his predecessors didn't even know was important.

Tennis has traditionally been a pleasure to retire from, into the yielding arms of some country club, where one helps nubile beauties with their backhands until one drops. Or so duffers like to imagine. In fact, mediocrity is intolerably painful for a star to be around in *any* human form, and it is significant that when something called the World Team tennis league tried briefly to popularize team play, the gaffers began cranking up again immediately for competition. Tournament tennis unfortunately allows only one winner; the rest are forgotten, and only an inspired crank like Ken Rosewall or Jimmy Connors finds it worth his while to grind his way eternally through the early rounds only to find the latest whippet from Scandinavia waiting for him. John Newcombe is our symbol here, a master of the semi-retirement and the half-comeback, who couldn't win and couldn't quit and bloomed through it all as a media man.

In some ways, the amateur track, field and water persons have the most orderly lives. First the sport, then the money. A Bruce Jenner has no place to go after an Olympiad, but must clutch his fame like the Olympic torch and hold it up as long as he can. The American mania for wooing people away from what they do well and turning them into TV announcers is a kindness for once, keeping these worthy young men off the streets. Mark Spitz may still be swimming somewhere, but the crowds have gone home. Dick Button skates alone. They must talk or perish. It is the only thing we'll still pay them to do.

Because his every move aches with mortality, ours and his, we tend to picture the athlete who hangs on as a sadder figure than he necessarily is. "Let us remember you the way you were," we beg Joe Louis, as he stumbles into Rocky Marciano's jackhammer right. But we *will* remember him the way he was. The last, indifferent years are forgotten, with Willie Mays and Babe

Ruth and Ray Robinson—or remembered as brave struggles, waged by extra-large spirits, with Fate.

The taste for old-timers' days* indicates that fans are not squeamish about old age. Joe DiMaggio still looks more like Joe DiMaggio than anyone else does, and any reminder is welcome. And old athletes serve at least two other purposes. One is that they testify to how much pro athletes really love their sports, even at the expense of *bella figura*. They would rather look bad than not play at all. Hank Aaron and Ted Williams wanted, like a kid in batting practice, to hit just one more. And a Namath or Simpson wants to play because 95 percent of his body still can, and that is what it is fashioned for.

The second thing old athletes do for us is give sports continuity, and the quality of a novel. Suppose, let us say, that some wave-of-the-future nut struts into the bar announcing that today's golf tour is so superior to yesterday's that any club pro could beat Bobby Jones: one has only to point to Sammy Snead, who won his last P.G.A. event at fifty-two against these highly evolved specimens but was never classed above Jones; tennis, and one mentions Rosewall or Pancho Gonzales; baseball, and Mr. Williams will do. The frangibility of track-and-field records, where breaking records is the whole point and essence, has misled people about the infinite improvability of athletes. Technique and equipment can obviously be improved—but the old boys can master that in a twinkling. Size, where size is important, can increase. (We may get more good heavyweights, yet lightweights remain eternally at par.) But the art of the thing, the eye and hand speed and the wit to use them, probably change at the more peaceful rate of genetic evolution; i.e., look for something every ten thousand years or so.

This, at least, seems to be the case with the Geniuses. A grand master, Ruth or Tilden, can be transported through time intact

*Back then, old-timers only had days, now some of them have whole seasons. Good for them. A few years back, Jack Nicklaus said he never planned to be a "ceremonial" golfer like Arnie Palmer; but when the time came, he didn't have to. He joined the Senior Circuit long enough to set it on fire, and now it's always there when he needs it.

and so can an old man playing darts in an English pub who can shoot the eyes off the board while his hand shakes and his beer spills.

And yet, and yet. An old boxer is a sad sight. In the first Spinks bout, Ali looked like an old man who's been told to go to bed against his will. And the later Joe Louis looked older than time itself. No other sport aims so directly at this, at aging the other man to the point of senility. There's courage in Ali, and that's always good to see. But I wish he'd knock it off, and become a young man again, while there's still time.

Index

293